Stephanie Edwards, *MA. MD of Customer 1st International, UK*: "What a brilliant read this was. The Halo and The Noose is a truly motivational and energizing read. The book inspires us to learn from individual life experiences and organisations will undoubtedly achieve business success through developing their people in this way".

John Griffin, *Business Consultant and Director, High Chem Industrials Africa, Nairobi*: "I've used extracts from this book as a basis for corporate training - they make a great impact with a wide range of staff and situations".

Mike du Plessis, *Head, Centre for Continuing Education, Cape Peninsula University of Technology*: "There is a definite and growing appreciation of story telling as an effective management training technique. This book covers the ground beautifully".

Rev. Peter Fox, *St Lukes Hospice Spiritual Counselor and Care Team Leader, BA (Hons), Dip Psychoanalytic Psychotherapy*: "The authors fuse their creatively different but complementing skills and competencies from their experiences in the corporate business and academic worlds to create this unique signature dish. It has all the taste, life-sustaining nutrients and stylish presentation that will leave you smiling long after you finish it. The stories told in this presentation are like the aroma of the dish-awakening the senses to our humanness and our souls quest to have another reference - a spiritual identity, beyond our capacity to define ourselves merely by what we earn. This book will remain in your memory and you will return to it as an appetising staple on your menu".

Rod Jones, *Group CEO of C3Africa, Customer Service and Call Centre Strategist and Consultant, Author, Trainer, Lecturer*: "In our lifetimes we have learned literally hundreds, if not thousands of lessons through the stories that we hear. Many of the earliest nursery rhymes that we were brought up on carry powerful messages and 'learnings'. Biblical parables and similar recounts form a common thread through virtually all ancient and contemporary religious and spiritual works and there are few who would challenge the validity of the ethical, moral and wellbeing-related lessons inherent in these writings. The jokes that we chuckle about on a daily basis or even better, the recounts of the after dinner raconteur may well leave us with a tears rolling down our cheeks or merely a comforting smile. Why? Perhaps because we recognise that in the story-telling, we have learned one or more valuable lessons. In business, we revel in story-telling. The conference presentations most frequently ranked as 'Exceptional' tend to be well-presented Case Studies... Are these simply Business Stories? We learn from them. And the lessons stick! In 'The Halo and The Noose' Graham Williams and Dorian Haarhoff have 'legitimised' the role that story telling can and should play in business today; from the boardroom to the shop floor".

David Taylor, *Director of Companies and Management Mentor*: "The stories in 'The Halo and the Noose' enchant and educate and will do so for many years whilst we remain in harness".

Louise van Rhyn, *BSc / MBA / DMAN (Doctorate in Organizational Change), MD of Symphonia, and University of Stellenbosch Business School lecturer*: "Wow! What an amazing resource and testimony to the power of stories. This book is a gift from South Africa to the rest of the world. I am SO excited about this publication and even more excited about having this kind of resource available for the Movement for Sharing Life Stories in South Africa".

The Halo and the Noose

*The Power of Story Telling and Story
Listening in Business Life*

The Authors

Graham Williams, CMC, B.Com Hons, B.A. is a certified management consultant, thought leader, speaker, executive coach – an associate of Change Partners, and author who has worked in a large number of countries and sectors around the world. An essential component of his 'motivational fingerprint' is to overcome severe organisational blockages by installing creative, healing solutions – from concept to implementation. He focuses on the use of narrative, anecdote and metaphor as critical contributors to successful business interventions. E-mail: centserv@iafrica.com

Dorian Haarhoff is a poet, writer and mentor who is steeped in story. A former Professor of English, he now runs his own business, Creative Workshops. He facilitates corporate story workshops for a number of companies in Africa and elsewhere, and acts as a writing coach for local and international clients. E-mail: dh53@mweb.co.za

Tony Grogan has been an editorial cartooonist for the Cape Times and other South African newspapers since 1974. His cartoons are noted for their perceptiveness, wryness and wit. He is also well-known as an illustrator. Seven books of his own work have been published and have become sought-after Africana.

Acknowledgement

We wish to thank David Taylor, Director of Companies and Management Mentor, for his support and generous assistance.

Cover design by Porat Jacobson

ISBN 978-0-9944028-8-2 Print
ISBN 978-0-9944028-9-9 ePub

Published and printed in Australia in 2016.

Published by Heart Space Publications
Website: www.heartspacebooks.com
E-mail: pat@heartspacebooks.com
PO Box 1085 | Daylesford | Victoria | 3460 | Australia
Tel: +61 450260348 (Australia).

To learn more about story telling for your organisation, go to:
http://www.haloandnoose.com

The Halo and the Noose

*The Power of Story Telling and Story
Listening in Business Life*

by

Graham Williams & Dorian Haarhoff

Illustrated by Tony Grogan

Foreword

People involved in business at all levels have time constraints. They are bombarded with data: electronic, printed word and voice, much of it unnecessary.

They need to find time to continue their education, particularly in their chosen business fields. There is so much to read and so little time and often little to capture the imagination. This book *The Halo and the Noose* is a very different type of business book. It covers the necessary theoretical aspects of business management, but the story telling captivates one.

We remember stories from childhood and some of the better fiction read in later years. The 100 stories and poems in *The Halo and the Noose* enchant and educate and will do for many years whilst we remain in harness. If you have taken very few memories away from this wonderful book, that of *Nasrudin's Donkey* is worthwhile relating to your children, your students, colleagues and very definitely to your boss.

David Taylor
Director of Companies and Management Mentor

To Lynette, for being who she is

To Elma, who connects many stories

A halo has to fall only a few inches to be a noose
Dan McKinnon

mutato nomine de te fabula narratur
(All you need do is change the name and it's about you, this story)
Horace

I see story as a honeycomb, a structure to hold the honey
Workshop participant

Contents

Section A
Why Stories in Business?

Section B
Kindling the Flame: Thirteen Ways Stories Work

Section C
Art and Craft: Story-telling Guidelines

Section D
Carrying on the Conversation

Appendices

Orientation

Stories can free us or trap us. They are like the two-edged sword. It depends on the telling, the motive for the tale and how we interpret the meaning. They can open us to new possibilities or keep us choked by or strangled in existing paradigms and orientations – whether these be about belief systems, values, religions, thinking styles, business and life journeys, strategies or behaviour patterns. Writer Dan McKinnon advises, "A halo has to fall only a few inches to be a noose". We acknowledge him for the book's title.

We also dedicate the book to those readers who seek the liberation of the halo and wish to escape the entrapment of the noose.

> *At a rural gathering a famous actor is invited to recite something. He chooses Psalm 23, "The Lord is my Shepherd". He recites grandly, eloquently, perfectly. At the end there is applause. Then one of the locals points to an elderly man. "He also knows that Psalm". So after much persuasion the old man gets up and recites in a quivering voice, making a few mistakes. As he ends there is a poignant silence. Someone asks the actor, "What was the difference between your rendering and his?" The actor responds, "I know the Psalm. He knows the Shepherd".*

So this book is for those who seek not academic knowledge, perfect performance and polished technique – but who wish to be released to bring all of themselves to their stories. To tell it from the heart. To live it. We wish that you will carry story into your thinking, conversations and presentations. This is profound but also simple and easy. The secret is to be yourself, be natural, move away from striving for perfection, and from comparing yourself to others, and competing. Not contend: the Chinese character for 'not' represents a bird flying up and away, and the character for 'contend' is from an image of two hands struggling for the same object.[1]

---

[1] Wing R. L. *The Tao of Power*. Aquarian/Thorsons, London. 1986.

Preface

Ever since I heard my first story I started looking
for you [1]
Rumi

Story telling in organizations is a growing focus for business related books. Many current books limit stories to examples of what factually happened in organizations. The emphasis is on telling success or motivational stories – 'war stories' of battles won, to generate and keep momentum during transitions, or to inspire workers to try harder, perform better, achieve more.

We believe that this book offers an expanded and more radical understanding of the nature and power of story listening and story telling. Its premise is that all stories are fictional whether they be work stories, life stories or imagined stories. Stories reach far beyond the literal into realms of imagery and open us to mystery. They include everybody in the conversation.

At the heart of the text is our belief that once we raise our Story IQ, we begin to hear and tell our work life in a new and vital way. We open up to transformation and new leadership paths. Like the lotus flower, we bloom and seed new beginnings at the same time. We reach into what may be murky depths and produce something of infinite beauty and worth. In the words of psychologist, James Hillman, "The first task is re-story-ing the adult... in order to restore the imagination to its primary place in consciousness in each of us". [2]

In writing this book we are aware that the written word lacks some of the electricity of the spoken word where teller, listener and story become the alchemy for transportation to a new world. We have endeavoured to bridge that gap by adding illustrations that may serve as illuminations, memory anchors, imagination catalysts or insight stimulators.

Of course, the spoken word, accompanied by gesture, body message, tone, pitch, volume, pace, pause and other verbal and non-verbal cues may be understood and interpreted differently at different times by different people. So too our written words and pictures in this book may be heard in many ways. That is your confusion, pleasure, right.

While the book offers techniques and practical applications, it offers (at a more abiding level) a way of being in business and doing business. The stories it tells offer us a steed or flying dragon, who knows its way though unfamiliar and sometimes dangerous terrain and senses where the treasures are hidden. These stories tell us how to ride that creature. What to feed it. And how to whisper to it.

The book's approach is multi-dimensional. It is about creating and connecting to inner and outer wealth in our lives, the lives of our colleagues and clients. About using our right cortex of pictures, daydreaming, colour, rhythm and patterning and our left cortex of words, logic, analysis and reasoning. And appreciating that our cortices are intertwined, supportive of each other and complementary.

We live in a participatory universe, say the physicists. Such is the nature of reality. When we 'story,' we participate in our lives in a way that grants access to the bigger us – the whole brain, where intuition, curiosity and vision dwell.

We believe that stories offer us a solar and lunar energy (for stories are about day and night, about substance and shadow). They recreate us and bring us alive and restore our enthusiasm, imagination and ability to act in an innovative and successful way.

The mythologist, Joseph Campbell, believed that as we look back over our lives, they resemble the plot of a Dickens novel.[3] Plot involves internal causation, played out in a web of relationships. All is connected. Stories open us to an understanding of the plot – the web of those interconnections. The echoes, the parallels, the guiding influences. The ironies where the surface water of the river appears to be moving one way, but the deeper current is moving the other way.

Fiction teaches us about this web of connection. As William Blake believed, "birds-nests, spiders-webs, humans-relationships".[4] As we work in the sense of the drama of story, we begin to appreciate the day-by-day drama. All stories are about drama. It means paying attention to what is happening – noticing nuance or changes, getting excited about the great storyline rather than only the bottom line. We begin to witness our own story. When we enter the great WHN of a story – What Happens Next? – we become curious about our own work lives.

Many business books draw their stories from the northern hemisphere or developed countries. Our stories, sourced from African and global cultures, from ancestor and animal, from literature and insight, from traditions or made up for the occasion, point to the great mystery of people at work. Work is a soul aspect that lies outside of ourselves, and mirrors back to us who we are, and what we can be. Or as Kahlil Gibran suggests, "work is keeping pace with the seasons of our journeys and lives".[5]

Story-telling is the language of Ubuntu (a person is a person because of other persons) for the language of story lies beneath all our languages. Stories form the bridge between cultures, genders, castes, floors. They help us to move beyond the stereotype towards the archetype.

Some CEO's feel that the conversation around their work is too small or too devoid of positive energy. We hope our book will inspire and equip you to trigger and enter the great conversations that ghost around stories. Some mentors, coaches and counsellors get lost in mechanical teaching. We hope our book will motivate you to truly awaken, motivate and guide others. Some individuals, managers and workers struggle to find purpose, meaning and enjoyment in their work-lives. We hope our book will be the catalyst that leads to greater self-awareness, self-management and self-realisation.

Emotional Intelligence and Social Intelligence are concepts increasingly used in business. We believe that the cultivation of Story Intelligence embraces and is integral to these two concepts. Social intelligence builds on emotional intelligence (mainly about managing one's own emotions) and is about being socially adept and managing interpersonal connections by good self-presentation, tuning in, building rapport, showing genuine empathy, influencing positively. (For an account of Emotional and Social Intelligence, see Appendix 1).

Much has transpired since publication in 2009 of The Halo and the Noose. The use of story in business has grown exponentially. It has moved far beyond future scenario construction, case studies and training illustration, triggering change. Areas of application now include knowledge management, sense-making and problem-solving, presentation formats, coaching, counselling, building resilience and agility, team development, developing character virtues, steering sustainability. Recent work we have conducted with organisations include the use of story and imagery for the development of Brand messages free of rhetoric and the promotion of products as heroes, improving the dynamics within diverse and dysfunctional teams, using biomimicry as a spur to creativity, conducting anecdote circles and metaphor elicitation in qualitative research ......

In the nearly 7 years that have lapsed since publication, 100 newsletters, 140 articles, a number of multi-media files and 6 further eBooks have been added to the simultaneously launched Halo and Noose web site. The resource site is designed for those who wish to continuously develop their story skills − practitioners, leaders, managers, trainers ..... The site's Quick-Finder facility enables members to instantly find what they seek. To illustrate, clicking on VALUES (under Developing the organisation, Response to Challenges) currently throws up 40 articles and newsletters that address the subject.

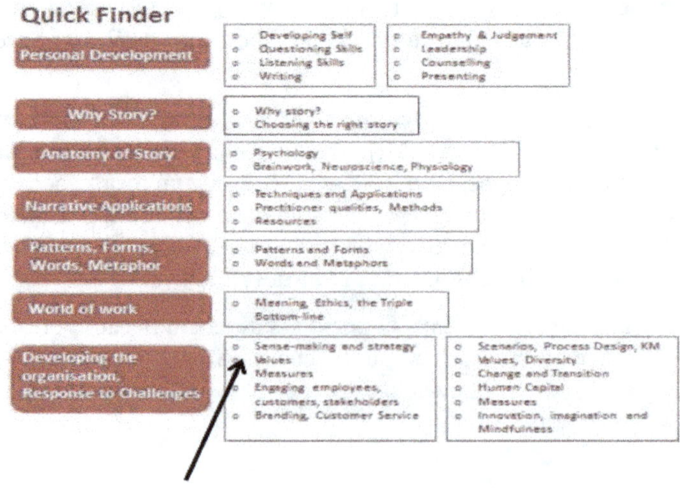

- **Values**
  ARTICLES
    - Leadership Lessons from leadership stories: Crossing the Alps
    - The Stone that Resists Fire: Warming the Corporate Soul - corporate governance principles
    - The Lion and the Ostrich – A Bushmen Story
    - Things are not as they should be……………
    - The Ripening of the Olive: a new metaphor for responsible capitalism
    - FROM VALUES TO VIRTUES: Living with purpose, meaning and flow. A concept whos time has come
    - THE DARK SIDE OF LEADERSHIP
    - Gratitude Versus Greed and a Rich Life
    - How do organisations become virtuous?
    - Paradoxically Nothing is Impossible, Outside is Inside, the Secular is Sacred
    - BEING IN THE LOVE ZONE
    - The Da Vinci Virtue of Corporalita: integration of body, mind and spirit
    - The Life, thoughts and works of Leonardo Da Vinci
    - A Case Study in Developing Organisational and Individual Values: G-Wiz
    - Fear Conquers Love
    - An interview by Marcella Bruner, Editor of Leadership and Change Magazine
    - Putting Proper Balance into the Balanced Scorecard
    - 4 Ways Leaders Lead by Employing Virtue-Clusters
    - Send in the Clowns
    - Agility Ability
    - Silver Coins: the Parable of the Virtuous Business
    - Fake Authenticity
    - Virtues or Vices in Business: guess which way the scales are tipping?

  NEWSLETTERS
    - Newsletter 66: Amazing Strategic Grace
    - Newsletter 68: Our working relationship with nature
    - Newsletter 70: Gift Giving
    - Newsletter 72: The Common Good, Shared Values and Cultural Neuroscience
    - Newsletter 75: Bringing Values to Life Using Stories
    - Newsletter 77: Developing Leadership Character for a Needy World
    - Newsletter 78: When the end justifies the means
    - Newsletter 1: Abraham the Atheist
    - Newsletter 16: Ethical Behaviour
    - Newsletter 17: Giving
    - Newsletter 47 WONDER
    - Newsletter 48 Going to fun from Monday to Friday
    - Newsletter 50 The Forgotten People
    - Newsletter 60: Bridges
    - Newsletter 61: I walk the line
    - Newsletter 62: 'Be the change you wish to see in the world'. Cliché?
    - Newsletter 64: Positively changing the world we live in

Because of the availability of all of this material, we have refrained from adding too much to version two of the Halo and the Noose, and confined ourselves to three key new chapters, another appendix, and some adjustment and addition to the content elsewhere. Including a number of new stories. From this additional material, readers gain insight into:

- Qualitative research with employees, customers, suppliers that goes deep, unearths information and feelings

- Diversity - in a world where migrations, movements, connections and interactions between people who differ, are rapidly increasing

- Higher purpose (at individual and organisation levels) as the route to effective engagement

- The emerging notion of spiritual mindfulness, and ethical guidelines for story telling

- Stories as containers of safe space and wisdom in a number of situations

- An instrument for assessing the level of story competence and degree of story application in an organisation

Developments in neuroscience, psychology and sociology support and reinforce our long-held contentions that story stimulates mindfulness and imagination, allows for emotional connections, triggers interest, engagement, facilitates insight, and builds memory.

We do not claim that story is a panacea for all business developments, practices and problems. We do believe that story is a very valuable contributor to most areas of business. Story should be used sensibly and appropriately in the knowledge that no rules apply.

Two companion monks came across a swollen, raging river on their travels. A pretty, young woman who had reached the same bank, asked them to help her cross the river.

Without hesitation the older and senior of the two picked up the woman and helped her across. The younger monk was aghast because his companion had broken a vow that they had both taken – never to touch a woman. He kept his disappointment hidden for a long time as they travelled on, and then blurted out, "What a poor example! How could you? You blatantly broke your vow!"

The older monk responded gently, "I put her down long ago. Why are you still carrying her?"

Here is a story to take us into the book and into Story Intelligence:

Nasrudin and the Ferry

Nasrudin owned a dilapidated ferry that took people across the river. There was a modern ferry that worked the same route. On this particular morning, the modern ferry was not operating.

A teacher in a pin-striped suit and shiny shoes approached Nasrudin. "Do you think this thing of yours will make it across the river?"

"I ain't sure," replied Nasrudin.

"Have you never learned grammar?" asked the teacher.

"No".

"In that case, you have wasted half your life".

The ferry took to the water and midstream ran into difficulty. The ferry rocked, taking in water.

Nasrudin turned to the teacher. "Have you ever learned to swim?"

"No," responded the teacher.

"In that case you have wasted your whole life because this ferry is going down".

Welcome to the great conversation. May the book enable you to swim.

---

[1] Barks, Coleman. *The Essential Rumi*, Penguin, New York, 1995.

[2] Hillman, James. "A Note on Story", *Reclaiming the Inner Child*, Jeremiah Abrams (ed.), Tarcher, NY, 1990.

[3] Campbell, Joseph. *Pathways to Bliss*, New World Library, Novato, California, 2004.

[4] William Blake. *The Marriage of Heaven and Hell*, The Complete Poems, Penguin, London, 1978.

[5] Gibran, Kahlil. *The Prophet*, Alfred Knopf, NY, 1923.

Section A
Why Stories in Business?

This section explores the many gifts that stories offer men and women at work. We raise many questions. What happens when we learn to listen? When we learn to tell? When we learn to engage with the stories of others? When we allow story to touch us at all levels of our humanity – physical, intellectual, social, emotional and spiritual or intuitive? What do stories have to do with leadership? With follower-ship? With the current constructs of business – customer service, ethics, missions, bottom lines, strategy, restructuring, transformation, empowerment, retrenchment, mergers, diversity, goals, team dynamics, values? With a meaningful career?

Story has been a part of the fabric of community since time immemorial. Stories contain moods and feelings and so can capture and engage, allow mind connections and associations (the very basis of our neurology). Thus story has the power to motivate, to move, to change or reframe belief systems (negative to positive, defeat to new beginning, hurting to healing, problem to challenge) and induce states (well-being, relaxation, contentment, determination).

"Story is a powerful means to conduct qualitative research, share feelings, beliefs, knowledge and wisdom"

---

[1] Metzger, Deena. *Writing For Your Life, a Guide and Companion to the Inner World,* Harper, San Fransisco, 1992.

Chapter 1
Why Stories?

*Africa breathes stories... In Africa things are stories, they store
stories, and they yield stories at the right moment of dreaming,
when we are open to the secret side of objects and moods* [1]

Ben Okri

Why is story so vital in business life?

> *A professor and an old peasant woman are discussing how it is that the world is*
>
> *held up in space and does not fall down.*
>
> *"Well you see," says the old woman, "the world rests on a giant plate".*
>
> *"Interesting. And what does the plate rest on?"*
>
> *"On the back of a giant tortoise".*
>
> *"And what does that tortoise rest on?"*
>
> *"On the back of another tortoise..."*
>
> *"And what does..."*
>
> *"Don't bother your head, professor. It's tortoises all the way down".*

And stories all the way down. Story is the foundation. Everything rests on story – one
way or another. Ultimately, it is story that makes the business world go round.

The Courage to Be

In our work with an organization, we told the story of Hans Christian Andersen's *Ugly
Duckling*.[2] We witnessed someone discovering – during the telling – that many of us feel

ugly inside at times, and that it's OK to find your own way to self-acceptance, and then becoming accepted and belonging to a team. We were thrilled to see people encouraged to move from being negative to becoming positive and determined after hearing about Lance Armstrong's overcoming of cancer and going on to win seven Tours de France, as told in *It's not about the Bike.*[3]

We have seen people inspired and motivated to tackle the seemingly impossible after being introduced to the lessons in *Touching the Void* of Joe Simpson and Simon Yates' tale of fortitude and courage.[4]

We believe that story is an integral, indispensable part of the life and growth of organizations and people in business, now more than ever.

When we were at junior school, an early reader offered us the story of *Chicken Licken* who feared the sky would drop on his head.[5] Sometimes the sky does drop on our heads. Often the unexpected arrives in our work and personal life. Random events. Weather patterns, human agency, natural causes. Sometimes they involve death – literal suicides or metaphoric. They bring changes and challenges. These events arrive beyond our control.

QUICK READ

Some insights offered in Touching the Void

Avoid doing the stupid and beware inadequate planning

When disaster strikes, you're basically on your own and have to rely on your own resourcefulness

The hero's journey follows a start, succeed, meet obstacle, fail, learn, continue, new obstacle, succeed, proceed cycle

We all need to find a higher spiritual meaning or treasure that carries us through the tough times

We must learn to allow our internal motivational voice to drive us forward and onward

When faced with a massive transition or challenge the move from despair/ lethargy/ helplessness comes from having a plan

In business we cannot procrastinate. We stand still but need to take action and make decisions – continuously, whatever the circumstances and no matter how great our uncertainty

We need to accept/let go of what we can't change

Sometimes the unknown is better than the known and leads to success. (We do not so much fear the unknown but the loss of the known). Sometimes we must counter-intuitively go down and deeper, and not up

We need a vision and intermediate, measured goals and realize them with a deter-mined obsession – taking one small step at a time

---

This is where the story enters. A story teaches me that what happens to me is one thing. How I react is another. The event and my response are not cause and effect. The wise ones, such as Einstein, tell us that it is futile to look for a cause and result in the same event. The events open up the choice of possible responses. This is the gift of story – the freedom to choose our responses. Victor Frankl, the therapist, who went through the death camps and saw the very worst that human beings can do to human beings, wrote *Man's Search for Meaning* based on his observations.[6] He believes the greatest freedom we have as human beings, is a freedom to choose how we will respond to a given set of circumstances.

> *Ryokan, a Japanese Zen monk, lived some 200 years ago. One night he came home from playing with children to find that a thief had broken into his home and stolen his meagre possessions. Ryokan sat down at his window and wrote, "The thief left it behind, the moon at my window".*

Ryokan exercises choice. Instead or focusing on what has been taken away, he rests his attention on what cannot be taken away.

Not all of us are as enlightened as Ryokan. Or as quick to get to that state of grace. Robert Frost writes:

> Ah, when to the heart of man
> Was it ever less than a treason
> To go with a drift of things
> To yield with the grace to reason,
> And bow and accept the end
> Of a love or a season?[7]

We may well go through a natural cycle of loss. Grief for the loss of job, for the loss of a loved one. After the period of grief, the choice opens for us. How will we respond to what has happened?

The sense of choice is enriched because we seldom know the full meaning or implication of what has happened. We often fall into the temptation to conclude a story before it is over – to prejudge the outcome. Another trap that the story reveals is that I can get stuck in the 'if only' of the past. In truth, I am in 'don't know mind'.

> *Every day a village Rabbi goes to the synagogue to pray. One day the local policeman accosts him. "Where are you going?"*
>
> *The rabbi responds, "I don't know".*
>
> *"What do you mean, you don't know? Every day you go to the synagogue. Now I'm going to throw you into jail for lying to me".*
>
> *As the cell door clangs shut the rabbi calls out, "You see, I don't know".*

Stories all the Way Down

Stories raise awareness, stimulate thinking, facilitate leadership, offer flexibility and possibility, nurture and engage. The telling of a story provides us with the opportunity to own and take charge of our own stories, beliefs, values and knowledge and share these confidently with others.

The Buddha was asked what his name meant. Did it mean enlightenment? The Buddha responded, "My name means I'm awake". How do we become awake? How do we become conscious? If we have not processed the stories imposed on us, then they live us instead of us living them. In our professional and personal lives, the unconscious, hidden stories drive us. We knee-jerk our way, not responding but reacting to previous stories. When we raise our story to consciousness, we are able to become selective. We can choose which parts of the story are a burden to our lives and which we want to grow and cherish. (The noose or the halo).

We are able to clarify and simplify our own thinking about issues, challenges, events. Story patterns can help us keep things simple. We know of a suicide where a CEO had left a note saying, "I could not simplify my life".

The sharing of story is not primarily about technique and skill. It is about being open, honest, *real*. The Velveteen Rabbit in Margery William's book, learns from the skin horse that we become real when others accept and value us, when we allow ourselves to risk and be vulnerable and give of ourselves unconditionally to others, and that the process can sometimes be painful.[8] "Does it hurt?" asked the rabbit. "Sometimes" said the skin horse, for he was always truthful. "When you are real you don't mind being hurt".

The telling of a story – about ourselves, our experiences, our feelings – directly or under cover of myth or fiction – gives us permission to show our passion in a socially acceptable way, and is a conduit for this expression. The telling of story helps us to take responsibility, clarify, become real, express what we believe in and value most, connect with others and reinforce that which makes us 'tick'.

Stories evoke connections with others and elicit responses. Stories trigger identification and response in the listeners. They become the glue for bonding people. People relate through the story and in that safe way, share the truths and values they need to share.

The Allegiance group have published findings that *engagement* (of both customers and employees) is one of our most powerful emerging business challenges. Investing in emotional attachment by means of empowerment, participation, dialogue, story telling – results in significant improvements in employee and customer satisfaction, loyalty, trust, retention, the bottom line.[9]

We cannot do without story at work. We are walking, talking stories. We are the stories we tell about ourselves and our workplace. We create our reality and confirm our identity through stories. Hidden or unprocessed stories can sabotage an organization, for an organization, like any individual, has its own story. Stories can erode our power or they can energise us to make choices and deal with changes.

We need to acquire story literacy. For the age and time of story in business has come. More about this is to be found in Chapter 22.

---

[1] Okri, Ben. *Birds of Heaven*, Phoenix, 1996.

[2] Estés, Clarissa Pinkola. "The Ugly Duckling" in *Women Who Run With the Wolves*, Rider, NY, 1992.

[3] Armstrong, Lance. *It's Not about the Bike :My Journey Back to Life*, McGraw Hill, NY, 2000.

[4] Simpson, Joe and Yates, Simon. *Touching the Void*, Vintage, London, 2004.

[5] Childs, S. *Chicken Licken*, Ladybird, London, 1999.

6 Frankl, Viktor. *Man's Search for Meaning*, Washington Square Press, Simon & Schuster, NY, 1963.

7 Frost, Robert. *A Boy's Will*, St. Martin's Press, NY, 1913.

8 Williams, Margery. *The Velveteen Rabbit*, Egmont, London, 2005.

9 Rhoads, Dr. Gary and Whitlark, Dr. David. *Discover Engagement: what is engagement and why is it one of the most powerful emerging business concepts of the 21st century*, www.allegiance.com/Library (14th February, 2008).

Chapter 2

Story Listening

The branches of your intelligence grow new leaves
in the wind of listening[1]
Rumi

Story telling in organizations is becoming a buzz word. But what of story listening? How do we listen to other people's stories? How to we listen to what is going on in the organization? How do we listen to someone who repeats information? I recall a friend who, when I checked out if I had told her a particular story, responded, "Maybe, but tell me again. I might hear something I didn't hear before".

The Ear of a Snake

The animals of Africa had a competition to see which creature had the most acute hearing. Most of the animals that had ears arrived. Elephant arrived with his big ears. So did Rabbit, with his ears twitching. Kudu came galloping to the meeting place in the middle of a great plane. Even the small-eared Hippo arrived to take part. Snake also arrived zigzagging his body along the ground. The other animals laughed at snake, "You have no ears. Go away". But snake said, "Let me hear what I can hear".

Lion said, "Let Snake take part. Let Snake go first". Snake lay on the ground. "I can hear a hippopotamus scattering his dung in a circle".

"Not bad," said Elephant. "You can hear as well as your cousin, the Lizard, who does have ears".

Snake raised its body into the air. "I can hear the wind in the distant forest uprooting trees".

"Impressive" barked Wild Dog. "I can hear that too". The animals were so busy watching snake that they forgot to listen to their environment.

Suddenly Snake spoke, "There is a hunter behind that tree. I hear him through the air putting an arrow to his bow. Now I hear him on the ground moving his feet". Sure enough, a second later a man appeared with an arrow in a taut bow. All the animals scattered and snake disappeared into the ground. The hunter's arrow flew into the empty air.

From that day on all animals honoured Snake for his hearing.

Deep Listening

When we were young, 'Cowboy and Indian' movies showed the Indian listening with his ear to the ground. Rumi, the thirteenth century Persian poet, talks of listening "with the deep ear in your chest".[1] This is listening without distraction, with total attention and mindfulness, with the purpose of understanding and learning and responding creatively, with the head and with the heart.

We all understand the way we respond when we feel listened to. But often in business,

---

CORPORATE WORKSHOP RESPONSES

Here are some responses to what was going on in a three hour workshop for a change management team in a large company:

"In listening to a colleague's story about his childhood, I realize what an effective tool this is to get in touch with humanness and influence change"

"A recognition that perhaps we haven't heard enough of the stories of others… about recognizing the constraints I put on myself… about courage"

"The tools I came searching for were with me all the time. Just listening to simple stories allowed me to go inside myself where the answers lie"

"From confusion to light to assistance to move further. I understand that timing and listening have now become the critical aspects in the way forward"

"Stories for me are tools to encourage the hidden – that which is not said but meant or implied"

"This morning has reaffirmed that the experience of a person is at the heart of the situation and that we should all participate in the story, as tellers and listeners"

"An eye opening session – to be prepared to listen to stories from others – more than telling them"

"If we communicated feelings maybe we would understand the difficulties in the personal journeys of our colleagues. This will also allow those tasked with 'driving the change initiative' to work together with others and mobilise effectively"

---

office deadlines, hidden agendas and corporate politics filter the kind of listening that encourages and initiates true dialogue. This doesn't allow individuals to let go of their narrow point of view and inhibits a sense of shared belonging, vision, commitment, harmony, engagement, readiness to move forward together, co-operation and achievement.

When you tell appropriate stories (work/life stories or fiction), if you listen to the responses, you will hear what you need to hear. The responses in the box came from hearing the same story which reveals the underbelly of how people really feel. Telling a story in a training workshop or a boardroom and asking people to connect it to their work situation, creates an opportunity to observe the body language and level of engagement of the participants. Here is one of the stories that elicited these responses.

> *Nasrudin, en route to market, loads bags of salt on his donkey's back. They come to a river. Nasrudin tries to tell the donkey to cross at the shallow causeway, but the donkey chooses to cross at the deepest part. The salt dissolves in the water. The donkey trips lightly up the other bank and trots off.*
>
> *Next market day, Nasrudin loads the donkey with bales of wool. Once again Nasrudin tries to tell the donkey to cross at the shallow causeway. The donkey once again chooses the deep part of the river. The wool absorbs the water. The donkey staggers up the river bank, the bags weighing heavily on his back.*
>
> *Nasrudin turns to it and says, "You thought that every time you entered the river you would come off lightly, didn't you?"*

The Nasrudin story reminds us of times when we follow a recipe for something that succeeded last time. This time it fails dismally. Times when we have neither read the river, nor the load on my back correctly.

What does the Nasrudin story suggest about listening? Is this a story about changing the relationship between the CEO (Nasrudin) and the personnel (the donkey)? (Or are the roles reversible?) Why is the donkey not responding to advice? How are we to read the body language of the donkey?

What action needs to be taken? Changing the route to the market? Finding markets where there is no river to cross? Developing more insight into likely behaviours? Training the donkey? Finding a new donkey? Changing from salt to wool? Building a bridge? Communicating more assertively? Working with new identities? Introducing punishment or reward?

Creating Space for Listening

In another workshop on story telling, one senior manager stated his needs. "I want to learn to tell a story so that middle management will buy into the changes and new structures we have put in place. They are resisting these changes".

We heard his frustration. Yet this is about telling not listening. About manipulation? There might be a serious reason why certain employees are not 'buying into' the new dispensation. In this company many felt anger. "We have been betrayed". Many were stuck. Colleagues had been made redundant and they mourned this loss and feared for their jobs.

It is possible to get stuck in this limbo. Carolyn Myss, intuitive healer, refers to being stuck in this way as 'woundology'.[2] How would it be if we allowed time to listen to such grieving? What is not grieved is given a shallow burial and comes to haunt us. The ghosts roam. When we do the grief work and people feel listened to, we give whatever needs attention a proper burial. Then we are able to move on.

Not that one necessarily needs to do anything about it or that one has the power to solve it. Paul Tillich, the theologian, said that the first duty of love is to listen.[3] Some psychologists feel that Sigmund Freud's greatest discovery was not of the unconscious but the power in the act of telling our story to an attentive listener. Proactive listening releases the one who is stuck to connect to their work in a new way, if they choose to do so.

Listening to Others

In listening to a story, we pay homage to and acknowledge the value of the other, gain new information and knowledge and perspective, learn, become motivated, find common ground and become enriched. Rilke says our listening ripens things.[4]

Here are additional ways in which this ripening happens. We become:

- a witness to the other person, to the legality of their viewpoint and the right to express it, we acknowledge their importance and worth. In the Hindu scripture, the Upanishads, there is a text. "Two birds, inseparable friends, sit in the same tree. The one eats the sweet fruit. The other watches without eating". When I tell stories, I become both birds – part of me passionately involved in the moment, while at the same time, another part develops the capacity to witness my life – not with judgment, but with compassion

- someone who draws on knowledge and information at different levels. This is perspective, information and knowledge about the story content, atmosphere, structure, context, the story teller, and the self – at all levels of being

- a student of those who know, especially at the lower levels. When the cleaner, service provider, former salesman now in the administrative office, delivery vehicle driver tell their stories from the point of view of their unique interaction with and understanding of the customer, we learn valuable lessons that we would not otherwise learn

- one who motivates colleagues – a feel-good, affirming event. Throughout the ages and from childhood, story captivates us and reminds us what is achievable by 'little people', who can do what others cannot. A line from the play *Les Miserable* says it all: "A flea can bite the bum of the Pope in Rome"

- someone who establishes common ground through identification and understanding

- a mirror of the self. Stories offer us the experience of others. In my imagination I can enter partly into their experience. As somebody in the office tells a formative story, we are given a glimpse through a window into the life of the person. We slip beyond roles into the wider life of the teller. And in so doing we relate at a deeper level.

Stories help us to know the kind of people we are.

We become a refining, building, enriching, dynamic colleague. The motto in Peter Shaffers' *Lettice Douffet* (of Lettice and Lovage) speaks of what stories do: They "Enlarge, Enliven and Enlighten!"[5]

People Listen to Stories

As soon as you start telling a story, the listeners go into 'story-mode'. In story-mode, if the story is well chosen, well constructed and well told (skills we can all learn – see Section C), people pay rapt attention. Jamie Smart, NLP practitioner, calls stories "The Ultimate Covert Communication Technique".[6]

Threads

> Listen.
> In every office you hear the threads
> of love and joy and fear and guilt,
> the cries for celebration and reassurance,
> and somehow you know that connecting those threads
> is what you're supposed to do
> and business takes care of itself.[7]

There is a resource in your company that you might not be hearing. It is the 'introverts', the shy ones, the ones who remain silent in a meeting, yet listen like the snake. Such people often see hidden connections. They connect the threads, bring new perspectives, have flashes of creativity and bring new insights to the group. Such people might not speak unless you ask them. Such people will not speak unless they know that their story will be heard, understood, accepted and valued.

---

[1] Barks, Coleman. *The Essential Rumi*, Penguin, 1995.

[2] Myss, Caroline. *Sacred Contracts, Awakening your Divine Potential,* Bantam Books, 2002.

[3] Tillich, Paul. *The Courage to Be,* Yale University Press, New Haven, 2000.

[4] Rilke, Rainer Maria. *Letters to a Young Poet,* Random House, UK. 2001.

[5] Shaffer, Peter. *Lettice and Lovage,* Andre Deutsch, London, 1998.

[6] Smart, Jamie. Salad Seminars Ltd. www.saladltd.co.uk. Leics. 2008.

[7] Autry, James. "Threads", quoted David Whyte, *The Heart Aroused, Poetry and the Preservation of Soul in Corporate America,* Doubleday, 1994.

Chapter 3
Leadership, Elephants and Matriarchs

It is only with heart that one can see rightly –
what is essential is invisible to the eye [1]
The Little Prince

The Leadership Challenge

Leadership is currently a hot debate. Theories abound. For example in their leadership studies section, www.psychology.about.com classify theories into a number of categories including: Great Man, Traits, Contingency, Situational, Behavioural, Participative, Transactional, Transformational, Synchronistic.

Story is a leadership ploy, a leadership technique. Here are two stories to open up a discussion about leadership and related issues.

God in all Beings

A chief who lived in the wilds, visited a guru who told him to see God in all beings. He returned to his village, which was in panic. There was a wild elephant rampaging in the nearby forest, smashing down the trees.

"We fear it will break down our huts and trample us to death," they cried.

"I will go and speak to the elephant. For God is in all beings. God is also in the elephant".

"No Chief, that is too dangerous," they pleaded.

The chief ignored their pleas and went to confront the elephant.

The elephant saw him coming and attacked, trumpeting and hurling him up into the nearest tree.

Battered and bruised, the chief returned to his guru and accused him. "You said I'm to see God in all beings".

"Yes, that is so".

"Look what happened to me". He told the story.

The guru asked, "Why did you not see God in the wisdom of your villagers?"

The Favourite

A guru has twenty disciples. One of them is his favourite. One day the other nineteen challenge their leader, "Why is this one the favourite?"

The guru responds, "Go into the forest everybody and bring back a chicken".

All twenty disciples return with chicken clutched under their arms.

The guru issues his second command, "Now, go where nobody can see you and kill the chicken".

The disciples disappear and return shortly. They have all killed the chicken, except the favourite. The chicken is still flapping under his arms.

The leader turns to the favourite and asks, "Why did you not carry out my instructions?"

The favourite responds, "I did carry out your instructions. You said go where nobody can see you. Now there is no such place. So I did not kill the chicken".

The leader turns to the other nineteen disciples and says, "That is why this one is the favourite".

What do these two stories suggest about leadership?

Change, Change and More Change

The world seems to spin faster and faster. Business leaders and managers are in the process of upgrading their skills to adjust to today's continually and rapidly changing world. In the late sixties, sociologist Alvin Toffler, in *Future Shock*, focused on the increasing tempo of technological change and how that acceleration itself effected the system.[2] A decade later Toffler followed up with another best-selling study *Third Wave*. It painted a portrait of a world being reconstructed by information.[3] How much more so in our decade.

Change, if you're not a wet baby, is still something that many avoid if possible. Even in cases of life and death a staggering 9 out of 10 effectively choose death by not changing their behaviour – according to new research shared at an IBM 'Global Innovation Outlook' conference. Just think of smokers.

Dr. Dean Ornish finds that non-physical, but psychological, emotional and spiritual dimensions came into play – so it's necessary to address feelings by changing frames of reference (for example accentuating joy not fear). Those who change are those who have kept up their brain machinery for unlearning and relearning.[4]

Business models, processes and technology are changing fast. No sooner has one wave of change receded than the next follows. For the business leader it's akin to being Hercules, grappling with the many-headed beast. Each time one head is cut off, another or more appear.

It's not unusual to find a product designed in the USA, made in Poland, marketed across the world, with post-sales service provided from a customer call centre located in India or Ireland. Businesses are becoming both 'bricks' and 'clicks'. 'Best practice' applies across geographic and industry boundaries.

Changes arrive uninvited, unannounced. Natural disasters wipe out structures. Stock markets crash. Companies merge and retrench. Change is the only certainty – accelerated change. You die or adapt, like the dinosaur or the elephant.

> *Abe rushes up to someone in the street.*
>
> *"Eve... I haven't seen you in years. You've changed. Your hairstyle, the way you walk, the way you dress".*
>
> *The woman retorts, "My name is not Eve. It's Sarah".*
>
> *Abe exclaims, "See, you have even changed your name!"*

The work habits of people are changing too. 50% of the workforce is non-permanent. And customers are getting choosier by the day. Their expectations are getting higher and higher. Society is getting more demanding of how business looks after the environment, contributes to social well-being, behaves as a good corporate citizen.

And on top of all of this, business must still make a profit.

Research is telling us that leadership must change...

The Adam Smith model of work and leadership is dead. No longer are employees just a 'factor of production'. No longer is a military-type 'command and control' style acceptable. No longer can the lone, charismatic 'person at the top' provide all the answers and direction.

But paradigms, or mental models, don't change quickly. For example, our computer keyboards still utilise a layout (QWERTY) designed over 125 years ago to slow down typing speed so as not to jam the typewriter mechanisms. We're a bit like a prisoner in a pitch dark cell. We cling onto the bars, peering obsessively at a faint glimmer of light, failing to inspect and explore the rest of the cell, not knowing that the door is open, and that by letting go we will be free. Paradigms are like that.

Hannibal's Secret

We need a brand new mental model of leadership. One that can respond to the ways in which society, customers, employees, processes, technology and doing the work of the business asks for nothing less than mobilising the whole person: their heads, their hearts and their hands.

The Whole Person

The two stories told at the beginning of this chapter perhaps offer clues.

How do we manage the change? Can we learn Hannibals' secret? He managed to move 30 000 men and 40 elephants from Spain across the Pyrenees and Alps into Italy, where his force stayed for 15 years, destroying over 400 Roman towns and villages. Is there a way in which we can lead our followers to meet the challenge, without destroying towns?

We believe that head, heart and hands competencies will make the difference:

Refer to chapter 23 Head, Heart and Hands Leadership for a more detailed discussion and for more stories. This model embraces the best of all the Leadership theories available to us.

About Elephants and Matriarchs

"Go to the ant thou sluggard…consider his ways and be wise".[5] Just as ants can teach us so can elephants. Elephants are hugely dependent on water for their well-being and survival. They drink up to 270 litres a day to help digestion. They spray it over themselves for cooling purposes and to get rid of unwanted parasites, and enjoy frolicking in water.

Some research indicates that in days gone by they were water creatures. They swim well and their lungs and kidneys develop in a similar way to many aquatic animals. When rain falls they hear it a long way off and go there. They are able to sense sub-surface deposits of water.

Matriarchs lead. These female leaders keep the family together, and make sure they are protected and have water always. They remember where water is to be found, for dozens of years and navigate and guide their community when there is drought. They use head (memory, intuition), heart (caring, nurturing) and hands (practical action), to ensure well-being, sustainability and the growth of their herd.

Perhaps we should consider the way of the elephant and of Ganesh, the wise elephant god in Hindu mythology. There is a story about Ganesh's leadership ability in Chapter 23.

---

[1] De Saint Exupery, Antoine. *The Little Prince*, NTC/Contemporary Co, 2000.

[2] Toffler, Alvin. *Future Shock*, Random House, NY, 1970.

[3] Toffler, Alvin. *Third Wave*, Bantam, NY, 1982.

[4] Deutschman, Alan. *Change or Die*, Fast Company New York. Issue 94, May 2005. ©2007 Mansueto Ventures LLC.

[5] Proverbs 6 : 6.

Chapter 4

Many Selves: Work as Love, Work as Service

Throw yourself like seed as you walk, and into your own field,
Don't turn your face for that would be to turn it to death,
And do not let the past weigh down your motion.

Leave what's alive in the furrow, what's dead in yourself,
For life does not move in the same way as a group of clouds;
From your work you will be able one day to gather yourself [1]

Miguel de Unamuno

Who Comes to Work?

A man visited his ancient grandfather in a rural village. One morning he watched the old man draw up water from the well hand over fist, the bucket attached to a rope.

He approached him. "Grandfather, I can devise a pulley which I'll suspend over the well. All you have to do is turn your wrist and the bucket of water will rise to the surface".

The old man thought a while then declined. "I don't think so. For then only my wrist will get exercise. My body will be left out of the work".

The young man went away shaking his head.

(For another version of the story see the Afterword)

The joy of stories is that they are alive and moving. In English, the word 'motion' hides inside the word 'emotion'. One way of moving a story is to continue it. We can add our own ending to them. We don't always need to stop the story at the point of conflict or irresolution. We can carry on to resolution or acceptance. Or in agreement to disagree. This is how story literacy operates.

In A *Ritual to Read to Each Other*, poet William Stafford reminds us, "It is important that awake people be awake".[2] Often we can bring only a part of us to work – the executive self, the efficient self. The money-earning self. While this might bring focus, it also can bring inattention.

Perhaps we need to see ourselves not as a single personality, but as characters in a story – a number of different selves in conversation. We carry aspects of both the grandfather and the grandson. We are also the well, the bucket and the water. The more selves I bring to work, the more present I am.

> *One day an earthquake shook the Zen temple. Parts of it collapsed. The monks were terrified.*
>
> *When the earthquake stopped the teacher said, "Now you have had the opportunity to see how a Zen man behaves in a crisis situation. You may have noticed that I did not panic. I was quite aware of what was happening and what to do. I led you all to the kitchen, the strongest part of the temple. It was a good decision, because you see we have all survived without any injuries. However, despite my self-control and composure, I did feel a little bit tense – which you may have deduced from my drinking a large glass of water, something I never do under ordinary circumstances".*
>
> *One of the monks smiled, but didn't say anything.*
>
> *"What are you laughing at?" asked the teacher.*
>
> *"That wasn't water," the monk replied, "you drank a glass of soy sauce".*

Stories engage all of us. Which means being present. What poet D. H. Lawrence said of thought, might well apply to story. "Thought is a man in his wholeness wholly attending".[3]

QUESTIONS FOR REFLECTION

Three workshop responses to the well story:

"What was the grandson's value system? Was the grandson genuinely interested in relieving the old man's burden? Or did he think that he was releasing his grandfather from physical labour and freeing up his time for other work – upgrading him to 'thought' labour?"

"I spend so much time stuck in an office chair. Apart from muscle work, how can we engage with our work? How can our bodies be present at work while we benefit from technical innovation?"

"What if the grandson had devised a gadget that assisted the old man, while honouring the connection to his body?"

Work and Love

The stressed executive is legion. The one who has a wage packet that turns many gadgets and opens many doors in life outside the office. Yet such a one has fallen out of love with his work. The traditional male greeting is, "What line of work are you in?" not "What line of love are you in?" The word 'love' is often absent from our work conversation. That's why we so like what is printed on the Primi Piatti restaurant staff overalls: "Work is love made visible"[4] (a Kahlil Gibran quotation).

There are many stories in which love and work are seen as opposing forces. Men leave the women at the hearth. Or vice versa. Or either leave children there. Work is divided into hierarchy. Unpaid work (such as cleaning the hearth and raising children) is seen to be at a lower level than salaried work, which is given more credibility. Two modes of desire in contest.

Freud believed that the purpose of psychoanalysis was to resolve this love-work conflict. If we separate these two forces, then work can become a means to an end – climbing the ladder, a digital bottom line. Martin Luther King Jnr reminds us that the end does not justify the means for the end is pre-existent in the means.[5]

Building the Work Community

Alfred Adler, one of the 'fathers' of psychoanalysis, saw the need to create community as one of our basic drives. The first community is bringing our own selves to work. When we do this, we begin to read work as a story. We become like the storyteller in Frank Delaney's *Ireland* who grows "larger in his chair as the black cloak swelled to the size of a conjurer's cloak and all the characters in the story sprang from its folds".[6]

This allows in love dressed for work. Our usefulness increases and as Carl Jung reminds us, "a person of genius is primarily a person of supreme usefulness".[7] The Romans believed in the idea of a genius. The genius, a personal spirit, arrived at birth. And it carried a person's full potential. How often do we see our work colleagues in this way?

Poet Rita Dove offers insight into the word 'genius':

> The genius was considered a birthright but it had to be nourished in order to survive... the ancient Roman was expected to make a birthday sacrifice to his or her genius. If one served one's genius well during life, the genius became a *lars*, or household god, after one's death. If one neglected one's potential, the genius became a spook, a troublesome spirit who plagued the living. [8]

As we begin to adopt such a fuller story, we dig the furrow, plant the seed and gather ourselves. And the harvest is richer.

Service Work

Here is a perspective on customer service:

> *A salesperson is trying to sell a television to a chief in an African village. The chief has an official storyteller in his tribe.*

> *"Chief, my television knows plenty of stories. This television knows more stories than your storyteller".*
>
> *The chief responds, "Yes, it is true that your television might know more stories than my storyteller. But my storyteller knows me".*

Basically, customer service value propositions consist of:

- *the rational* – the hard task, process, equipment, material, tangible aspects

- *the emotional* – those far more important soft interpersonal, emotional, relating aspects of interactions and transactions: people-things like empathy, responsiveness, assurance.

Together, the rational and emotional make up the customer experience.

Most firms get their balance wrong. Employee development and engagement must major in providing the emotional aspects of customer service. This is what the leading service providers do. This is what customers want.

Here is a classic customer service research story:

> *Library personnel offered library users the lowest possible human interaction (no acknowledgement, no greeting, no eye-contact, no smile). Upon leaving the library, users rated service as poor: citing bad lighting, inefficient cataloguing and numbering.*
>
> *When librarians interacted with users with warmth (the only factor that changed), upon exiting, users rated the customer service as good – this time citing good lighting, convenient cataloguing and numbering.*

Unconscious emotional responses formed and conditioned their perceptions of service and in particular the material, physical aspects. This highlights the value of emotional competence as a key service delivery aspect.

In the myth of *Tristan and Iseulde*:

> *After fighting a great battle, wielding his sword with valour, the mortally wounded Tristan is laid in a small boat. There is no sail. No oars. He has only his harp for comfort. He drifts from close to King Arthur's Tintagel across the Irish Sea. Irish fishermen hear his harp's soft melodies and he is rescued, healed.*[9]

The sword represents one half of our human nature. The rational, decisive, powerful, efficient. The harp represents the values of relating, nurturing, empathising, feeling, affirming. The yin and yang in balance.

So too with effective customer service delivery. If the balance is lost, we get into trouble. Tristan lets his heart rule completely. He and the King's bride to be, Iseulde, drink of the love potion meant for the King. They fall deeply in love and big trouble follows.

In effective service delivery our emotional interactions must be supported and balanced by sound, slick business processes, the right physical environment and appropriate enabling technology.

One of us tells this story:

> *I had only one hour to spare between the end of a conference at the Ritz Carlton Hotel in Atlanta and leaving for the airport. I was keen to buy a saxophone. I mentioned this to the receptionist at lunch time. By the close of the conference she had organized my checkout, arranged for three music stores to remain open in case I called, given me clear directions, and arranged transport.*

> *Not only did she go the extra mile to facilitate my purchase, I'm sure that my details on their database will elicit a follow-up inquiry the next time I stay there. And I will. I changed from being just another customer to an advocate, someone who champions their cause, recommends them to others whenever possible.*

In all work, especially service work, "There must be more to life than to be a cog in someone else's great machine, hurtling God knows where".[10] (Charles Handy).

Inside Out

> *A rabbi gave away a ring to a passing beggar. A friend who witnessed this transaction asked the rabbi, "Do you know how much that ring is worth? I saw one like it in a shop window for 2000 Talents".*

> *The rabbi chased after the beggar and stopped him in the street. "My good man, the ring I gave is worth 2000 Talents. Now, don't you sell it for anything less".*

Ultimately we must be aware that a true service ethic comes from within, and that some introspection is necessary. It's a two-pronged process of doing and being. Like the Roman God, Janus, we must look in two directions at the same time: search for meaning both 'out there' and 'in here'.

To continue in a direct service role when this is really 'not you' becomes debilitating and mentally exhausting. Oriah Mountain Dreamer's probing question is relevant here: "What sustains you from the inside when all else falls away?"[11] What is your primary motivational thrust, your source of significance and self worth? Is it dependent on adoration, recognition, role, possessions, a relationship, reward? Or have you moved beyond prosperity, status and power to servant-hood as a path to meaning? Are you uniquely designed with giftedness in the area of service – giving – caring?

Customers intuitively know the difference between real and false. We cannot pretend to be interested, to empathise, to be service-oriented. Indeed, when giving service, we're far more likely to suffer stress and even burnout if we mask feelings and are incongruent. So the sooner our behaviours match right motive, values and attitude, the better. As a start point it's important to become aware of this, and also to see that, although customer service is not something new, it does carry the seeds of higher meaning in our service endeavours. And to want to embark on the service journey, and to have a plan for reaching the 'destination': achieving meaning through service.

Some final suggestions for searchers:

> "Nothing gets fixed until we choose to fix ourselves".[12]

> "Learn your theories as well as you can, but put them aside when you touch the

miracle of the living soul. Not theories but your own creative individuality alone must decide".[13]

And finally:

"Work is not primarily a thing one does to live, but the thing one lives to do".[14]

For a continuation of the discussion and for more stories, refer to Chapter 26 Meaningful Work.

[1] De Unamuno, Miguel. "Throw yourself like seed", Bly Robert, et al, *The Rag and Bone shop of the Heart*, Harper Collins, 1992.
[2] Stafford, William. "A Ritual to Read to Each Other", Bly Robert, et al, *The Rag and Bone shop of the Heart*, Harper Collins, 1992.
[3] Lawrence, D. H. *Selected Poems*, Penguin, 1989.
[4] Gibran, Kahlil. *The Prophet*, Alfred Knopf, NY, 1923.
[5] King, Martin Luther Jnr. *A Testament of Hope*, Harper Collins, 1990.
[6] Delaney, Frank. *Ireland*, Time Warner Books, London, 2004.
[7] Jung, Carl. *Psychological Reflections*, Pantheon Books, NY, 1953.
[8] Dove, Rita. "To Make a Prairie", *The Writer*, Boston, Jan., 1995.
[9] Bedier, J. *Romance of Tristan and Iseult*, Dover, NY, 2005.
[10] Handy, Charles. *The Empty Raincoat*, Arrow Books, 1994.
[11] Mountain Dreamer, Oriah, *The Invitation*, Thorsons, NY, 1999.
[12] Lundin, Stephen C., John Christensen and Harry Paul. *Fish! Tales*, Hodder & Stoughton, London, 2002.
[13] Jung, Carl. *Psychological Reflections*, Pantheon books, 1953.
[14] Engstrom, Ted W. and Mackenzie, Alec *Managing Your Time*, quoting Sayers, Dorothy, *Creed or Chaos?*, Zondervan, 1967.

Chapter 5
Story Circles

"The beginning and the end are one" - Heraclitus

Story is being deliberately and increasingly used in organisations

Story is a wonderful means of gathering information about facts and feelings. Far more areas of the brain are activated when a story is told, compared to the sharing of data or information. As psychologist Pamela Rutledge eloquently explains, *"Stories are about collaboration and connection. They transcend generations, they engage us through emotions, and they connect us to others. Through stories we share passions, sadness, hardships and joys. We share meaning and purpose. Stories are the common ground that allows people to communicate, overcoming our defences and our differences. Stories allow us to understand ourselves better and to find our commonality with others. Stories are how we think. They are how we make meaning of life".*[1]

Small wonder then that business is rediscovering the power of story-telling and story listening. Allowing the right and left brain team to get cracking.

Story circles have a long history

Throughout the ages there have been attempts to capture this power. Since we first gazed at the sun and moon, man has found meaning in circles. Inner circles and the family circle, punk imagery, the Buddhist wheel of life, eternity rings, the Celtic cross the Taoist yin-yang, a Hindu mandala, prayer circles, halos, nooses. In circles we see infinity, cycles, a container, the eternal, unity. And we have always gathered in circles to make sense of life:

- In First Nation's culture, *"Whoever holds the talking stick has within his hands the sacred power of words".* (Carol Locust, Ph.D. Native American Research and Training Center, Tucson, Arizona)

- A special table in King Arthur's Camelot was round instead of rectangular. This meant that everyone who sat around it was seen as an equal. (The word democracy means people + purpose).

- In very early 17th century French salons people from all walks of life, men and women, gathered to carry out the art of conversation (telling, listening, questioning). Pioneer Madame de Rambouillet, *"showed what it meant to be sociable in the most refined way....provided one knew how to take part in a conversation".*[2]

- On assuming leadership of the Zulus, Shaka instituted a new tradition called *Ukuxoxa impi* (talking about battles). Round a fire, each warrior would tell about momentous situations and outcomes during battles. A principle of ubuntu is that everyone has equal worth, has an equal say.

More recently (in the 1990s) we've seen the advent of Café Table Conversations: *"The World Café creates a space for collaborative inquiry in which participants continually exchange knowledge, discover shared meaning, access collective intelligence, generate new knowledge, deepen trust, and experience new levels of creativity that are energizing and exciting.*

The entire experience fosters a strong sense of shared commitment and ownership of the outcomes of the process". [3] People are seated informally, café-style – to look into a concern or challenge facing their community or organization. After a certain time of conversing, sharing, recording, they change tables. Ideas and insights are carried to the next table. Finally a 'plenary session' pulls together actions that have emerged during the process.

A modern process

And new ways of using story to gain an understanding of underlying reasons, opinions, and motivations, to make sense of issues in a coherent manner, to provide insights into problems, to help to develop ideas, to gather strategic knowledge, to support qualitative research, are emerging. In his wonderful book about story, *The Circle of the 9 Muses,* David Hutchens refers to the Art of Hosting a story circle.[4]

In simple terms, the process involves having a clear intention, majoring on listening and sharing (of experiences, values, feelings – not opinions and judgements) in a safe place of trust, and having a minimum of rules or guidelines.

David: *"The Rule of Two Feet. My colleague Graham Williams uses this, and it is a recurring principle of Art of Hosting methodologies. The rule of two feet is a dramatic statement that says, 'You don't have to be here. Your presence is an act of free will, and we want this event to include people who want to be a part of it. At any point, if you feel like there is more value to be found elsewhere, you're welcome to leave'. What a bold statement! And yet, it establishes an enormous amount of trust, neutralizes any feeling of coercion, and increases the commitment in the room: Simply by remaining present, the participants are testifying to the relevance of the event".*

He continues: *"When you say, 'Tell me about a time', you move people's awareness to a linear, time-based continuum which is exactly where stories live. This prompt is historical and encourages people to scan over the timelines of their experiences for a specific event and the cascade of events that followed. Notice how the language in these examples reinforces that we are looking for a specific event:*

> *Tell me about a time you were proud that you made a difference for a customer.*

> *Tell me about a time when a team failed because people couldn't let go of their old ways of thinking. What happened?*

> *Tell me about a time when you felt you were being truly vulnerable as a leader. What happened?"*

The Danish organisational story catcher Toke Paludan Møller says that when true listening takes place *"then the collective story surfaces. It is unstoppable. So even though people come into the room with consciousness fragmented, when listening arises, the story being told reconnects us to the collective".*[5]

After the event, the context, logic and emotion inherent in the stories that are shared, are analysed in order to make sense of the issue. The outcome or finding is carried into an intervention

Types of Story Circle

There are a growing number of powerful narrative inquiry methodologies for groups. We like using:

- Anecdote Circles. Anecdote.com.au have produced what is in our opinion the best guide to hosting an anecdote circle, usually of peers, in order to gather information, conduct research – either internally or with customers.[6] Recently, we used this methodology to steer the way an international Fast Moving Consumer Goods company gleaned from the staff ways forward in their pursuit of sustainability.

- Storyboarding.[7] The River Set is a flexible tool, enabling work from a single card depicting a section of a river, to continuums of cards – with different continuums representing the complete river: past and future, real and imagined. Participants (individuals or groups) construct a common narrative of their history, envisaged future, obstacles they might face on the way. The River set is produced by Gali Salpeter an Israeli storyteller, drama and narrative therapist. In The *Virtuosa Organisation* we tell of the use of this tool to develop a vision and change programme for embracing a culture change in a company using vales and virtues as the basis of their being and doing.[8]

- Metaphor elicitation. Using the story circle format, we've been able to unearth deep feelings usually not easily expressed, to get to grips with dysfunctional dynamics in departments of organisations. *The Zaltmans tell the story of Oticon (who sell hearing aids internationally as part of their product range). This was a market where 80% of the hearing impaired (a huge untapped market) refused aids, citing cost and inconvenience reasons. Metaphor elicitation showed that the real reasons were being seen as being flawed or decrepit not socially acceptable – 'as glaring as a large, bright red neon sign'. As a result Oticon's new devices were smaller, with a high-tech look – and their highly successful advertising switched to containing metaphors of freedom, transformation from imprisonment to normality, and attractiveness. For example a state of the art hearing aid flying out of a cage - the messages being 'set yourself free' and 'nothing should hold you captive, not even hearing loss'.[9]* Metaphor elicitation is a reminder that "*Words and pictures are yin and yang, married they produce a progeny more interesting than either parent*". (Dr Seuss). In addition to metaphor we've used archetypes to describe product and consumer-group attributes as part of a Branding intervention designed to move a company away from seeing their products as the heroes of their advertising and public relations stories – with the accompanying rhetoric - and towards dialogue and stronger emotional connection.

We hope that this overview of story circles shows that organisational leaders have at their disposal some wonderful means to engage their people, customers and suppliers in deep, meaningful sharing – in a natural, authentic way.

Rumi the Sufi poet told the ancient story of an elephant and blind men. Each man felt a different part. To one a leg was assumed to be a pillar, the tail felt like rope, and ears like a huge fan. Yet another thought the elephant's trunk was a branch of a tree ..... Each one was right in their own way but only by putting their different views together could the complete picture be seen.

---

[1] Rutledge, Pamela Brown PH.D., M.B.A *The Psychological Power of Storytelling* Published on January 16, 2011 by in http://www.psychologytoday.com/blog/positively-media

[2] Zeldin, Theodore *An Intimate History of Humanity* Vintage 1994

[3] A World Café Hosting Guide http://www.empowermentinstitute.net/lcd/lcd files/WorldCafeHostingGuide.pdf

[4] Hutchens, David *Circle of the 9 Muses: A Storytelling Field Guide for Innovators and Meaning Makers*
John Wiley & Sons, Inc., Hoboken, New Jersey 2015

[5] Baldwin, Christina *Storycatcher: making sense of our lives through the power and practice of story* New World Library Novato, California 2005

[6] Anecdote (Callahan, Shawn; Rixon, Andrew & Schenk, Mark) *The Ultimate Guide to Anecdote Circles: a practical guide to facilitating storytelling and story listening* www.anecdote.com.au

[7] Salpeter, Gali *The River Guide Book* www.storyandtherapy.com 2011

[8] Williams, Graham; Haarhoff, Dorian & Fox, Peter *The Virtuosa Organisation: the importance of virtues for a successful business* Knowledge Resources 2015

[9] Zaltman, Gerald and Lindsay *Marketing Metaphoria* Harvard Business Press, Boston. 2008

Section B
Kindling the Flame: Thirteen Ways Stories Work

The stories people tell have a way of taking care of them. If stories come to you, care for them. And learn to give them away where they are needed. Sometimes a person needs a story more than food to stay alive [1]

Barry Lopez

In this section we offer thirteen interconnected ways of opening our understanding to stories, their patterns, their power. This section provides a guide through work-land, mounted on the steed or the dragon of story.

But we need to choose that horse or dragon carefully and learn how to ride it.

Stories can trap us or help break us out of the self-constructed prisons of time, perception, rivalry, performance and habit. If used with wisdom, they create "trialogues" rather then merely dialogues. There is you, me and the story as an enriching third point of reference. Stories direct us to vast untapped resources within the company. Stories bring life to business people. In a lot of ways they promote self-help, rekindle the flame.

Hidden stories can sabotage us while stories made conscious can rekindle our ability to visualize and vitalize. Stories give birth to new realities. When we make stories conscious, and attend to the language we use (for stories move beyond business speak), they open up choices, offer growth and facilitate transformation. They offer us a universal form of communication. Stories offer us vocabulary to read the wheel of fortune when it spins our way and a context to place blame, failure and dark days.

James Hillman's interest in story, "is as something lived in and lived through, a way in which the soul finds its life".[2] Our intention is to introduce you to such stories and the process involved as we contemplate them. We illustrate the use of story in key business processes such as vision, purpose, virtues, values, effective coaching, focus, spiritual mindfulness, transition, teamwork, achieving customer service excellence, gaining the right information and knowledge in order to stimulate world class performance harness the richness of diversity. Leaders and workers, how to manage time, money, energy, people, technology, processes, their own beliefs, thoughts, emotions and actions.

Stories are never static, always dynamic. Stories retold are like a river, for you are in a different river each time you step into it. Buddhist author, Thich Nhat Hanh, makes the point in his *Going Home,* that our notions cannot ever become permanent, fanatical standpoints – "You know that three years ago you had a notion of the Buddha, and now after three years of practice you have another one".[3]

As the song says: "When we were small and Christmas trees were tall", then "Now we are tall and Christmas trees are small".

The Section also explores how stories assist with time management and supply the energy needed for success. We offer insights into how stories operate in mentoring, coaching and counselling and clarify the differences between these three modes.

---

[1]   Lopez, Barry. *Crow and Weasel,* North Point Press, NY, 1990.

[2]   Hillman, James. "A Note on Story", *Reclaiming the Inner Child,* Jeremiah Abrams (ed.), Tarcher, NY, 1990.

[3]   Hanh, Thich Nhat. *Going Home: Bringing Christ and the Buddha together in Daily Life,* Rider, Riverhead Books, Penguin Putnam Inc, NY, 1999.

Chapter 6

Myths: Minor and Major

*I took it upon myself to get to know my myth, and
I regarded this as the task of tasks...
I simply had to know what unconscious or
preconscious myth was forming me* [1]

Carl Jung

World Views

*An anthropologist, stalking through the forest in India, comes across an ancient
sage dancing in a clearing. He stops and watches from behind a tree. The old woman
strokes a tree then bathes herself in moonlight. Unable to contain his curiosity, the
anthropologist steps from his cover and with a puzzled look on his brow asks.*

*"Pardon me, old woman, but what are you doing alone in the forest?" With an even
more puzzled look the sage replies, "Pardon me young man, what makes you think I'm
alone?"*

Ken Wilber in his book, *No Boundary,* reminds us that every time we draw a boundary
between us and other people or forms of life, we create a potential battle line.[2] For the
anthropologist, human beings are inside the circle of belonging and relationship, while
nature and the planets are outside. For the old woman, all is animate and included in
the circle of belonging. Her circle is wider, her paradigm more embracing.

Hidden Stories

Carl Jung once asked himself, "What is the myth I am living?" He found he could not
answer the question. Jung implies that people unconsciously live out myths (*mythos*

35

= large story/belief system) that influence their behaviour. The age into which we are born, the culture we live in, the economic climate, the state, parents, teachers, religious authorities, corporate giants, advertising campaigns tell us who we are. We live out the stories they have prescribed for us – what our role is – what our culture has proclaimed about leadership, race, gender, social standing, office rank. In many cases these providers of our myths have never explored or made conscious their own myths inherited from previous generations.

A myth is a formative story. Like the movie screen it can be larger than life. A legendary narrative, usually of gods and heroes, or a theme that expresses the ideology and world view of a culture. A guiding story. It contains elements of fiction.

Sometimes we are aware of that large story. More often, it is an imposed story that involves hidden belief or an unconscious drive that influences choices and behaviour. Myths drive companies as they do individuals.

A man employs a younger woman. They take on the role of father and rebellious daughter. How did he end up in such situation? The hidden unprocessed story might well be that in his parents' marriage, an age difference dictated that roles in that marriage would involve the themes of fathering and rebellion.

Making Stories Conscious

A young girl asks her father, "Is it true, that when we are asleep, we can wake up?"

Her father responds, "Of course it is".

"Then," says the girl, "it must also be true that when we are awake, we can wake up more".

(See chapter 17 for another application of this story).

Teacher trainers often observe that once they are in the classroom, student teachers revert to the way they have been taught. In most cases this was a repeat of an outmoded authoritarian pontificating. They became tin pot dictators. Often when we overreact to a situation, the roots of that reaction are in the unprocessed past. Perhaps this is what T. S. Eliot, the poet, means when he writes, "Every moment is a new and shocking revelation of all we have been".[3]

So the first thing these students needed to do was to tell the story of their own learning – the formative years. Once they had raised this story by its hair from the murky waters, they were able to process it. Select. Discard. Innovate. Many of them began to teach in a new way.

Another way out of this dilemma is to exchange minor myths for major ones.

Minor Myths

The word, 'myth' is problematic in that we use the same term for two entirely different concepts.

When somebody proclaims, "Our way of doing business is superior" or "Men are better than women at business" or "This is the way we do things in this Company", "Big is beautiful", "Technology will save us", they are indulging in minor myth making.

In this sense, a myth is a prejudiced belief, a superstition, a group lie. It operates through inclusion and exclusion. I'm in. You're out. I draw a boundary around my group at the expense of another group. Such myths work 'top down'. They consolidate the tribe, whatever the CEO thinks the tribe to be. This kind of mythology can dominate a company. It declares who are the chosen people. Corporate examples of living somebody else's story abound. Stress can be defined as living somebody else's story.

Two South Africans, writer Ezekiel Mphahlele, and psychologist Chabani Manganyi, in conversation in the early eighties, argued that we see each other through keyholes.[4] They were referring to the strategies of the apartheid state, which locked doors between people and denied them access to each other's experience. The business world, inheriting such a legacy, can operate in a similar way.

In this sense minor myths constitute an ideology. They deal with answers, not with questions, and uncertainty. Linguist Terry Eagleton argues that, "Ideology is a kind of contemporary mythology, a realm that has purged itself of ambiguity and alternative possibility".[5] In minor mythology there is no room for alternative paths to understanding. No room for explanations that we have not thought of, for minor myths presume that everything is knowable. They're a bit like the personal 'belief bubbles' and limiting beliefs described in another chapter.

If we have not processed such minor myths, then they live us instead of us living them. In our professional and personal lives the unconscious, hidden stories drive us. We knee-jerk our way, not responding but reacting to previous stories. Once we have raised the company myth to consciousness, we are in a better position to choose what kind of myth we want to live by.

Major Myths

There are many myths – some of them more than five hundred years old – about Anansi, the spider, a folk hero among the Ashanti of West Africa:

> *Anansi has six sons, each named after a special gift. One day, off on an adventure, he falls into a river and is swallowed by a fish. The first son, See Trouble, detects that his father is in danger. Then Road Builder cries, "Follow me" and leads his brothers to their father. River Drinker sucks up the river, while Game Skinner splits open the fish. More trouble arrives. A falcon swoops down and takes Anansi into the sky. The brothers call to Stone Thrower, "Hurry". Stone Thrower knocks his father out of the falcon's claws. The last son, Cushion, provides his father with a soft fall.*
>
> *That night Anansi finds a great globe of light shining through the trees. In consultation with the God of All Things, he rewards his six sons with the gift of the moon. None will possess it, but they all will enjoy it.*

Myths such as this are major myths. Creation myths are in the same category. One of the Owambo myths from Namibia is that people originated out of a tree stump. Australian aborigines believe the ancestors created themselves from clay and climbed out of the earth. Other cultures cherish beliefs about the ancestors and the after life.

Many Greek myths deal with the lives of the gods. Some of them, such as the story of Demeter and Persephone, explain how it is that we have spring and winter. Plato in his *The Symposium* tells a story of how the sexes came to be. In its simplified form:

> *Once there was a creature with both sets of genitals. The gods feared this creature so one suggested that it be split in two. The two halves would be so busy finding each other they would no longer be a threat to the gods.*[6]

We are in the realm of major mythology. Major myths deal with the cosmic questions that surround the human journey at the beginning of the twenty first century – questions about origins, identity, passage and endings. In admitting that so much is unknowable, these myths stress our common heritage as beings who all suffer, deal with evil (our own and other people's) and death.

Another African myth tells how death came into the world:

> *God sent the chameleon with a message, "Tell people they can live forever". But the chameleon was so slow. God got angry and sent a snake with another message. "Tell people they have to die". The snake got to us first.*

We are all included in these stories for major myths widen the circle of belonging.

The old woman in the forest story has a wider ecological view of how things are related and connected. She belongs to a network of relationships. We could say she has a more developed Mythological IQ. Were she the CEO of a company, she would understand that when we do business, the physical, social and ethical environments are involved. Her bottom line would be more encompassing than that of the anthropologist.

We could say she has been born again. A second birth involves taking charge of the hidden story, and working with principles of inclusion, transparency and vision. She would tune the company's daily business so that it resonates with the larger local and global story.

Anansi the CEO

The Anansi spider story also offers insights into a new way of doing business.

The Ashanti were and still are skilled artisans working in metal and fabric. They weave significant symbols such as the sun, moon, the web of the cosmos and Anansi the spinner, into their art. Were their creation Anansi a CEO, he would know the gifts of his employees, name them and call them into being. And in times of trouble they would move and act – deftly and with sureness and determination.

Joseph Campbell in *Pathways to Bliss*, says, "Your bliss can guide you to that transcendent mystery, because bliss is the welling up of the energy of the transcendent wisdom within you. So when the bliss cuts off, you know that you've cut off the welling up; try to find it again. And that will be your Hermes guide, the dog that can follow the invisible trail for you. And that's the way it is. One works out one's own myth that way".[7]

Major myths open us to the spider web of connections that enhance the work we do.

---

[1] Jung, Carl. Quoted in Keen, Sam and Fox, Anne Valley. *Your Mythic Journey*, Tarcher, NY, 1989.

2 Wilber, Ken. *No Boundary, Eastern and Western Approaches to Personal Growth,* Shambhala, Berkeley, 1979.
3 Eliot T. S. *Four Quartets,* Harcourt, 1968.
4 Manganyi, Chabani. *Looking Through the Keyhole*, Ravan, Johannesburg, 1981.
5 Eagleton, Terry. *Literary Theory*, Blackwell, 1983.
6 Plato. *The Symposium*, Penguin, London, 2003.
7 Campbell, Joseph. *Pathways to Bliss,* New World Library, Novato, California, 2004.

Chapter 7

Archetypes: Gods and Office Giants

The first original model of which all other
similar persons, objects, or concepts are merely
derivative, copied, patterned, or emulated [1]
Carl Jung

Live in the nowhere that you come from,
Even though you have an address here [2]
Rumi

An Alphabet of Archetypes

Masilo's Adventures by Bob Leshoai is an African fairy tale with certain *Jack and the Beanstalk* parallels.

> *Young Masilo leaves the poverty of the village and sets out to find what is at the end of the rainbow. En route he carries an old woman across three different rivers and she rewards him with three stones to use when he is in trouble. At the end of the rainbow he finds a cave lined with gold. He encounters the Ogre and his wife.*
>
> *The Ogre wishes to eat him, but Mrs. Giant helps him escape. Running away, he's able to use the three stones to create three obstacles between him and the pursuing giant – a huge tree, a mountain, and a river. The Giant chops down the tree, digs through the mountain, but drowns in the river. Masilo returns to the village in triumph and the villagers fetch Mrs. Giant who brings with her the wealth of the cave.* [3]

In this story we have a hero, an old magical woman, a malevolent giant and his benevolent wife. These are archetypal figures. Here is a list of some of these energies that inhabit human beings:

ADDICT ADVOCATE ALCHEMIST ANGEL ARTIST ATHLETE AVENGER BULLY BEGGAR CHILD CLOWN COMPANION CRONE DETECTIVE ENGINEER FATHER FEMME-FATAL FOOL GAMBLER GARDENER GOD GODDESS GUIDE HEALER HEDONIST HERO/INE JUDGE KING KNIGHT LEADER LOVER MARTYR MAGICIAN MOTHER MYSTIC NETWORKER MENTOR MEDIATOR MESSIAH MISER MONK/NUN NYMPH PERFECTIONIST PIONEER PIRATE PRIEST/ESS PRINCE/SS PROSTITUTE QUEEN REBEL RESCUER SCRIBE SEEKER SERVANT SLAVE STORY-TELLER STUDENT THINKER THIEF TRICKSTER TRAVELLER VAMPIRE VICTIM VIRGIN WARRIOR

As you run your eye across this list, you might become aware of certain Greek or Roman gods, mythical figures, literary characters, historical persons, newspaper celebrities, entertainers, film stars, co-workers and people you meet in your private life. Names might come to mind – Aphrodite, King Arthur, Midas, Macbeth, Nasrudin, Florence Nightingale, Elvis Presley, Joe in customer service, the beggar on the street corner. Some of these figures have featured in the stories in this book.

Archetypes can be viewed as aids to explaining and understanding our own and other people's nature and behaviours. They are innate, imprinted drivers within each of us and our self-development role is to filter, appropriate, steer those already-present drivers to best effect.

Each archetype has a dark side and a light side – so for example, the King can be a tyrannical ruler or a servant of his people, the Mother can be a smotherer or a nurturer. Each archetype may be comprised of sub-types, so for example, the child may be an orphan, a wounded or neglected child, or playful and happy.

In general terms, although men have a female side to them, and vice versa (Yin and Yang) the male needs to develop a balance of King, Warrior, Magician, Lover and the female needs to be Goddess, Nymph, Mother and Crone. The Warrior in us achieves actualization when he lays down his sword, the Nymph actualizes when love of power is surpassed by the power of love. Archetypes can also apply to situations, states of mind and climate.

BUSINESS TYPES – RESEARCH FINDINGS

DARK ENERGIES IN THE WORKPLACE

Dramatic, grandiose, charismatic, publicity-seeking, narcissistic

Suspicious of outside forces, competition, people, and fanatical about analyses studies, information processing

Detached, cool, inwardly focused, reclusive

Depressive, formal, bureaucratic and hierarchical, inflexible

Compulsive need to be in control of others and events at all times, obsessively thorough, manipulative

In business we also desperately need the wisdom and creativity of the crone and the magician, the determination and perseverance of the warrior, the caring of the mother, the coaching, guiding, supporting skill of the Gaelic *Anamchara* (a word meaning soul-friend).

We need also be aware that leaders are human. They have feet of clay. In *The Leadership Mystique*, Manfred Kets De Vries outlines how different leadership styles (forms of archetypes) can be successful, but can also lead to failure in organizations if applied in excess and if they become neuroses or pathologies.[4]

"Fish start to smell at the head".

You might also become aware of the energies that operate in your life. If you were to ring three from the archetype list, which would they be? There is a connection between how I live my life and conduct business and some of these archetypes. Working with them – which are present? which are absent? – is another way of becoming conscious of the influences that shape my choices and behaviour. Where do I need more balance by developing an archetype, how do I embrace my dark side in order to lighten my approach to life, people, business?

Jung and the Archetypes

The pantheon of gods is a ready source of archetypes:

> *The gods were debating where to hide the secret of life so that human beings would not be able to find it. One god said, "Why don't we hide it underneath the mountain?"*
>
> *Another god responded, "No, human beings are clever. They will dig up the mountain and find the secret".*
>
> *"Well, how about underneath the sea?"*
>
> *"No, human beings will drain the sea and find the secret".*
>
> *Then one god said, "I have an idea. Why don't we hide the secret of life inside the human being? That is the last place they will think of looking".*

Carl Jung coined the word 'archetype' (from the Greek *archetypos* -first of its kind). He believed that humans have a collective unconscious – a distant memory common to all people irrespective of their gender, language, country, culture. This memory includes the archetypes. The collective, shared unconscious consists of "deposits of the constantly repeated experiences of humanity... a kind of readiness to reproduce over and over again the same or similar mythical ideas...".[5] From such a shared memory, concepts such as the hero and heroine arrive in human life. Archetypes transcend time, place and culture.

A movie theatre is a fine place to study archetypes, as these stars and their circumstances are projected onto a screen larger than life. Nor do they age. Actors such as Marilyn Monroe, Clark Gable. Movies depicting the siege of Troy, the Mafia or a heist. In the movie *The Motorcycle Diaries*, Che Guevara's early journey is characterized by the two friends portraying their lover and trickster archetypal energies. When Guevara swims across the river to be with his leprosy colony patients and friends, overcoming his asthma and achieving an unheard-of feat, his gesture epitomizes the warrior. At the end of the same scene, the response by the gathered crowd to his wave is the moment that he becomes recognized as servant-king.

Zorba the Greek's dance at the end of that movie is in a sense a celebration of his contentment at being a serving king who can evoke warrior, trickster and lover qualities when needed. Is Don Quixote a bumbling idiot when he tilts against windmills or a true warrior because his chosen reality 'on the inside' is what infuses his life with adventure, fun, passion and questing?

Stereotypes

A stereotype originally meant a duplicate impression of an original typographical element.

> *A bored professor finds himself next to a blond on a long flight. He suggests, "Why don't we play a guessing game? We ask each other questions and if the other doesn't know, then he or she pays $5.00". "No," she says, "I want to rest. "I'll make it worth your while," insists the professor. "If you ask me a question and I don't know the answer, I'll pay you $50.00. And if I ask and you don't know, you only pay me $5.00". The woman agrees. "I'll go first. What has six legs and is green in the morning, has three legs in the afternoon and turns yellow and has one leg in the evening and turns pink?"*

> *She sits back and the professor takes out his laptop.*

> *He phones a few friends on the card phone. Hours later he wakes her up and admits, "I don't know". He hands her a crisp $50.00 note. "What is the answer?" he asks. The blond takes five dollar note from her purse and hands it to him.*

Jokes often work on stereotypes. A stereotype is a generalization, a simplification about a person or group of persons. Based on gender, class, race, nationality, sexual orientation or social background. They are often a generalization used in a prejudicial sense to justify discrimination against a particular group of people.

The instantly recognisable nature of stereotypes mean that they are useful in advertising and sitcom. Yet when we see our colleagues as stereotypes, we are seeing them as stock characters in a soap opera.

Archetypes are not stereotypes. A stereotype involves a stuck image of somebody. An archetypes invokes a moving energy.

Who is in Charge?

> *An intellectual was pontificating in a tea house, airing his knowledge. He pronounced on any subject that came up, his thoughts running in patterns. He spoke ad infinitum of logic and reason. He showed off a book he had written, "It's in here," he declaimed.*

> *Nasrudin, who was the only other person in the tea house who could read, took the book and thumbed through it. As he turned the pages, the intellectual shouted*

out, "You're holding my book upside down, you imbecile".

Nasrudin responded, "Since it is one of the archetypes which seems to have produced you, it seems to be the only sensible thing to do, if one is to learn from this situation".

Sometimes we feel that these giants have taken over – these characters that operate in our myths. People sometimes say, "I don't know what came over me. I just went ballistic". Addiction could also perhaps be defined as being taken over by an archetype. Patterns that we are not aware of, for example our attitude around money as exchange and relationship, influences us more than we would like to admit.

We are in the realm of the gods for we can view the gods as archetypal figures. Tad Crawford writes, "When a corporate president reorganizes a company to increase profits, he or she is operating with the archetypal energy of Zeus". Hermes governs commerce – "the market research, the product design, the advertising campaign and the determination of a price change".[6]

When somebody calls a board meeting, or a round table discussion, or refers to the boss as Atilla the Hun or says, "I went as cold as ice", the archetype is evoked. Typical archetypes in business may be Apollo (logic, order, harmony), Zeus (charisma, entrepreneurial leader), Athena (teamworker, shared goals advocate), Dionysus (creative individualism).

A knowledge of Greek and Roman mythology might be a useful addition to a business school curriculum.

Carolyn Myss's *Sacred Contracts* might well be another useful addition to the boardroom bookshelf.[7] Norman Shealy, Professor of Energy Medicine, writes in the foreword, "In *Sacred Contracts* you will explore your archetypal relationships with your career, finances, use of power in general, ... creativity, relationships, death and victimization". Myss offers a comprehensive list of archetypes, their positive and shadow attributes and examples from film, fairy tale, literature, religion and myth of characters who have manifested these energies. Her entries under the King/Emperor/Ruler/ Leader/ Chief include King Lear, *The Godfather* movie, Chief Seattle, Haile Selassie, Ethiopian Emperor Priam, King of Troy.

Sometimes we feel a colleague has been caught in an impersonal force. Trapped in an archetype. A boss for example, who like Marlon Brando in *The Godfather,* is a dynamic leader, and has time for nothing but work. Born to lead, he might have conquered his way to the top. He's tough, decisive, goal-oriented. Overbearing and inflexible.

Myss suggests we make contracts with ourselves around our specific archetypal issues. There might be energies in these blue prints to be controlled or harnessed. As always, a knowledge of our deeper selves opens us to opportunities, choices and new stories.

---

[1] Jung, Carl. *Psychological Reflections*, Pantheon Books, NY, 1953.

[2] Rumi, ed. Coleman Barks, *The Essential Rumi*, Penguin, NY, 1995.

[3] Leshoai, Bob. "Masilo's Adventures" Stephen Gray, ed., *Modern South African Stories*, Donker, Johannesburg, 1983.

4 De Vries, Manfred Kets, *The Leadership Mystique*, Financial Times/Prentice Hall, Great Britain, 2001.
5 Jung, Carl. *Psychological Reflections*, Pantheon Books, NY, 1953.
6 Crawford, Tad. *The Secret Life of Money*, Allworth Press, NY, 1994.
7 Myss, Caroline. *Sacred Contracts, Awakening your Divine Potential,* Bantam Books, NY, 2002.

Chapter 8

Reading Time

I wasted time and now does time waste me[1]
Shakespeare

The Clock God

The Lilliputians believed that Gulliver's watch was his God, because he did nothing without first consulting it.[2]

In de Saint Exupery's novel, the *Little Prince* visits a minute planet.[3]

> *There is only enough room on it for a street lamp and a lamplighter. The lamplighter puts out the lamp and immediately lights it again. Puts it out. Lights it. The lamplighter laments that in the old days, in between putting out and lighting up, he had time to relax. But every year the planet spins more rapidly and there is no time.*

Most of us experience the lamplighter's plight. We have a continuing battle with:

- proper use of limited time and energy resources

- a constant tension between order and chaos in our lives

- self-control in a world where it is easy to be event-controlled or other-controlled

- feeling imprisoned by, a slave to work, meetings, deadlines, and what has been called the tyranny of the urgent.

How do we seek a good rhythm, a flow, a focus on the important and serious, and a good balance of quality leisure, social, family and work activity? In attempting to manage our lives, we can lose perspective, and put too much weighting on 'time management'.

Our suggestion is:

- don't view time management in a narrow, 'technical' sense only. We also need personal mastery of our energy levels

- make a decision to take responsibility for *our own* time and energy management. Too many of us allow others or events to dictate time – for the wrong reasons (fear of the consequences of saying no, trying to please others because of poor self-esteem)

- find ways to improve without becoming uptight.

See Appendix 2 The Tyranny of the Urgent – Managing Time and Energy. You may wish to complete the questionnaires. It gives you a 'reading' on your personal time and energy management.

Two Kinds of Time

'Time is running out', 'Meeting deadlines', 'Time lines', 'Time management'. Time is possibly one of most common words in business speak. We tend to approach time in an exclusively linear way. Working in stories opens up other ways of reading time. Opening up different rhythms. The Romans distinguished between *nunc fluens* – the fleeting moment and *nunc stans* – the timeless present. There is something timeless about stories.

Once there was a woman who often walked backwards. As a baby she had often crawled backwards. The rest of the tribe always walked as normal folk do, looking ahead of them. But this woman walked backwards to the river to collect water and backwards to her hut. When planting furrows, she walked backwards too. She did not look over her shoulder. It was slow going but she persisted. Her work was thorough. She seldom spilt water and she dug a straight row.

When the others asked, "Are you not afraid you will trip over an unexpected obstacle?" she answered, "It is possible but I still feel safer this way. More present".

When they asked her, "How do you know where you are going?" she responded with what to them was a riddle. "The way I walk, tells me where I have been and where I am. Where I am, tells me where I am going".

Though most people avoided her, she was the friend of the humming bird, who flew backwards and of the mother-of-pearl caterpillar who, when threatened, walked backwards in a travelling wave.

And as she walked the river path, she would drag a stick in the sand making patterns. On her way back she would tread on those patterns and her feet would erase them. The next day she made fresh patterns. Occasionally she did trip over something unexpected in her path but she got up again.

Time came when she wanted to marry. There were several suitors. Local men (frontwalkers) were intrigued by her. She rejected them all. She chose a man from a neighbouring tribe who sometimes walked in circles. She chose him as he did seem more balanced, more flexible than those of the tribe who hurried along.

Together they became wise. People began to consult the couple about the past and about the future. And how these were contained in the present.

Walking Backwards

"Gregor, however, had no practice in walking backwards, and, to tell the truth, it was very slow going for him. If Gregor had only been able to turn around".[4]

When we think in linear mode of the present and the past in relation to our bodies – behind or in front – we tend to put the past at the back and the future in front. Our language reflects this. We say, "I have put the past behind me". "I am looking forward to my future". Our sundials are anti-clockwise, or 'backwards'.

South African Koi San culture reverses this. People say, "The past is in front of me because I can see it. The future is behind me because I cannot see it. And I am walking backwards through my life".

We often use a backward walking exercise in workshops. People step into the garden and put their noses close to a mark on a brick wall or a leaf or a flower – some point of reference. They spend a minute or so looking intensely at the object. Then, while fixing their eye on this object, they take a dozen steps backwards. Then stop. And observe again what they have been looking at.

It is good to change our point of focus, to see things from a new perspective, and to get critical insights. Taiichi Ohno, who in the 1960s trained Toyota managers by making them stand for a long time on one spot on the factory floor, said to them, "Observe the production floor without preconceptions".[5]

Stuck on a Story: The Past

What does this exercise say about the way we view the past?

In Charles Dickens's novel, *Great Expectations*, Miss Havisham is a symbol of the emotional arresting of time. This eccentric elderly woman lives in seclusion with her adopted daughter, Estella. Deserted on her wedding day, she lives in the past, wearing her yellowing wedding dress. Cobwebs surround her. All the clocks in her estate are stopped on the minute she discovered that her fiancé had left her.[6]

WORKSHOP EXPERIENCES

Here are a few responses to the difference between 'close-up' and 'distance':

"The object is smaller"

"It is no longer in focus"

"I lose detail but gain context"

"The object became an important reference point in the journey backwards"

"I need both ways of looking to connect to the object"

Sometimes when a person has experienced a trauma, they're still standing up against the object emotionally, although they might now be standing twenty years away from that event. We can get stuck in emotional time. Once we worked alongside a social worker who facilitated a workshop for bank personnel who had experienced heists and hadn't moved on to once again becoming fully functioning. Part of our function was to help reintroduce the ticking of the clock.

Here linear time is helpful. Time lines. Time as progression. So once again its 'both and' not 'either or'.

But often we limit our concept of time to the linear (even in the workshop exercise). In English we lump all concepts of time under one word, whereas the Greeks acknowledged two gods of Time – Chronos and Kairos. Chronos is tick-tock time. Clock time. Measured time. Time laid out in a past-present-future line. Kairos is time as in the moment, an occasion. Time as qualitative. Indivisible. Kairos cannot be measured or counted. Kairos keeps on redefining time. This is the time that poet T. S. Eliot talks of in *Four Quartets*:

> Time present and time past
> Are both perhaps present in time future,
> And time future contained in time past...
>
> Time past and time future
> What might have been and what has been
> Point to one end, which is always present.[7]

This way of seeing time, suggests that the past is not fixed. It moves as I move. As I reflect on my life, the nature of the reflection can be determined by where I'm standing. This is why I need to reinvent myself, not get stuck on old stories and old ways of telling. There is a way in which the present can change our response to the past. Often our response to the same version being told over and over again is boredom. It becomes hard to listen for something new in the story. It is possible to be stuck in a story.

Authors Sam Keen and Ann Valley Fox in *Your Mythic Journey* suggest, "To remain vibrant throughout a lifetime we must always be inventing ourselves, weaving new themes into our life narratives, remembering our past, re-visioning our future, re-authorising the myth by which we live".[8]

Ken Wilber in *No Boundary* argues that a person, "demands a real future ahead of him... a real past behind him, and this he engineers by pretending that memory gives us a knowledge of past events instead of being part of his present experience".[9]

Patrick Harpur in *The Philosopher's Secret Fire, A History of the Imagination,* suggests that, "the art of memory reminds us that memory is a dynamic place, a theatre, where the images we store take on their own life, interacting like the gods and myths of which they are composed. They create new connections and new imaginative configurations".[10]

The Future

It is also possible to get stuck on the future. Stress and fear push us out of the present moment. We plan. We over plan. Predicting outcomes. Corporate prophecy. Goal chart gazing. These are fine if we balance this linear mode with other ways of reading time. This next story contains another possibility:

A Never-Ending Story

A farmer's horse runs away. His neighbour commiserates, "How terrible". "You never can tell," the farmer retorts. The next day the horse returns with a wild horse. His neighbour responds, "How wonderful". "You never can tell," the farmer says.

The third day the farmer's son rides the wild horse. The horse throws him and he breaks his leg. The neighbour laments, "How terrible". "You never can tell," is the farmer's refrain.

On the fourth day the soldiers recruit all the able-bodied men for the war. But they leave the son with the broken leg. And the neighbour says... and the farmer responds...

There is no end to this story. I often fall into the temptation to conclude a story before it is over – to prejudge the outcome. Another trap that the story reveals is that I can get stuck in the 'if only' of the past. In truth, I am in 'don't know mind'.

If we are open to our work story, then we can become excited, because we do not know how the story will progress. Sometimes what seems to be disaster turns out to be benign. Like the old weekly cowboy serial at the movies, where each episode ended on a cliff hanger as the carriage with horses out of control hurled towards the cliff. Or sometimes, as Shakespeare's Lear discovered, "Oft with the best intent we incur the worst".

As we walk backwards or in circles, metaphorically, stories call on our freedom to choose what kind of story we want to follow. A potential disaster? Or opening up the gap for a new story to arrive when all seems lost. The next story illustrates another element of this. Creating a gap (Kairos time).

Teaching the King's Horse to Sing

A peasant, accused of some misdeed, is brought before the King who happens to be passionate about horses.

The King shouts, "I will cut off your head".

The peasant pleads, "Please, Oh mighty King, spare me".

"Why should I spare you?"

"Give me one year. In that year I will teach your favourite horse to sing".

The king shrugs, "What have I to lose? If in a year's time, you have not taught my favourite horse to sing, then I will cut off your head".

As the peasant leaves the king's presence, walking backwards, a friend who has overheard the conversation remonstrates, "Are you crazy? You will never teach the king's horse to sing".

"You never know. I have twelve months. During that time the king might die. I might die. The horse might die. Or I might just teach the horse to sing".

Circular Time

It is possible to read time as we do the seasons. The Israeli Nobel Prize winner, S. Y. Agnon, tells a story of a rich merchant, at the peak of his fortune.

On the way to market he loses a wallet under a bush. On his return he finds it with all his money intact. He breaks into irrepressible grief. At that point his fortunes decline, his life falls apart and he is left destitute. On his way to visit a friend he stops at a bath house. In an altercation with a beggar, his clothing is ripped. At that moment he begins to laugh wildly.[11]

One possible interpretation is that the merchant believes in the wheel of fortune. Life is so good it can only decline. Life is so bad it can only get better. His approach to time might be more circular than one composed merely of deadlines and targets.

Stories open up the moment as they introduce us to wider readings of time. They embrace both past and future in that moment. Unlike Gregor in Kafka's *Metamorphosis* who changes into a bug, we can learn to walk backwards. And in circles. And when appropriate forwards or backwards in a straight line.

---

[1] Shakespeare, William. *Richard II.*

[2] Swift, Jonathan. *Gulliver's Travels,* Barnes and Noble, NY, 2003.

[3] De Saint Exupery, Antoine. *The Little Prince*, NTC/Contemporary Co., 2000.

[4] Kafka, Franz. *Metamorphosis,* Crown, 2003.

[5] Toyota Traditions, www.toyota.co.jp, 24th May, 2008.

[6] Dickens, Charles. *Great Expectations,* Allen and Unwin, London, 2000.

[7] Eliot T. S. *Four Quartets,* Harcourt, 1968.

[8] Keen, Sam and Fox, Anne Valley. *Your Mythic Journey*, Tarcher, NY, 1989.

[9] Wilber, Ken. *No Boundary, Eastern and Western Approaches to Personal Growth,* Shambhala, Berkeley, 1979.

[10] Harpur, Patrick. *The Philosopher's Secret Fire, A History of the Imagination,* Penguin, London, 2002.

[11] Agnon, S. Y. *Book that was Lost and other Stories*, Schocken, NY, 1996.

Chapter 9
Silent Stories

The young farm-child
Interrupts rice husking
To gaze at the moon [1]

Basho

What am I leaving out?

One night an old monk, deep in contemplation, feeling stuck and wanting to grow in faith, asked for a sign.

A voice dropped a question from the heavens, "What are you leaving out?"

The monk was puzzled by this response. He woke a younger monk and asked the question, "What am I leaving out?"

The sleepy monk responded, "Me" and fell back asleep.

Still puzzled, the monk wandered outside the monastery and looked up at the night sky with the question in his mind. The night sky said, "Me too". He tripped and fell with his face into the mud and the mud said, "Me too".

What am I leaving out? Who am I not inviting into the conversation at work? Perhaps the farm boy in Matsuo Basho's poem, shelling the husks, might have something to say to me about what is happening on the farm. About the 'bigger picture'. Or about the 'smaller picture'. We have a need to develop both a bird's and a worms' eye view, abilities to see the bigger picture and also the role of and interconnectivity of constituent parts.

In every company there are stories that fall between the cracks – stories that are not being told. Sometimes the person does not feel important enough or that it is their place to share the information that they observe and the knowledge and life experience they possess. A waiter might have stories about customer service that the manager does not have access to. Yet when the restaurant management plans a meeting about improving service, perhaps nobody asks the waiter to attend. The cleaner might observe something of significance in the reception area but does not speak. A woman employee might withhold knowledge and information because men dominate the conversation.

When the boss is present, people may lapse into a tacit agreement mode, rather than speak out and offer a different viewpoint. They might fear ridicule or sanction. Conformity may be a more valued cultural element than diversity – of thinking style, relating behaviour, viewpoints.

Sometimes a story is withheld for selfish reasons – the leading sales person may resist sharing her secrets of success because of no perceived reward, perhaps even a "disbenefit". The withholding of the story might also have to do with perceived rewards – creating a power base that excludes rivals.

> *A farming community was growing crops for a local competition – the highlight of the year. Farmer Jacob who was out of a particular seed, asked Farmer Reuben on the neighbouring farm for some.*
>
> *Farmer Reuben gave him his best seed. Farmer Benjamin, observing this, asked, "Why are you doing this? Don't you want to win the competition?"*
>
> *Farmer Reuben responded, "You have forgotten the wind factor. Whatever I give him, will blow back into my face".*

Midrash

Around every story, there are stories that are not being told.

In the Jewish tradition, there is the idea of *Midrash*. *Midrash* involves fleshing out a story we only have the barest details for – the bones of the story. An example of this might be the story of Lot's wife in the Old Testament. She turned around and gazed at the city God had told them to leave. She was turned into a pillar of salt. *Midrash* might involve creating the story of Mrs. Lot – what was in her mind and why did she turn around?

Here are a few lines from a poem *The Salt of the Earth:*[2]

> her eyes circled the city of Sodom
> that had been hearthstone.
> they swept like the reed broom
> wielded before leaving.
> she hunted under the sleeping mat
> for a memory shaped
> by the weight of their bodies.

When we see people only in their roles at work (the secretary, the janitor, the boss) there is an opportunity to *midrash*. Often a bigger or smaller picture brings deeper understanding of what extra value such people might be able to bring the company.

Stories, like other conversational activity exercises, explore the nature of stereotypes, prejudice, the richness of diversity. Yet they explore at a more effective level. When we only know the role of a colleague but nothing of the experience that gives them their energy, a form of *midrash* might well be to create a space to explore work memories of other times and other places. This can help integrate newcomers into a newly created or existing organization, assist two companies merging, each with a separate history and culture and foster understanding in an international company.

One effective exercise involves asking participants to draw a childhood memory of them doing some kind of work as a child. Remunerated or not remunerated. Ask them to use their non-dominant hands. This takes care of the 'I can't draw' feelings of incompetency some of us have. It also invokes powerful visualization, relaxation and playfulness. For a few reflections on this process see Exercise Feedback box below.

Such a *midrash* can put the flesh on the skeleton that comes to work. *Midrash* is akin to the neuro-linguistic programming technique called reframing.

There is a William Stafford verse from, 'A Ritual to Read to Each Other'.[3]

> If you don't know the kind of person I am
> and I don't know the kind of person you are
> a pattern that others made may prevail in the world
> and following the wrong god home we may miss our star.

The Conversation: Dominant and Hidden Stories

There is a school of therapy called Narrative Therapy. Stories carry the power to heal us. The other side is that stories can keep us stuck in our dysfunction. Dominant stories might suppress other stories which, if privileged and given air time, have the power to create new realities. As writer Salmon Rushdie reminds us, every story is an act of censorship.[4]

Here is a possible scenario. The person with the drinking problem (talking to his narrative therapist), cites a week of not drinking.

> "Did anybody witness this?"

> "Yes my wife was there".

> "Let's call her in to tell what she observed".

EXERCISE FEEDBACK

"Suddenly a new understanding arrived in my eyes. I caught a glimpse of Mike's personal history. He is no longer just a function"

"This exercise gave me such insight that I rearranged some work descriptions"

"A year later, this particular exercise was still impacting on how we relate to each other"

In this scenario, a story that is not being told, is given space. If the husband and wife's alternative story can be told, the dominant story (drunkenness) can be challenged and the person motivated to change their behaviour.

In Colorado in the nineties, the State authority ran a sobriety campaign to reinforce good behaviour. The thrust was to 'catch' and reward sober motorists. They were congratulated, given gifts, balloons for the kids and thanked. Many motorists responded positively to this approach.

This too is a kind of *midrash* that can be practiced in the boardroom as a reframing of problems and challenges, in order to provide a new angle, a new perspective.

When we listen to all possible stories we get a composite picture. Confusing the part for the whole or adopting a narrow view (perception for reality, if we can ever know it) is one of the definitions of heresy.

We particularly like two points that Tony Manning makes about conversation within organizations in his book *Making Sense of Strategy*,[5]

- that strategic management is conversation

- leaders can limit their people or foster their growth (raise the strategic IQ of the firm) by determining the size of their conversations.

This conversation informs, focuses attention and effort, triggers fresh insights, lights up the imagination, energizes people and inspires performance. What the leader constantly and passionately talks about and promotes as the organization's conversation material, is what people will pay attention to. This will assume importance, become serious, assume priority.

Choose your topic or subject (or 'story' if you like) – if you, as the leader, talk about costs (or productivity or customer service or innovation or whatever) all the time – then what you have chosen to talk about will echo through (inform) the organizational conversation – which will become costs (or productivity or customer service or innovation or whatever).

Conversely if you state, for example, that customer service is important but then never talk about it, this is clearly an incongruous statement destined to remain unheard (a *midrash*) by the organization at large.

Restrict your staff to small, petty conversations and you gain nothing. You could lose important stuff like trust. Give them access to information, treat them like adults, and let them have big conversations (by telling their story in context), and the chances are that extraordinary things will result.

Business conversation is about topic and size:

- what is told

- how much is told.

Letting go is about much more than letting work go to others. It is operating from a basis of trust, confidence and respect, which allows for letting go of the fear of losing control, of achieving perfection, of worry, of getting the credit for something.

Silence Around the Obvious

> *Nasrudin and his donkey moved between villages in neighbouring countries. The first time he crossed the border he was dressed in rags. When he crossed a few day later he wore a new shirt. Haran, the suspicious customs official, mused, "I'm sure he is smuggling something".*
>
> *Days later Nasrudin crossed the border in a new kaftan. The donkey sported a cloth bridle. Haran searched Nasrudin but found nothing. The next time Nasrudin had added a hat to his outfit and the donkey wore a bridle of fine leather.*
>
> *Haran searched Nasrudin and he searched the donkey. Nothing. He sighed and let Nasrudin pass.*
>
> *This continued over the years until Haran retired. One day Nasrudin came out of his mansion in the town centre. Haran was sitting at the fountain. He called out, "I can no longer arrest you. Satisfy an old man. Those days when you crossed the border... what were you smuggling?"*
>
> *Nasrudin confessed, "Donkeys".*

Stories are about paying attention so the obvious may be revealed. This means paying attention to:

- the edges of the story (creating story opportunities for those employees whose wisdom is not being sourced)

- the centre of the story (that which is not seen, because it is right in front of our noses).

May entering the silence around stories increase the range of our telling and listening.

---

1   Basho, Matsuo. *Matsuo Basho, The Master Haiku Poet*, Macmillan, London, 1983.
2   Haarhoff, Dorian. *Tortoise Voices*, Mercer, Cape Town, 2001.
3   Stafford, William. In Bly, Robert, Hillman, James and Meade, Michael, *The Rag and Bone Shop of the Heart*, (eds), Harper Collins, NY, 1992.
4   Rushdie, S. *Shame*, Viking Press, NY, 1985.
5   Manning, Tony. *Making Sense of Strategy*, Zebra, Johannesburg, 2001.

Chapter 10

Stories, Prisons and Belief Bubbles

*I could be bound in a nutshell and count myself
the King of infinite space* [1]
Shakespeare

The Prison House: Three Stories That Can Free Us

A Son's Ashes

A man returns home to find that thieves have set fire to his house. His son had been at home at the time. He sees the charred remains of a body. The father grieves the death of his son and puts the ashes in the locket. He wears this around his neck.

Now what happened, was that the thieves did burn down his house but they abducted the son. The charred remains could have been the body of a passing tramp. The son escapes his captors and finds his way home. He knocks on his father's door.

"Here I am father. I'm home".

The man looks at the youth then looks at the locket around his neck. Holding the locket in his hand, he says, "Nonsense. You are an impostor. My son died in the fire. Go away".

The Caged Bird

Rumi, the Persian mystic, tells this story.

The merchant has captured the bird and takes it from the forest to the city. One day the merchant informs the bird, "I'm going back to the forest. Is there anything you desire?"

57

"Yes," says the bird, "Give me my freedom".

"I will not do that. Is there anything else you wish for?"

"In that case, will you tell the other birds what has happened to me?"

"Yes I will".

The merchant arrives at the forest and calls all the birds who assemble on boughs nearby.

He tells them, "Your fellow bird is in a cage in the city".

As soon as the forest birds hear this news, as one they fall down off the boughs, senseless to the ground.

In some trepidation, the merchant returns to the city and tells the caged bird what he has seen. As soon as the bird hears this story, it falls off the perch to the bottom of the cage and lies there senseless. The merchant opens the cage, picks up the bird in his hands and puts it on a shelf, prior to burying it.

At that point the bird recovers, flaps its feathers and flies into the air, calling out, "Tell my fellow birds, I thank them for the message they have sent to me, via you, my jailer".

The Design in the Carpet

A jeweller is in prison unjustly. His captors allow him his tools and he fixes many things for the warders. His wife visits him and brings him a prayer rug. The man is disappointed because he wants a file or a hack saw.

However, since he has the prayer rug, he lays it out in the centre of the bare cell. Every day he kneels on the rug and bows down as he prays. Days pass. Weeks pass. He begins to concentrate on the pattern in the carpet.

Then one day new evidence arrives that the man is innocent. When the warder arrives with the news, he finds the door open and the cell empty. Days later, the warder meets the man in the street and engages him. "You are free to go... but tell me, how did you escape?"

The jeweller responds, "As I concentrated on the pattern in the carpet, I understood that it was a design of the lock system that was keeping me in prison".

A couple of years ago one of us travelled to Robben Island with twenty four secretaries. We heard stories of the prisoners studying in their cells, their minds like Hamlet's, ranging through the world. The workshop theme was around freedom and the ways that we imprison ourselves. We are physically free to roam, yet our minds imprison us. Our belief system, our perceptions put us behind bars. As someone said, "we are birds looking for a cage".

Reflecting on the stories

Stories like these open conversations that range the world. A story is an octopus with multiple tentacles. Here are a few observations from workshop participants.

A Son's Ashes

"In my culture the father made two mistakes. One was not to recognize his son. The second mistake was that he did not say, "I do not believe that you are my blood son, but you do not have a father and I do not have a son. Come inside".

"I can tell you exactly how that story played out in our company". She spoke of someone who brought an alive, innovative idea. The company rejected it because they wanted to stay with the old dead idea. So the man left with his idea and founded a thriving business.

The Caged Bird

 "The birds including the caged bird, all believed in the power of community. The caged bird connected to his community and was able to use their advice to escape".

"I believe in communication. It's rooted in the word community. The merchant was willing to carry a message... to communicate. There is hidden power in this".

"Because the merchant who represents a leader, willingly carried a message, was flexible, he unwittingly became an agent for liberation. His own liberation too. His unconscious belief became operative".

"This story offers a different approach to getting unstuck – trying other options. Challenging other people's beliefs".

The Design in the Carpet

"The wife was the clever one. She offered the means to get out of the prison, but the jeweller had to work out how it connected to his skill".

"We don't always get what we expect – what is obvious. But he stayed with the process, paid attention and turned it to his advantage".

Belief Bubbles, Belief Blocks

In Christopher Marlowe's *Doctor Faustus*, Faustus sells his soul to the devil for 24 years of longer life. At the end of the play, when the clock is striking the hour for the devil to claim his part of the bargain, Faustus in panic cries, "I will leap up to my God. Who pulls me down?"[2] The answer is himself. Faustus is trapped in a perception. The primary sin is not that he has made a pact with the devil, but that he thinks that he has sinned beyond the grace of God.

Personal beliefs are ingrained, conditioned views about ourselves. They are not always true. Something like anxiety – fear of something not real that may not happen or be. If you listen to daily office conversation, you will hear people expressing their belief system. Predictions. Self worth. Assessments. Flexibility. Availability. All day colleagues reveal where they are coming from. Their beliefs, interpretations, hopes, needs, fears. What they expect to happen to them probably will – either empowerment or victimization. "I don't deserve this relationship", "I'll never make the money to own that", "I'm not a nice person".

A 'belief bubble' is like a balloon that expands or contracts to take in or let out air. It is light, responds to the breeze and floats in the atmosphere. It is open to 'both and' rather than 'either or'. We are getting a composite picture.

A belief block or limiting belief is a heavy thing with clearly defined borders. It exists in a world of 'either or' – I'm right and you are wrong. Or in a negative statement or mind-set or unconsciously held belief: I am not worthwhile. It blocks us from other ways of reading events and opportunities. An actor will get stage fright and forget his lines if he believes that this will happen.

Another belief block is when people believe in a world of only facts. Unlike Einstein who was a 'belief bubble' person. He once commented on a colleague who would not become a great scientist because his ideas were not crazy enough. When a belief becomes rigid or when we confuse perception for reality, we incarcerate ourselves. In his *Going Home*, Tich Nhat Hanh cautions that our notions and belief systems should be flexible.[3]

Fiction writers work with two premises – 'what if' and 'let's pretend'. Both of these entertain a pliable belief system. They invoke the possible and are open to change. In the 1950's I remember my mother bringing home clothes from the department store 'on appro'. She would try on the garments, keep one that she liked and return the others. It is possible to try on beliefs on appro. This is one way of expanding the 'belief bubble' and keeping the shape flexible. We try on new realities and if they enhance us, we keep them. If not, we discard them.

Fictional Identities

As human beings, we own a fictional identity. We love stories because we are stories. The Psalmist suggests, "We spend our years as a tale that is told".[4] We process our dreams and daytime reality as a story.

When we tell our stories or state our beliefs, or even act out our unconscious beliefs, we select what will happen to us. Selection is fiction. If I am in a particular mood, I can find correspondences to that mood in the past and then I will align those events in the telling. Oom Schalk Lourens, Herman Charles Bosman's persona, suggests, "It is not the story that counts. It is the way that you tell it".[5]

When we suggest that we are fiction, sometimes people respond that a certain event did happen. We need to separate what happened and how we tell it, because we are 'how we tell it' creatures. Here is a scenario we often witness in workshops. If you ask someone to tell a late comer what has been going on, a third participant, puzzled and surprised, might interject, "What workshop have you been in?"

My history professor's favourite quotation was "*Quot Hominen Quot sententiae*". So many people so many opinions. So many beliefs.

A few years ago one of us asked Tanzanian teachers to share a break-through career moment – a moment of inspiration in which they celebrated their calling. Here is one person's experience:

> *"One night in a pub a man approached me. 'You taught me 25 years ago'. I vaguely remembered him. 'You taught us Macbeth. You used to put on the accents of the*

characters'. I nodded. 'I will never forget the day you put on a purple cloak and you came down the spiral staircase and you recited Lady Macbeth's speech, "was the hope drunk wherein you dressed yourself?"

The teacher continued: "I never put on a purple cloak and there wasn't a spiral staircase in that school. But I must have taught in such a way that this student created it as his reality. I touched his imagination. That is my breakthrough moment".

In one of those old famous movie lines from Gigi, Maurice Chevalier sings to his woman:

"We met at seven".

She responds, "We met at eight".

"I was early".

She responds, "You were late".

"Ah yes, I remember it well".

Memory is a trickster figure. Our perception of the organization's history and what cultural behaviours are expected can entrap us.

A couple approach a therapist for marriage counselling. First the husband shares his version. The therapist nods, "You're right". Then the therapist listens to the wife's version and comments. "You're right".

There is a trainee student with the therapist, who asks, "How can you say to both the husband and to the wife, "You are right?"

The therapist turns to the student and says, "You know, you too are right".

A 'belief bubble' opens me to other stories in the company. Other versions. Other possible future scenarios. Other ways of doing things around here. Cultivating a 'belief bubble' mind raises the story-telling, story-listening consciousness of the company. The SIQ. When this happens, a conversation is possible. We can then share our perceptions of reality and break our shackles. We can grow and change our beliefs and set ourselves free by identifying them, challenging them, creating new more robust beliefs. And grow a bigger balloon.

Thais use a word *michadhitti*. Loosely translated it means an inappropriate, narrow view. They also talk about *sammadhitti* – having a more holistic view, a better paradigm. This is the gift of story. Once again the halo or the noose.

---

[1]   Shakespeare, William. *Hamlet.*

[2]   Marlowe, Christopher. *Doctor Faustus.*

[3]   Hanh, Thich Nhat. *Going Home: Bringing Christ and the Buddha together in Daily Life,* Rider, Riverhead Books, Penguin Putnam Inc., NY, 1994.

[4]   Psalm 90 : 9.

[5]   Bosman, Herman Charles. *Mafeking Road and Other Stories,* Human and Rousseau, Cape Town, 1947.

Chapter 11

Money as Story, Money as Symbol

Love makes the world go round and money oils the spokes
(old saying)

Silver Stories

The miser visits a rabbi to complain how miserable he is. The rabbi takes him by the shoulders and places him in front of a mirror.

"What do you see?" he asks.

"I see myself," mutters the miser.

The rabbi steers him to the window and asks, "What do you see now?"

The miser responds, "I see people and trees".

"The difference," says the rabbi, "is the silver on the mirror".

One of the exhibits at the Sciencentre Museum in Durbanville, Cape, is a rectangular frame with two chairs on opposite sides. Inside the frame are slats of glass, much like a Venetian blind. A silvered surface alternates with a slat of plain glass. If you sit opposite someone you see part of your face and part of the other person's – a little like the matching faces and work clothing you might have worn as a child at play – baker, farmer, business magnate, cop.

This chapter looks at the possibility of 'both and' rather than 'either or' when it comes to bottom lines. Stories encourage us to think symbolically rather than to be stuck in literal interpretations. When we do this, the word 'rich' takes on additional meaning. If we approach money through the symbolism of story, this could lead us to a deeper connection to ourselves and others as we explore inner and outer riches.

62

Exchange Systems

The history of money makes for a fascinating read – grain, white deer skin, tobacco, sea shells, the teeth of dogs, giant stone statues, the feathers of birds, minted coins, printed paper, plastic cards have all been used for exchange. The micro chip might be the next currency. Currently a number of alternative exchange systems are emerging. In one such system people work with the unit called Talents and do community bartering.

Paul N. Malherbe, author of *A Pragmatic Approach to The Creation of Value, Enrichment and Prosperity,* attempts to "show how the marginalised billions might be given some real hope without harming the basis of prosperity".[1] He succeeds admirably by spotlighting the importance of earned *exchange*, entitlement and opportunity as *the* basic principle of economic well–being.

Malherbe postulates that value and wealth (both material and intangible) are created through perceived fair, win-win exchanges between two parties (but which carry benefit for all involved along the 'production of value' line). He expounds on 31 such exchanges – types that satisfy the whole person. It is clear that this exchange principle is likely to remain and even increase in importance as digital communication and interaction possibilities multiply and globalization advances.

The word money is derived from a name of the Roman goddess Moneta (Latin for mint or coins) which evolved into the old English *mynet* (money). Moneta was one aspect of the fertility goddess Juno. Fertility implies times of feast and times of famine – which in turn might explain the bulls and bears of the stock market. The mythical origins of money as coming from the gods is still present in currencies such as the US dollar, which carries the inscription – in God we Trust.

Tad Crawford in *The Secret Life of Money, How Money can be Food for the Soul* explores the symbolism of money through a number of stories. "Money speaks to us of life and death, of the fertility of the natural world, and of our own natures".[2] Some currencies bear traces of this symbolism. The Grim Reaper appears on one of the Swiss bank notes. The big five appear on South African notes, for example, the lion on the R50 note.

Money Mystique

> *The God, Dionysus, granted King Midas of Asia Minor one wish. Midas wished that everything he touched be turned to gold. Dionysus warned Midas of the dangers but the King insisted. King Midas was thrilled with his new gift and turned everything he could to gold, including his roses. His food and wine were also changed to gold. Then he kissed his beloved daughter. She too turned to gold.*
>
> *The desperate Midas asked Dionysus for help.*
>
> *Dionysus told Midas to bathe in the Pactolus River. As soon as Midas touched the river water, the golden touch was washed down steam in the current. The gold settled in the sands of the Pactolus River and was carried downstream to Lydia, one of the richest kingdoms in the ancient world and the source of the earliest coinage.*

Like so much else in our work lives, money is a form of energy. Energy implies movement and flow, yet so often we get stuck around money issues. As in the Midas story, when the energy freezes, the flow stops – between Midas and his roses, his food and wine and his daughter. It is the river that reintroduces the flow. The word currency comes from the Latin *(currens)* for flow and is related to the current of the river. Possessing wealth does not confer wealth. Wealth in the flow, in the cycle or circulation of energy. Millionaire Andrew Carnegie believed, "There is no class so pitiably wretched as that which possesses money and nothing else".

Our attitude to money can be a minefield. The topic is shrouded in secrecy, superstition and controversy. Like Midas we see gold or money as elixir of future happiness. Many people measure their worth by their income. Books on how to make a million or how to attract money, crowd the bookshelves. The possible shortage of money raises fears of being destitute, of not being able to provide for our family. Workers strike over wages. How much we earn remains one of the taboo subjects at dinner parties. Or in boardrooms. Some unlisted organizations that seek transparency will up-front their earnings. This is becoming mandatory.

The oft misquoted Biblical text, "money is the root of all evil", shows our suspicion of the power we give this force. The actual reading "the love of money is the root of all evil", suggests that it is attachment as in the Midas myth, that causes the problems.

The Clay Digger's Fortune

The circulation of wealth in the context of relationship can bring great benefit. Here is a story that might appeal to a country rich in wheat fields, or one where wealth has been based on minerals taken from the earth.

> *A poor clay digger unearths a stone of great wealth. The local villagers say it is too big for them to exchange and he must go to the town. The townsfolk say it is also too big for them to exchange and he must go to the city across the waters. At the port he strikes a bargain with the captain of a ship. He shows him the stone and tells him he will pay for his passage once he has sold the stone in the city. The captain agrees. They sail away and during the voyage, the captain and the clay digger become friends.*

> *Then one afternoon while he is sleeping, the clay digger puts the stone on a table. The cabin boy enters, scoops up the tablecloth and shakes it out over the railing. The stone falls into the sea. The clay digger is distraught when he discovers his loss. But he decides not to tell the captain but to carry on as if he still has the stone. After all, the transaction will only happen once they have docked.*

> *A few days out of the port of the city, which happens to be the wheat capital of the area, the captain approaches the clay digger and asks for a favour.*

> *"Conditions for buying wheat are just right at this very moment. But as captain of the ship, certain rules do not allow me to buy wheat. May I buy it in your name? When you pay for your passage, we can also do the wheat transaction".*

> *That clay digger readily agrees as he would like to help his friend. The secret transaction is concluded and the captain radios ahead and buys many bushels of wheat. The ship docks two days later. As the captain steps from the ship onto the gangplank, he slips and falls down in between the ship and the quay. He drowns.*

The clay digger who has lost the stone, inherits the wheat and the wealth that comes with reselling it.

In workshops participants debate this story at great length, questioning the morality of the clay digger. Some judge him for not disclosing to the captain that he lost the stone. Others say that his silence was wise or that the captain had not yet performed his part of the bargain to deliver him safely to the shore. Some people say he was faithful to the relationship. Some talk of the irony of unexpected losses and unexpected gains. Timing seems to play an important role in the story.

Legals and Extralegals

What distinguishes the 'haves' from the 'have nots' in societies, is money. If the 'have nots' had more, markets for business would be so much bigger.

Hernando de Soto in his *The Mystery of Capital* points out that the ordinary 1st World person doesn't have any real difficulties in being able to enter into a contract, arrange insurance cover, organize services, raise loan monies and access capital.[3] Legal instruments exist to prove who they are, where they live, what they can offer as security, where accounts may be sent and collections made, where services may be delivered.

If, however, you are an 'extralegal' – one of those who lies outside of the formal system, then you are effectively barred from any form of capital – access. For example, for the deprived to obtain legal authorisation to build a house on state-owned land in Peru would take 207 administrative steps, and to obtain legal title a further 728 steps. In the Philippines, 168 steps involving 53 public and private agencies are required in order to legally purchase a dwelling built in a settlement. In Egypt to acquire and legally register a lot on state owned desert land can take up to 14 years. No wonder that 5 million Egyptians have built their dwellings illegally.

The point is that if formal systems bar you, you set up your own system – an unofficial system of exchange and money creation. Eventually it will be legalised, as in all developing and ex-communist countries everywhere (if European and American history is anything to go by).

In 18th century France, for example, more than 16 000 smugglers and clandestine manufacturers were executed within a 10 year period. In Spain, England and elsewhere there were many similar legal/extralegal clashes. In Germany also outside of the formal law whole districts could be found in which plenty of houses were being built, though there was no one in the district qualified to build them. In the USA squatting was an early American tradition as the West was 'settled' and developed by the new migrants. Between 1785 and 1890 Congress passed over 500 different laws in attempts to regularise the property system.

A wealthy lawyer and an impoverished cook, both dying of AIDS in hospital, become friends. The cook's death is approaching. One day the lawyer asks the cook, "Have you made a will?"

The cook responds, "I have nothing and nobody to leave it to".

His lawyer friend remonstrates, "That is irrelevant. By making a will you are saying, "I was here. I existed".

So the cook makes a will. In it he leaves his favourite recipe to his lawyer friend.

So in South Africa and elsewhere, roll on more and better communication about money, possessions, symbols and personal exchange between the haves and the have nots. Somehow we are in this together. Roll on a generosity mind-set.

Jesus, master story teller, in his parable about the servant who is cleared of his debt by his king, then demands from others what they owe him, points to the imperative to give and forgive and to let go of a 'you owe me' mind-set. This applies to both monetary and other issues.

---

[1] Malherbe, Paul. *A Pragmatic Approach to The Creation of Value, Enrichment and. Prosperity*, Author published, Cape Town, 2000.
[2] Crawford, Tad. *The Secret Life of Money,* Allworth Press, NY, 1994.
[3] De Soto, Hernando. *The Mystery of Capital,* Bantam Press, NY, 2000.

Chapter 12

The Sixty-Cycle Hum: Stories and Technology

Communicating Through Technology

In Jan Phillips' book *God is at Eye Level, Photography as a Healing Art,* she tells the story of how as a young novice, she was asked to leave the convent for a "lack of religious disposition". She left a close friend, Lois, behind.

> *Jan was not allowed to communicate with Lois, neither phone her, nor write to her. As Lois's birthday approached, Jan bought a simple Kodak Instamatic and began to take photographs – footsteps in the tide, a shadow on a locked church door, toppling sand castles. She sent the photographs to the convent. Lois was allowed to look at the photos in the novice director's office. Jan Phillips became a photographer, working with more sophisticated camera equipment.*
>
> *Jan Phillips used technology to communicate her story.*[1]

Good management of information and technology is crucial to the story of business success. Managers used to concentrate on their products, their money and the productivity of their people. They still do, but these days there is much more emphasis on technology, both within the organization and in terms of a vast array of connections to the outside world.

So in business, there's a move into

- more data mining

- information gathering and manipulation

- more information and communication technology convergence and usage

- more on-line behavioural research.

And perhaps a danger of moving away from story?

More knowledge about the interface between an organization and its customers does bring many blessings and advantages. So many companies are developing customer relationship management systems as they are seen as a way to create more meaningful and lasting relationships. In other words they now possess the means to create stories which supply the human faces behind technology.

A Balancing Act

Goethe kept a model of a steam engine and its track from Liverpool to Bath on his desk as a symbol of the hope for technical progress. One of the driving myths of the Enlightenment and Industrial revolution was that technology meant progress and gains for humanity. The greatest good for the greatest number. We are no longer so sure. Many of us do not predict a more fulfilled life for our children because of greater technology.

One spin off of technology is that it can separate the worker who made the product from the person who uses his product. Refer to the story of the 4th century BC Chinese sage Chuang-tzu in the Afterword.

We need to keep the proper balance between technology, business processes, people competence and customer communication and partnering. When these things get out of kilter, friction and sub standard performance result. We miss the service boat.

INFO SHEET

Service technology can be used to facilitate better customer and employee relationships, that is, new stories by:

Increasing convenience. Web browsing and price comparisons, live and cyberspace self-service transactions, tracking the progress of orders, effecting bank transfers, processing a mortgage application, speeding up the supermarket checkout, making an entertainment booking

Reducing paper. Forms (leave applications, loan requests, employee record changes), company news, performance information, events, policy and operating manuals, business results information, making insurance claims, doing flight bookings, doing automatic stock replenishment

Democratisation – in the form of easier and freer communication, using open internal polls to garner customer and employee opinions, managing aspects of 'virtual teamwork', conducting ongoing motivational climate surveys, capturing customer feedback

New training methods, for example e-Learning which stimulates self-directed learning

Knowledge management – the appropriate, efficient sharing of solutions (for example applications, sales, fault correction) captured on a data base accessible to service providers and customers

Consider also that

- information networks make it difficult to hide trade secrets. An average two year lead time in the 1950s is now closer to two months. The time taken to get information to the global market is similarly reducing, as the lifetime of new technology shortens. Without diminishing its importance, we believe that gaining a competitive edge through information technology is going to become more and more difficult

- as Francis Fukuyama[2] points out, "trust does not reside in integrated circuits or fibre optic cables… thus it is far from clear that the information revolution makes large, hierarchical organizations obsolete or that spontaneous community will emerge once hierarchy has been undermined".

Research into Japanese interaction with robots is showing that subjects are more likely to look an android in the eyes when answering questions than they do when interacting with humans – perhaps because of the subtleties and sensitivities of normal conversations and norms of behaviour there. The writer predicts that people might well develop emotional responses to lifelike robots.[3]

In the Theodor Seuss Geisel books, (*Dr. Seuss*), there are many fancy gadgets roaming the landscape, performing amazing tasks (e.g. a zoom-zoom-ka-boom machine). In Seuss Landing, a theme park in Orlando, structural steel has been used to bring alive the crazy constructions that Dr. Seuss illustrated in his books.[4]

Incidentally narrative literature such as Dr. Seuss's *The Lorax,* has been used to teach management ethics in organizations.[4]

Of course we must use technology creatively, but let's not put all our faith in it. As in the story of the grandfather at the well and his grandson's proposed invention. We have all seen polished power point presentations that falter as faulty electricity or a missing plug the size of a golf ball disrupts timing and loses the audience.

This story of the woman dissatisfied with her husband, set in the year 2500, illustrates how advanced technology can disappoint.

> *The woman decides to replace herself with a robot so identical to herself that the husband will never know the difference. When the job is done, the manufacturer points out that there is one small difficulty: instead of a heartbeat, the robot has a sixty-cycle hum – like that of electric motors, fluorescent lights.*
>
> *So the plan is that when the robot first gets together with the husband, it will record and adapt his heartbeat. That night the woman sneaks off for a night on the town after releasing her identical duplicate robot to go to the husband. When she sneaks back in after her night out and checks with the robot to see how things went, she is told that it couldn't detect the husband's heartbeat. All it could pick up was a sixty-cycle hum.*

A group of technicians were pondering the question whether computers would ever replace human beings. They fed the information to the computer and it responded, "That reminds me of a story".

Our machines are technical stories that exist to serve the greater story.

---

1 Phillips, Jan. *God is at Eye Level – Photography as a Healing Art,* Theosophical Publishing House, Adjar, India, 2000.

2 Fukuyama, F. *Trust,* Penguin Books, London, 1996.

3 *The Economist*, "Better than People", December 24th 2005 – January 6th 2006.

4 Greenwood, Michelle. "The study of business ethics: A case for Dr. Seuss", *Business Ethics, A European Review*, Vol. 9 No. 3, July, 2000.

Chapter 13
Clowns, Boats and Camels Naming, Blaming, Teams and Diversity

No blame (recurring phrase in
the IChing, the Chinese book
of Wisdom)

Clowns, Boats and Blame

An exhausted rabbi, travelling late at night, arrives at an Inn. The innkeeper apologizes, "I'm sorry there is no room".

"Please, I am desperately tired and must leave early in the morning. Do you not have somewhere where I can lay my weary head?"

"Well," says the innkeeper, "There is a clown sleeping in a double bed. You can share the bed with him".

Early in the morning, the innkeeper wakes the rabbi. He dresses in the dark, pays his way, thanks the innkeeper and steps out into the street. As dawn comes, he notices people giving him peculiar looks. Then he catches his reflection in a shop window. He is dressed as a clown.

The rabbi exclaims, "That stupid innkeeper. He has woken the wrong man".

In this story the rabbi encounters another part of himself in the night – dream life – which he refuses to recognize. His response? To blame the innkeeper. Often blame arises in a knee-jerk reaction. The need to pin fault on to somebody else.

Early one misty morning a boatman is making his way up river. He sees the prow

71

of a boat appearing out of the mist, pointed towards him. He calls out politely, "I have right of way".

There is no response. The boat still keeps on coming towards him. The boatman calls out more stridently but still the boat approaches. The man then shouts abuse at the inconsiderate person in the other boat.

Then the boat slips out of the mist, missing his boat by a hair's breadth. As he raises his oar in rage to assault the other boatman, he sees that the boat is empty.

Cosmic Trouble

Sometimes when things go wrong, our default setting is to find someone or something to blame (character disorder) or we blame ourselves (neurosis). There might be occasions when somebody needs to take responsibility. But often difficulty and hardship and suffering are a given. There is no one or nothing to blame. The Buddha said in this life we would know ten thousand joys and ten thousand sufferings. Theologian Teilhard de Chardin spoke about "the tears that are in all things".[1] This is trouble at the cosmic level.

Therapist Wayne Muller was asked to convene a commission in California to sort out problems around teenage delinquency. He walked into a cycle of pain and blame. Storekeepers blamed the schools. Teachers blamed the parents. Parents blamed the teenagers. Some blamed the shopkeepers. The teenagers blamed the police. The police blamed the teenagers, teachers and parents.[2]

Muller said he would only work in this situation, if the principle that 'pain is nobody's fault' was adopted. He met with representatives from every group in the community. Once people were released from blaming, they began to collaborate – teachers, police, juvenile offenders, parents, probation officers, gang members and students. Once they all acknowledged their pain without needing to pin it on to anybody, they began to work as allies. The group came up with creative approaches to community issues. Strategies they collectively created, ten years later were still in place.

Failure as Opportunity

In Arthur Miller's play *Death of a Salesman,* Willie Loman commits suicide. At his grave, his son, Happy, cries out, "He had a good dream. It's the only dream you can have – to come out number-one man". Charley, the neighbour, laments, "He's a man way out there in the blue, riding on a smile and a shoeshine. And when they start not smiling back – that's an earthquake".[3]

Sometimes we allow words to create our reality. Failure is one of those words. Perhaps it is a word that we pick up in our school reports and it lingers through our lives. "I am a failure".

A more generous approach might be to read failure as a learning opportunity. The scientist builds failure into his experiments. Thomas Edison, whom some consider inventor of the phonograph, motion pictures and the light bulb, was approached by his frustrated workers. "We've done this particular experiment and we can't get the light bulb to work". Edison's response? "At least we know another way in which the light bulb doesn't work". Edison also said, "The successful person makes a habit of doing what the failing person doesn't like to do". Luck often arises from perseverance in what others consider failure.

Camels and Teamwork

A wealthy, elderly man owns seventeen camels. He calls his three children to divide his inheritance. He tells them, "My Firstborn, when I die you will have half my camels. My middle child you may have one third. And you, you young scoundrel, you may have one ninth".

The old man dies and the children gather round to divide the camels. This seems to be an impossible task. They don't want to cut up the camels because they're fond of them, so they visit the old wise woman in the village.

She speaks, "Unlike your late father, I am but a poor woman. I have only one camel. But you may have it". The children thank her for her generosity and return home.

Now the division is easy. The first born says, "I am due half so I will take nine camels", the middle child says, "I am due a third so I will take six", and the youngest says, "I and am due a ninth so I will take my two".

When they go to the camel kraal, they find that once they have taken their share, the old woman's camel is still there. For nine and six and two equals seventeen. So they return the camel to the old woman and thank her for her help.

The father is the kind of team builder we admire.

The Forest is Not the Office: Team Building

We have never believed in those popular corporate events that promise to build teams as people learn to abseil, tackle obstacle courses, go paintball shooting or white-water raft together.

We don't believe the pseudo logic that says,

> "Because I trust you to find your way through this forest, you will lead equally well in the marketplace".

or

> "I trust that you won't let me fall here, therefore I trust that you will not let me down, not engage in corporate politics, and do what is in my best interest in the workplace".

or

> "I have faith in your judgement and direction-finding in the great outdoors and so I know that your judgement and decision making at work will be as good".

Jon R. Katzenbach and Douglas K. Smith get it right in their *The Wisdom of Teams – creating the high performance organization*.[4] Essentially, teams at work produce collective work products, foster personal growth and get performance results through:

- applying their technical, problem solving and interpersonal skills

- being mutually accountable to each other and to their work delivery

- being committed to the approach of the team, a meaningful purpose and specific and well understood goals.

This happens even if they don't like each other and haven't bonded at a team-building event as described above! By focusing on performance and team basics – as opposed to trying to 'become a team' – most small groups deliver the performance results that require and produce team behaviour.

On rare occasions or during projects, people working together in a team enjoy a marvellous sense of purpose, learning, relating, creativity and belonging. We need to belong. It is a basic human need. Not only at work, but in every part of our lives.

Ugly Ducklings

In her best selling work *Women Who Run With The Wolves*, author, story-teller and Jungian analyst Clarissa Pinkola Estés refers to this Hans Christian Andersen story as a "psychological and spiritual root story", one that contains a fundamental and vital truth about the human condition.[5] She tells the story in a chapter entitled: "Finding One's Pack: Belonging as Blessing".

We all find ourselves lost, bewildered, lonely, not nurtured, ostracised, wandering and outcaste at times and need to find where we belong, where we have our home, where we connect with beautiful strangers who are like ourselves, where we find our identity and soul companions.

We need to come out of our dark cold nights of the soul and feel alive. We need for spring to come. We need to feel acknowledged, welcomed, accepted, esteemed. We

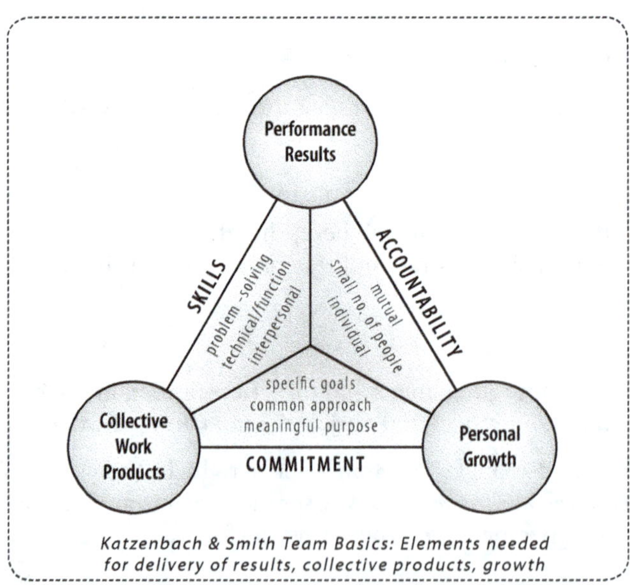

Katzenbach & Smith Team Basics: Elements needed for delivery of results, collective products, growth

need to be in that place and with those kindred spirits where we are able to find meaning, express our creativity, share our talents, achieve and learn and grow.

We need to be part of an all encompassing story. Part of a team that appreciates our individuality.

Diversity

And this belonging can transcend artificial differences.

The hordes of people fleeing war and distress in Syria and other places has led to many stories. Stories of Cultures Clashing. Difficulty and Disaster. Courage and Cooperation.

Neuroscientist Richard Crisp reminds us that we *do* have hardwired prejudices and a tendency to stereotype. This fear-based, 'protective mechanism' keeps us from adapting to a new person or outgroup, and leads to resentment, friction, and conflict. He also points out that we can activate cooperation. He shows how, throughout history, where groups have seen the potential benefit in cooperation, this has set off creativity, innovation and progress. In the long run *"... diversity in our social ecologies nurtures a more creative, resilient and adaptive culture".*[6]

Migrations take many forms. As the global village becomes smaller countries, market places and workplaces are fast becoming more connected and more diverse. This represents either a stumbling block or an inclusion opportunity. Performance may be strangled or unleashed, a halo or a noose.

Deeply appreciating the other (across a divide) is the platform on which some call CQ (Cultural Intelligence) is built.

Diversity takes many forms. Clearly different perspectives have a major bearing on how different people will view and approach different issues, solve problems, make decisions (and view each other, get frustrated with each other. Think gender, ethnicity, religion, culture, language, class, education, wealth, thinking style, personality type, age, lifestyle, experiences, psychological space and distance, the temporal dimension ..... Now that's an interesting one!

QUICK READ

Different perspectives on time

A PAST perspective may be seen to be the repository of incredible tradition, wisdom, and heritage. Because 'there is nothing new under the sun' we can learn from the past, and avoid repeating mistakes. Everything has arisen in the past therefore it is the determinant of what is now and will be. The past is something that can't be changed – it's over and done with – so why bother. Full of negatives – the source of our pathologies, faulty beliefs and conditioning, suspect memory. Dwelling on the past will get us nowhere.

> PRESENT. The present moment is all that we have really. Today determines and informs tomorrow and provides proper perspective on the past. Being in the present we can create a future that is emerging right now. The present is only a bridge between the past and the future. This conveys a necessary urgency. Actually it's so fleeting that every nano second that passes is a move from present to past ….
>
> Those who are able to imagine the FUTURE become equipped to handle the complexities and challenges of today. We must focus on the future and think long-term so that we can begin to do our duty and leave the right legacy for future generations. The future is uncertain, unknown, unpredictable – we don't know if disaster or something glorious beckons – so why bother?)
>
> (And Quantum physicists offer another view on time, other than tick tock time)

Social scientist André Laurant, Emeritus Professor of Organisational Behaviour at INSEAD, discovered an amazing phenomenon: that the best and worst performing teams have in common their multi-cultural make-up. The best teams rely on the difference and uniqueness of their members to create something better than can be produced by a mono-cultural team. But people who fear difference and put their energy into conforming produce little of note and do even worse than mono-cultural teams. *"He offers useful guidelines which harness cultural diversity and shows decision makers around the world how differences can become a source of synergy and competitive advantage when they are recognised, understood and appreciated".*[7] Richard Rohr offers this perspective, worth pondering: *"Negativity works in many immediate and seemingly good ways. It unites a fear-based group far more quickly than love does".*[8] Let's harness the richness of diversity in the teams that we put together, and remember poet Maya Angelou's words in, "Human Family".[9]

> I note the obvious differences
> between each sort and type,
> but we are more alike, my friends,
> than we are unalike.

There Are No Clones: Diversity Richness

> *A sculptor heard via a clairvoyant that he was soon to die. He dashed to his studio and created eleven statues – all an exact likeness of himself. He hid among the statues and froze. The Angel of Death arrived to fetch him and was greatly confused. God did not make clones.*
>
> *The Angel returned to God and told him what he had seen. God laughed and whispered in the angel's ear. The Angel returned and walked up and down the rows.*
>
> *"This is brilliant work," he observed. "Perfect, except for one small flaw".*
>
> *The sculptor jumped out and asked, "Flaw? What do you mean, flaw?"*

Anthony de Mello tells a story about a Brother tasked with scribing who is irritated by the never ending noise of bullfrogs at night. When he reaches an understanding of the Divine's love for the bullfrog, he begins to hear the music of the bullfrogs.[10]

Stories help foster belonging, introduce a positive flavour to team dynamics, allow the building of acceptance and trust – so that members move beyond blame, embrace diversity, create harmony, become more committed.

Stories create bridges between people.

Bridges

Bridges are an appropriate metaphor for our times.

> *Two turbulent, fiercely independent Mexican artists, Diego Rivera and Frido Kahlo, who deeply loved and were married to each other, lived in adjoining houses in San Angel, Mexico City. The architect designed a home made up of two separate concrete blocks linked by a narrow bridge that joins the rooftops. A red block represented Diego, a blue one Frida. The bridge that united them was the bond of love.*

Bridges speak to the crossing of barriers, forging connections, and peace-making.

> *In 2014 South African Kumi Naidoo, then Head of Greenpeace International, and Francesco Starace, CEO of Enel, were nothing short of enemies, waging bitter court battles. Greenpeace accused coal plants in Italy of killing people. They've become friends and partners. Together they are fighting global warming. Starace has promised to close 23 coal plants in Italy, and not develop planned new coal mines (in Italy and Chile). Enel Green Power is initiating and running renewable projects in Brazil, India, the USA and elsewhere.*

A pearl of wisdom: *"You are you and I am I and if each of us follows our own story, the world machine will keep on humming. But we have been inattentive to the cosmology that holds our lives together. How do our individual and communal stories shape our lives in the larger order of things? What holds us together despite our differences? We need a larger story that can include diversity and difference, and in which our local stories can thrive. Stories create meaningful lives; they provide cohesiveness and direction".[11]*

By building bridges, exchanging stories, getting to know one another we avoid what Nigerian novelist Chimamanda Adichie calls *'The danger of a single story'.[12]*

"You never really understand a person until you consider things from his point of view, until you climb into his skin and walk around in it" - Harper Lee (To Kill a Mockingbird)

---

[1] Teilhard de Chardin, Pierre. *The Appearance of Man*, Collins, London, 1965.

[2] Muller, Wayne. *Legacy of the Heart, the Spiritual Advantages of a Painful Childhood,* Simon & Schuster, NY, 1993.

[3] Miller, Arthur. *Death of a Salesman,* Penguin, 1998.

[4] Katzenbach, Jon R. and Smith, Douglas K. *The Wisdom of Teams: Creating the High Performance Organization,* Harvard Business School Press, Boston, 1993.

[5] Estés, Clarissa Pinkola. "The Ugly Duckling", in *Women Who Run With the Wolves,* Rider, NY, 1992.

[6] Crisp, Richard The Social Brain: how diversity made the modern mind Robinson Great Britain 2015

[7] Laurent, Andre http://www.speakers.co.uk/our-speakers/profile/andre_laurent

[8] Rohr, Richard Rohr Daily Meditation 25th December. 2015 Wisdom Lineage Summary: *Perfect Love Casts Out Fear*

[9] Angelou, Maya. "Human Family", in Simpkinson, Charles and Anne, *Sacred Stories,* Harper, San Fransisco, 1993.

[10] De Mello, Anthony. *The Prayer of the Frog,* Gujarat Sahitja Prakash, Anand, India, 1989.

[11] Delio, Ilia *The Unbearable Wholeness of Being: God, evolution and the power of love Orbis Books, 2013*

[12] Adichie, Chimamanda *The danger of a single story http://www.youtube.com/watch?v=D9Ihs241zeg*

Chapter 14

The All Devourer: Story and Strategy

If you wish to make God laugh, tell God your
plans for the future
(Old saying)

The Essence of Strategy and Strategic Execution

A Sufi arrives at the crossroads with a candle, a lamp and his woollen wares. He lights a lamp and sets it down. Then he lights a candle and places it at some distance away. He spreads his woollen scarves around the candle and waits for customers.

A passer-by asks, "Why are you not selling under the brighter light?"

"That," says the Sufi, "is to attract the moths".

Where to place the lamp, the candle and the merchandise? We see strategies as being about the how of doing what an organization needs to do – the broad, consistent, behavioural and action options that are chosen – in order to realise its vision.

How to position itself in the marketplace (the crossroads) to be both different and better in areas where it wants to excel. How to choose, gain and retain its customers. How to reach its 'personal best'.

Each organization needs its own unique set of strategies. "Only rarely does the template for one company's strategy fit the needs of another company, even if they're serving the same market".[1] It is important to have a good strategy story, but even more important to execute it well.

79

Bushmen and A Bushman Story

Here is a version of a Bushman folk tale that speaks to strategy. In Bushman folklore, Mantis is a super-being – a very human sort of god.

Mantis is caught stealing sheep and severely punished and beaten. He dreams of revenge, but when he shares his dream he is ignored. Mantis refuses to listen to wise counsel and against better advice he asks Porcupine, his trusted adopted daughter, to call upon her real father, the All-Devourer (bush fire), to 'eat' the people's sheep.

And the All-Devourer voraciously eats and swallows the veld, the food, the water, the shelter, possessions, sheep. The All-Devourer fire scorches and burns Mantis – his hands, his ear. And devours him, then Kwammanga (Porcupine's husband who is a part of the rainbow).

Porcupine weeps bitterly. She speaks to Young Mantis, son of Mantis, her brother and Kwammanga, her son – the All–Devourer must be beaten. Porcupine puts a heated spear into their noses to teach them to withstand heat. Young Mantis's eyes water and Kwammanga's eyes stay dry. They go to fight the All-Devourer.

The All-Devourer scorches their ears. But they withstand the heat, and thrust spears into him, and all that he has swallowed pours out. And he dies.

Young Mantis is thirsty. His wife, Dassie the rock rabbit, tells him to drink sparingly, but he gulps down lots of water, collapses and nearly dies. Dassie beats him on his shins to waken him and admonish him. Porcupine gives her son Kwammanga water and he drinks properly and recovers well.

Bushmen Stories and Business Strategy

Bushmen are steeped in story:

I must first sit a little

I listen, watching for a story I want to hear

I sit waiting for it, that it may float into my ear.

These are those stories (for) which I am listening with all my ears

While I sit silent I must wait listening behind me

As if I have travelled a long road and then sit down,

And I wait for a story to travel after me

Following me along the same road...

When my three names, Jantjie, /Uh-ddoro and //Kabbo

Float along to my place

I will turn backwards to my feet's heels on which I went

For a story is the wind.

I will turn backwards with ears to my feet's heels, on which I went, for a story is the wind.[2]

When the Bushman tribe is under threat, a strategic solution is to burn the land, having first buried its own water supply underground in ostrich eggs so that it can still survive where others cannot.

In modern business how do we outwit circumstances and ensure our survival? How do we withstand and overcome severe heat when necessary – for example a hostile corporate raid or a painful transition or restructuring? Who are our identified strategists, our carefully chosen warriors for certain tasks? Who has 'been there, done that, wears the T-shirt' and can impart wisdom and contingency plans gleaned from past experience (for example the storing and burying of water in ostrich eggs)?

How do we combine strategy and heart, improve our execution-ability? Who will be our warriors? What resources do we need to use? How do we develop the disciplines of assessing situations, solving problems, making decisions, carrying out those decisions – turning plans into actions? How do we make the needed changes, mobilise the necessary resources? Survive, prosper, sustain?

Strategy, Experience and Structure

God and the Devil are watching a group of survivors crawling through the desert. They stumble across an oasis. There are date palms, shelter from blazing sun and abundant water.

The Devil mutters, "These people have found paradise".

God turns to the Devil, "I suppose your work is over now".

"On the contrary," responds the Devil, "I will help them organize it".

There is a peculiar relationship between experience and the structures we build and strategies we put in place to contain or express that experience. And to ensure that it continues. People who have, say a religious experience, inevitably construct a dogma. Often when another experience presents itself, the response is to measure it against existing dogma instead of changing the dogma to suit the experience. When a river

---

READING

Versions of the story above and other Bushman tales, with many lessons for organizations, are beautifully told in

The Mantis and His Friends – Bushman Folklore [2]

Specimens of Bushmen Folklore [3]

Stories that Float from Afar [4]

There is much to learn and digest

---

course changes, the map becomes obsolete and needs to be redrawn. Stories help us with such redrawing as they are true to shifting experience. They reflect where we are.

Stories and Future Scenarios

Strategic planning inevitably involves storytelling, as we think ourselves into an imagined future. We try to gauge external and internal changes in our economic, social, personal and political life. In the business world strategic planners are legion.

We suggest that a greater consciousness of stories strengthens such planning.

The heart of the story is contained in the three words 'what happens next?' This is what keeps us curious as to the outcome. Stories offer open-ended possibilities. They call forth our creativity and imagination.

Many of the stories told in this book can be used for strategic planning. Beyond them are sequels that can be imagined, that is, what happens after the story ends? How successful is the Sufi's lamp and candle plan in selling his woollen merchandise at the crossroads? What happens when All-Devourer has regurgitated all he has swallowed? What happens when people who formed a community in the desert find themselves in an oasis?

We enter the future echo of the story. This is a form of ripening. Poet Wendel Berry reminds us:

> Our hair turns
> white with our ripening
> as though to fly away in some
> coming wind, bearing the seed
> of what we know.[5]

As you develop your storytelling powers, so you will develop the witness who watches the story developing. This witness, moving ahead of us, showing the way, has an intuitive knowledge of the future. This witness is the strategist.

---

[1] Whitney, John O. and Packer, Tina. *Power Plays*, Simon & Schuster, NY, 2000.
[2] Bleek, W. H. I. and Lloyd, Lucy. C. *The Mantis and His Friends – Bushman Folklore*, T. Maskew Miller, Cape Town. 1923.
[3] Bleek W. H. I. and Lloyd, Lucy. *Specimens of Bushmen Folklore*, George Allan and Unwin, London, 1869: Facsimile reprint, Cape Town, 1911.
[4] Lewis-Williams, J. D. (Ed) *Stories that Float from Afar*, Texas A&M University Press 2000.
[5] Berry, Wendel. In Bly, Robert et al, *Rag and Bone shop of the Heart*, Harper Collins, NY, 1992.

<h1 style="text-align:center">Chapter 15
Four Riddles
Cooks, Suitors, Stones and the King's Reward</h1>

Encoded Stories

Often challenges at work are like riddles. Something that defies an approach that previously worked. Something missing in the puzzle. Defying left-brain logic.

Riddles and proverbs play an important role in many oral cultures such as the Ovambo in Namibia. Stories are encoded in riddles.

This chapter offers you four riddles. There are no right responses. Perhaps each response has merit. Stories like this encourage us to think more laterally and go beyond the obvious. We suggest that you treat the four stories as a whole, read them through, think about them and then look at various possible responses.

The Choice of Cooks

There is a competition to find a new cook for the King. There are two candidates. The King instructs them, "One of you can cook on the first night. And the other one can cook on the second night".

On the first night, the first cook prepares a sumptuous banquet. The three course meal greatly delights the King. The next night the second cook prepares exactly the same banquet.

Which cook does the King choose? And why?

The Three Suitors

Three princes request the hand of the princess. She dies before she can choose.

The first prince goes off to live with her father, the King. "He would have been my father in law," he reasons.

The second prince lies on the grave for two days and cries his eyes out.

The third prince goes travelling. On the first night, he enters a cottage and sees an old man throw a child into the flames. The old man assures him, "There is no harm done". He waves his hands and chants a few words. The child steps from the fire unharmed.

The third prince hurries back to the graveyard. He waves his hands and chants. The princess comes back to life and steps out of the grave.

Which prince does the princess choose as her husband? What reasoning and emotions motivate her choice?

Black and White Stones

A young woman lives happily with her father in a cottage on a beach, famous for its black and white stones. One day the local tyrant, without reason, (tyrants – corporate or other – don't give reasons) takes her father and throws him into jail. The young woman requests an audience with the tyrant. Because she is beautiful, he agrees to meet with her "on the beach of black and white stones".

When they meet, the tyrant explains, "This is how it works. I will pick up two stones from the beach – a white stone and a black one – and put them in my bag. You close your eyes, put your hand in my bag and select a stone. If you choose the white stone, then I will release your father and give you 1000 gold pieces. If, however, you choose the black stone, then I will behead your father and you must be my concubine".

The tyrant stoops down, picks up two stones and drops them into his bag. The young woman notices that they are both black stones.

What is she going to do? Complete the story. What insights do you gain from the completed story?

The King's Reward

The King wishes to reward his three favourite subjects for their services. He tells them, "You may have what your heart desires. Ask and I will grant".

The first responds, "Oh King, I want wealth".

"Granted," says the King.

The second says, "Oh King, I want half your kingdom and I desire to marry your daughter".

"Granted," says the King. (He's that kind of King).

The King then turns to the third subject and says, "Whatever you ask, I will grant you".

The third subject looks into the eyes of the King and says, "Oh king, I want audience with you three times a day".

How does this third request differ from the other two? Is the third subject's request self-directed or aimed at serving the king?

Workshop Responses

In workshops there are many different responses to these riddles. For stories reflect where we are. We bring our individual experience to them. Refer to the box for some participant responses.

In the King's Ear story, if one substitutes the word 'God' for the word 'king,' then this opens up the idea of having a conversation with God three times a day – a ritual encounter. If we take out the word King and substitute the word 'creativity' we now have a ritual commitment to engage in our creativity. If we substitute the word CEO then this asks for the availability of the CEO.

In Sophocles's play, Oedipus became ruler of Thebes by answering the riddle of the Sphinx. "What walks on 4 feet and 2 feet and 3 feet and has only one voice, when it walks on most feet it is the weakest?" Oedipus correctly answered, "Man" and became the King.[1] How we feel, think and act determines our responses and creates our destiny. In our work and lives.

Story riddles engage the whole person – they get the physical, intellectual, emotional, creative, social and spiritual juices flowing.

---

[1] Sophocles, *Oedipus Rex*. Preston House, Clayton, 2004.

The Choice of Cooks

Some people choose the first cook, because he showed originality and took the risk of pleasing the King or not pleasing King.

Others choose the second cook, because he too risked. Presumably, since he was a cook, he could have prepared an entirely different dish to please the King's palate, but he deliberately chose imitation – an art in itself. And yet not imitation, because the same ingredients in the same dish will turn out differently on a different day and certainly when another cook is in charge of the combining, simmering and the mixing.

Some people say the King being the King, probably would have chosen both cooks. In the version we heard, the King chose the second cook because he said, "You know the meaning of repetition". If you have problems with the word 'repetition,' you can substitute the word 'ritual'. What new dimensions to the story open for you?

The Three Suitors

Some people choose the first prince, because he shared commitment to family and did not only think of himself. He wanted to comfort her father, who lost his daughter. Others reject the first prince, because he was trying to ensure his own future.

People who choose the second prince, respond to his grieving. This choice raises the question of appropriate grief, necessary grief. And timing. Did he lie there for two days or for two years? The people who have walked the way of grief, say a certain passing of time is necessary before they can move on. If he lay on the grave for three days, then this would be appropriate. If he lay there for ninety weeks, then he might be stuck.

Those who choose the third prince, argue that he is the one who was able to apply something he experienced. He brought the princess back to life, so she owes her life to him. Others argue that this could make for an imbalance and dominant relationship.

In the version we heard, the King chose the second prince, because "He was the only one who, through his grief, showed how much he loved me".

Black and White Stones

This is how the story continues:

The young woman closes her eyes. Swiftly she digs into the bag, encloses one stone in her fist, takes it out and promptly drops it on the beach.

"I'm terribly sorry," she apologizes. "But we'll know which stone I dropped by the one that is left in the bag".

Workshop participants suggest, "Clever. She does not put the tyrant down. She beats him at his own game". "She allows the tyrant to save face". "If she stays in the bag – the box – she is stuck. If she takes in the wider environment – the beach – she finds the solution".

The King's Ear

How does the third subject's approach differ from those of the other two?

People talk about the materialism of the first two choices and what drives them. When it comes to the third subject, people say that he wants a process. This, of course, is hardest for the King to give. His time. Some say, "If he has the ear of the King, he will end up with half the kingdom and the princess and land and the wealth". Others suggest, "He feels he has something to give the King. So he engages in an ongoing conversation".

Chapter 16

A Higher Purpose, Dreams, Visualization, Play and Imagination

You could travel from your inner man into your
outer man. By a journey of that sort this becomes
a place where you find gold [1]

Rumi

If a story is the house – a structure above ground – then underneath it there is a basement. The basement contains four building materials – dreams, visualization, play and imagination. This chapter is about honouring these four visitors so our work life can be animated and enriched.

Dreams

> *Once Chuang-Tzu dreamt he was a butterfly, fluttering around... Suddenly he woke up... But he didn't know if he was Chuang-Tzu who had just dreamt that he was a butterfly, or a butterfly now dreaming that he was Chuang-Tzu.* [2]

We use the word 'dream' to cover both our daytime hopes and our night time realities. John Lennon's *Imagine* is an example of this.

> You may say I'm a dreamer
> But I'm not the only one
> I hope someday you'll join us
> And the world will be as one

So is Martin Luther King Jnr's oft quoted speech:

> I say to you today, my friends, that even though we face the difficulties of today and tomorrow, I still have a dream... I have a dream that one day this nation will

87

rise up and live out the true meaning of its creed – we hold these truths to be self-evident that all men are created equal. I have a dream that one day … the sons of former slaves and the sons of former slave owners will be able to sit down together at the table of brotherhood.[3]

We will deal with this kind of dream under visualization, which in a sense is a dream made specific and concrete. The future visualized in the present or as Lady Macbeth puts it, "I feel now the future in the instant".

Let us focus on the sense of dream as the night time story. We process our dreams in narrative form. In the drama of a dream you find atmosphere, plot, setting, characters, action, conflict and form.

> *In a dream, a messenger told a village Rabbi, "If you go to the city and dig under a tree at the emperor's castle, you will find hidden treasure". The second night he had the same dream and the third night. So he went to the city. But the castle was heavily guarded so he couldn't get in.*
>
> *Every morning the rabbi walked around the castle. One day the captain of the guard asked him, "Old man, what are you doing walking round and round the castle?"*
>
> *The rabbi told him the story.*
>
> *The Captain laughed, shook his head and said, "Dreams are foolish things. I had a dream about a poor rabbi who came from a village like yours. He dug up his own hearth and found a treasure hidden there".*
>
> *The Rabbi thanked the Captain, walked the long road home, dug beneath his fire place and found the treasure.*

Sigmund Freud called dreams the royal road to the unconscious. The *Talmud* tells us, "A dream that is not understood is a letter that is not opened". Dreams offer guidance, an understanding of what is really going on in our private or business lives and a symbolic way of processing this information. Since dreams are related to the context of our lives at a particular moment, they sometimes offer clues or solutions about how to deal with particular problems.

> *Elias Howe, inventor of the sewing machine needle, was struggling with design – how to incorporate a needle in his machine. (In the conventional needle, the point and the eye are at opposite ends). In a dream he was being chased by savages carrying spears. He noticed that at the head of the spears there were eyes. He woke with the machine needle design.*

Dreams can be very simple and clear. A longtime friend who is suffering from advanced multiple sclerosis, Dave Smal, and called Sipho (The Gift) by the predominantly Xhosa staff at his place of care, was recently very comforted by a dream in which he saw a tablet saying, "Romans 8 : 18"

Many Southern African groups honour the importance of dreams in traditional healing. The Dinka of the Sudan had an animistic understanding of dreams. They believed that memories and day dreams were external to oneself, as external as surrounding nature.

This suggests that such dreams can shape our business landscapes. Robert Louis Stevenson, author of *The Strange Case of Dr. Jekyll and Mr Hyde,* who dreamt many scenes in the book, described the "little people" in his dreams, who helped him with stories.[4]

Dreams obviously can help us address the emotional life of the workplace. Spanish poet Antonio Machado writes:

> Last night, as I was sleeping,
> I dreamt – marvellous error!
> – that I had a beehive
> here inside my heart.
> And the golden bees
> were making white combs
> and sweet honey
> from my old failures.[5]

The simplest way of gaining access to our dreams and beginning to work with them, is keeping a Dream Journal. Writing for five minutes at the instant of waking. Especially when we are facing big decisions in the 9-5 world. Dreams are shy. If we do not pay attention to them they tend to disappear. And if we say we will write down the dream at a more convenient moment in the day, often when we try to recapture a particular dream, it has disappeared and left no business card.

Another way of dealing with dreams is to suppose that all features of the landscape, objects, motifs and characters carry aspects of the dreamer in symbols that are peculiar to that dreamer.

Dreams can be a drive to action as writer Delmore Schwartz reminds us, in his short story, "In Dreams Begin Responsibilities".[6]

Visualization

Martin Luther King's dream was of the type that became a reality, an inspiring and measurable vision of the future that provides clear purpose and serves as a rallying point. This is vital in business organizations. People need a clear picture of where they are going if they are to commit to getting there.

> Alice: "Would you like to tell me which way I ought to go from here?"
>
> "That depends a great deal on where you want to get to," said the cat.
>
> "I don't know where," said Alice.
>
> "Then it doesn't matter which way you go," said the cat.[7]

When working with groups formulating a vision, I sometimes hand out blow pipes (pea shooters) and wadding balls to participants without instruction. Their immediate instinct is to shoot at each other, randomly chosen targets, or nowhere in particular. I then, without words, place an archery-type target on the wall. Immediately, *everyone* focuses on and aims at the target. People need something to aim at.

In *Man's Search For Meaning*, psychiatrist and author Viktor Frankl draws on his Auschwitz concentration camp experiences during the 2nd Word War to illustrate the veracity of vision.[8] People need meaning and a future to hang on to when the going gets tough: "Any attempt to restore a man's inner strength in camp had first to succeed in showing him some future goal".

Mohammed Ali, perhaps the greatest boxer of all time, latched on to the power of visualization when he chanted:

> Float like a butterfly
> Sting like a bee
> Your hands can't hit
> What your eyes can't see.

We need in business and in our personal lives to reframe the context and content of what we are doing, what we believe in, the words that we use or where and what we want to be.

By visualizing a goal, event, achievement, state, we have already taken the first step towards positively approaching and reaching what we wish to happen.

For the individual, it would be silly to go to a railway ticket office and ask for a ticket without being able to name a destination. Sadly, this is the case for many. We either don't know or our vision of what we want to be and do is skewed by parental and societal conditioning. We strive for self-esteem and personal identity through power, position, possessions .....

Typically we see ourselves ("man") as a superior being who has dominion over and can control all else – other sentient beings, systems, ideologies, the earth itself, space ... Or we are overwhelmed by the vastness of the universe and all that happens in it. We feel powerless. Insignificant. As Nobel Physiology/Medicine Prize winner Jacques Monod would have it, *"man at last knows that he is alone in the unfeeling immensity of the universe".*[9]

A third view is of 'we', an appreciation of the interconnectedness (immediate and intimate) of all things. This sentiment resonates with findings in Gestalt psychology, Integral Theory, the Collective Unconscious, Systemic Thinking, Rhizomes (Systems Biology), Chaos Theory, Quantum Physics and Neuroscience. It also resonates with aspects of Hindu, Buddhist, Shamanic and the Judeo-Christian mystical tradition. We are an integral part of a much bigger whole, and that whole is also within us.

Foremost Catholic scholar Ilia Delio also speaks about the emerging new consciousness of interbeing as we continue to evolve, explaining, *"If being is intrinsically relational, then nothing exists independently or autonomously"* and *"Integral thinking is thinking the whole and the parts as wholes within the whole. The lines of analysis are not linear but contextual".* She speaks of the evolutionary miracle of interdependence and integration, *"Bees and ants, for example, are unable to survive in isolation, but in great numbers they act almost like the cells of a complex organism with a collective intelligence and capabilities for adaption far superior to those of their individual members".* Delio's clarity when describing the noosphere - *"a level of shared consciousness that transcends boundaries of religion, culture and ethnicity"*, the complex evolutionary mind-brain-body system that is spiritual consciousness, and how we are evolving towards greater unity of love and shared virtues, is breath-taking.[10] Here is food for contemplating purpose.

For the organisation, especially in a time where there is great emphasis on serving, sustaining and nurturing people and planet and economic well-being, purpose has assumed new importance. The best purpose statements are clear, simple, not limited in scope nor time:

- Sounds True: *'to disseminate spiritual wisdom'*

- Southwest Airlines: *'we exist to connect people to what's important in their lives'*

- *Pirch*, Atlanta: *'the reason we exist is to create inspired moments in people's lives'*

New research shows that organisations driven by a higher purpose secure superior engagement from their employees.[11]

And purpose flows out of contemplation, reflection and mindfulness, *"Purpose and values are central to mindfulness. Almost inevitably, practising mindfulness calls leaders (and each of us) to ask how they are spending their energy and their lives".*[12]

Play

A skilled archer came to a village. As he walked around he noticed that somebody had been practising shooting at a number of targets. Whoever it was had drawn his targets in chalk. The archer was impressed for the arrow had left its mark in the middle of every target.

He asked who the marksman was and was directed to a hut where a small boy was playing with his bow and arrow.

"Did you score all those bull's eyes?"

The boy nodded.

EXERCISE

Here is a right–brain exercise:

Think about an instance of success or failure that was significant to you. Identify the emotions that were present. What picture do you see and hear:

       Bright and colourful?

       Light and warm mood?

       Lots of movement?

       Are you in the picture or watching?

       Close to the action or distant from it?

       Loud noise?

Now deliberately change the picture to the opposite of all of the above elements and notice how your feelings about the event change, what new emotions surface.

"How did you do it?"

"Easy" answered the boy. "First I shot the arrow. Then I drew the target around it".

Carl Jung believed that adults should be involved in serious play. He practiced what he preached.

> *One day in the grounds outside his home, he was playing in nature, busy constructing in miniature a bridge over a stream. A peasant passing by, looked on in amazement and observed, "Is that not the world famous doctor? It doesn't look like it".*

As children, a great deal of our learning was doing exactly what Jung was doing – playing in scale. We love scale, whether it be a miniature Dutch town, a doll, a model train, a ship in a bottle or the architect's scale model of the building to be.

Another form of play involves the idea of a twin. We imagine that as we bubbled out of our mother, another stream bubbled from the same source. This is our twin. For those who are twins consider a triplet.

Playing around with a hypothetical twin's story, can be a road to 'the companion self'. That part of me that accompanies all I do – the part that Carl Jung called the twin. As Ray Bradbury, the writer, suggests, "I do not write. The other me demands emergence constantly".[13]

Who is 'the other me'? Anthropologist and writer, Jean Houston, answers this question as she shares a childhood experience that changed her life.[14] Her father wrote scripts for various radio personalities. One client was Edgar Bergen, the ventriloquist who had a famous puppet called Charlie McCarthy.

> *Once she went with her father to deliver a script to Bergen, who was staying in a local hotel. As they entered his room Bergen, with his back to the door, was deep in conversation with the puppet, Charlie, perched on his knee. Jean's father coughed and Edgar swung round.*
>
> *"You caught me. I was asking questions and Charlie was answering".*
>
> *"But Edgar," Jean's father responded, "those are your words coming out of the mouth of the puppet".*
>
> *"Yes, but I have no idea where the answers are coming from".*

Imagination

During her trial one of Joan of Arc's accusers asked, "You say you hear the voice of God. How do you know this is not just your imagination?" Joan of Arc responded, "How would God speak but through the imagination?"

The poet, Coleridge, regarded what he called primary imagination as "the living power and prime agent of all human perception".[15] Imagination and the ability to form images of the past, present or future is as natural as breathing. Our dream and waking life is filled with images. Some of these, like the images that came to Macbeth, shake us nightly. Others offer us energy and enthusiasm.

productive – is contained in the stories that we construct. Theologian Richard Rohr in *Hope Against Darkness*, reminds us:

> Imaginal knowing, the only way that the unconscious can move into consciousness, happens through fantasy, through dreams, through symbols ... and through well-told stories. It happens through poetry ... the words that create the image that in turn creates a new awareness – that is in us already. [16]

We need to allow these four consultants – dreams, visualization, play and imagination – into the board room. They are the prompts to a story with a quadruple bottom line.

---

[1] Barks, Coleman. *The Essential Rumi*, Penguin, NY, 1995.

[2] Chuang-Tzu. *Chuang-Tsu – Inner Chapters*, Random House, NY, 1974.

[3] King, Martin Luther Jnr, *A Testament of Hope,* Harper Collins, NY, 1990.

[4] Stevenson, Louis. *The Strange Case of Dr. Jekyll and Mr Hyde*, Norton, NY, 2002.

[5] Machado, Antonio. In Bly, Robert, Hillman, James and Meade, Michael, (eds) *The Rag and Bone Shop of the Heart*, (eds), Harper Collins, NY, 1992.

[6] Schwartz, Delmore. *In Dreams Begin Responsibilities,* New Directions, 1978.

[7] Carroll, Lewis (Charles Dodgson). *Alice's Adventures in Wonderland* and *Through the Looking Glass,* Barnes and Noble, NY, 2005.

[8] Frankl, Viktor. *Man's Search for Meaning*, Washington Square Press. Simon & Schuster, NY, 1963.

[9] Monod, Jacques (translation by Austryn Wainhouse) *Chance and Necessity: an essay on the natural philosophy of modern biology* Collins London 1972

[10] Delio, Ilia *The Unbearable Wholeness of Being: God, evolution and the power of love* Orbis Books 2013

[11] Hurst, Aaron (CEO of Imperative Group, Inc.) & Tavis, Dr Anna (Adjunct Professor of School of Professional Studies, NYU) *Workforce Purpose Index 2015* https://www.imperative.com/index2015

[12] Sinclair, Amanda *Possibilities, Purpose and Pitfalls: Insights from introducing mindfulness to leaders* Journal of Spirituality, Leadership and Management, 2015, vol. 8, no. 1, pp. 3-11 http://www.slam.org.au/wp-content/uploads/2015/07/JSLaMvol8no1_Sinclair.pdf

[13] Bradbury, Ray. *Zen and the Art of Writing*, Bantam, NY, 1995.

[14] Houston, Jean. *Trialogues at the edge of the West, Chaos, Creativity and the Resacrilization of the World,* Inner Traditions International, Rochester, 2002.

[15] Perry, S. (ed.). *S T Coleridge- Interviews and Recollections*, Palgrave Macmillan, 2001.

[16] Rohr, Richard. *Hope Against Darkness*, St Anthony Messenger Press and Franciscan

Chapter 17

Five Creatures and a Blue Guitar: Coaching

They said, "You have a blue guitar.
You do not play things as they are".
The man replied, "Things as they are
Are changed upon a blue guitar" [1]
Wallace Stevens

Flow Zones and Bubbles : The Purpose of Coaching

Onami, a great wrestler in Japan had a problem. When he performed in private he could beat his teacher, but when he performed in public, even his students could throw him. So he went to his teacher who lived in a temple next to the sea.

The teacher said, "Your name means great waves. So tonight, Onami, I want you to listen to the waves".

The teacher left, leaving Onami alone with the sound of the sea. At first he was distracted, then he began to focus on the waves. A wave rolled into the temple and took away the flowers in the vase in front of the statue of the Buddha. Then another wave rolled in and took away the vase. A third wave took away the Buddha statue.

In the morning Onami rose and went into the wrestling ring. There was no one in Japan who could defeat him.

When Ernie Els lines up a putt he is able, as other top athletes do, irrespective of their sport, climb inside a 'bubble' and focus without distraction on sinking the putt. At that moment he is operating in his flow zone. A 'bubble' of total attention, concentration and most importantly, relaxation combined with harnessed energy.

This is what Onami achieves and what top coaches teach their winning performers. Czikzentmihali introduced the notion that we are all at any one time in one of three zones: the flow zone, the panic zone (a place of anxiety, negative energy, disorientation, dysfunction), or the drone zone (where we are listless, bored, drifting without purpose).[2] Roger Bannister on being the first person to run a sub four-minute mile, described the feeling of being in the zone this way: "I discovered a new unity with nature. I had found a new source of power and beauty, a source I never dreamed existed".[3]

We all need to learn to get inside our flow zone bubbles when we need to achieve without wasted effort – whether sales persons, leaders, coaches, service providers, other workers. We need to be aware, attentive, concentrating, focused, de-stressed. Refer our chapter on Mindfulness.

The *Walkie-Talkie*: Coaching

As children, some of us created a *walkie-talkie* by speaking into an empty tin linked to another empty tin along a piece of taught wire. Imagine a coach at the other end of the line who is in constant communication.

Coaching is arguably, together with contact centre service providers, the fastest growing profession in business. "Coaching is a conversation, a dialogue, whereby a coach and *coachee* interact in a dynamic exchange to achieve goals, enhance performance and move the *coachee* forward to greater success".[4] So coaching is a supportive, nurturing, two-way interaction, where both parties are continually learning and looking ahead in order to define what they want to achieve and then achieving those required results. It's just like a story. Coaching is a unique relationship.

Coaching is *not*

- mentoring, which is a longer term relationship, usually with an older, more experienced person on an 'elder brother' basis. Greek mythology tells how Odysseus asked Mentor to look after his son; to share learning, to give of himself. Coaching may be short-term or take place sporadically

- therapy, which is depth analysis in order to lead the person to emotional and psychological healing. Coaching seeks to find out what works, and to use that to get better future results. Of course, coaching conversations may include the need for purpose and meaning, overcoming blockages and procrastination, building self-concept and esteem, dealing with life problems, understanding self and others

- management with a smile, which may when appropriate add to the workplace dynamics and climate, foster praise and encouragement, but does not positively develop the other person

- cheer-leading, which is about inspiring. Coaching may inspire, but it is also about realistically assessing and addressing weaknesses as well as strengths

- disciplining and counselling, which is directed towards an immediate 'problem employee' or workplace incidents that are outside of policy, in order to eliminate causes and achieve conformance rather than focusing on building new skills over time in order to get genuine, positive improvement. Or directed at giving advice

- training, even individual on-the-job training, which is more time-consuming and is focused on the trainer imparting new knowledge and skills rather than the continuous and consistent transfer of new skills and behaviours and ensuring their practice so as to develop new habit patterns, on a *coachee*-led and more democratic basis. *Coachees* learn to *do* things differently and to *be different.*

In paying homage at his former coach's funeral, a moment of catharsis where he is able to forgive and accept, former football hero Neely Crenshaw says, "Once you've played for Eddie Rake, you carry him with you forever. You hear his voice, you see his face, you long for his smile of approval, you remember his tongue lashings and lectures".[5]

> *Neely and other former players gathered for a vigil to the enigmatic Rake to relive his motivation and inspiration and his teaching that to think of losing was never an option, that you never ever quit. They recall his bullying and manipulation, his behind-the-scenes compassion yet inability to express emotion. They again feel moments of regret and sheer hate at being forced into making unwanted changes, moments of exhilaration and being totally in the maximum achievement zone, and what it is like to experience rare team greatness. They contemplate his influence on their lives way beyond the football stadium.*

In every field of endeavour, sport, business, balanced living, coaches carry enormous power – power to make or break others. With this power comes great responsibility. In addition to higher level skills, a coach requires the highest standards of integrity, ethics and values, and a deep-seated drive to serve others.

Five Creatures: What Makes a Good Coach?

Competencies required by effective workplace coaches are, broadly speaking

- to know themselves, have a positive attitude and be other – oriented

- to nurture others with sensitivity and motivate and inspire by role – modelling

- to communicate and relate assertively (both warmly and to good effect!)

- to have good observation and listening skills and see what is required, know how to get there (this also implies a future-orientation) and then go for it unreservedly

- to use a coaching process that works, and gets the required results in the right way.

These broad qualities could be supported by humility, authenticity, mindfulness and kindfulness, curiosity, wonderment, courage, resilience, appreciation of diversity, non-dualistic thinking, self-reflective and self – determining ..... Challenging!

Coaches are leaders, yet coaching takes place downwards, upwards and sideways in organizations.

What should you keep in mind as you go about your coaching duties? We think you should have a picture in your mind of land, sea and air – of five living creatures:

Elephant

Some don't know that learning, change and growth is beneficial. James Belascoe, a Professor of Management at San Diego State University, illustrates the power of conditioning that can be so deep that people cannot even conceive of needing to change or be different in any way.[6]

Trainers shackle young elephants with heavy chains to deeply embedded stakes. In that way the elephant learns to stay in its place. Older elephants never try to leave even though they have the strength to pull the stake and move beyond.

Mussel

The mussel decides where it is going to settle and then stays there.

After making that decision, the mussel cements its head against a rock and stays put for the rest of its life. I've discovered that many people are like that.[7]

People need to have a good reason to embrace change, to move out of their comfort zones, to become involved, to be and to perform differently.

The good coach understands this and gives people a view of the future, personal benefit, explanation and encouragement to participate in the coaching process. The good coach does not simply tell people where and how to improve and then impose solutions. The good coach also knows that people are individuals and that change is more threatening to some – and formulates an approach and process and selects his/ her coaching techniques accordingly.

Dolphin

Gregory Bateson tells a story in his book *Steps to the Ecology of Mind* about the time he was involved in studying the communication patterns of dolphins at the Marine Research Institute in Hawaii:

He watched the trainers teach the dolphins to do tricks for a paying audience. On the first day, when the dolphins did something unusual, such as jumping out from the water, the trainer blew a whistle and threw the dolphin a fish as a reward. Every time the dolphin behaved that way, the trainer would blow the whistle and throw the dolphin a fish. Soon the dolphin learned that this behaviour guaranteed a fish; it would repeat it more and more and come to expect the reward.

The next day the dolphin would come out and do its jump, expecting a fish, but none was forthcoming. The dolphin would repeat its jump fruitlessly for some time, then in annoyance do something else such as rolling over. The trainer then blew the whistle and threw the dolphin a fish. The dolphin then repeated this new trick, and was rewarded. No fish for yesterday's trick, only for something new. This pattern was repeated for 14 days. The dolphin would come out and do the trick it had learned the day before for some time, to no avail. When it did something new, it was rewarded. This was probably frustrating for the dolphin.

On the fifteenth day it suddenly appeared to learn the rules of the game. It went wild and put on an amazing show, including eight new unusual behaviours, four of which had never been observed in the species before. The dolphin had moved up a learning level. It seemed to understand not only how to generate new behaviours, but the rules about how and when to generate them.[8]

One further point: during the 14 days Bateson saw the trainer throwing unearned fish for the dolphin outside the training context. When he questioned this, the trainer replied, "That is to keep my relationship with him. If I do not have a good relationship, he is not going to bother about learning".[8]

For the coach as for the story teller, the learning that is taking place may not always be visible to you, but it's happening all the same, sometimes at levels higher and more profound than you expect, so don't falter in your efforts and keep on persevering.

Eagle

Coaches can become deeply involved with the individuals that they coach. Even when coaching teams, it is possible to become absorbed and not see the wood for the trees. In the interests of obtaining perspective and of looking ahead, cultivate in yourself an eagle's view of what is happening in the organization and the contact centre. See the bigger picture. Don't lose sight of where the business needs to be

going. Don't become sidetracked by peripheral issues, problems and activities.

Tortoise

And finally, be like the tortoise, not in the sense of being slow, but in the sense of being sure and thorough. And of being aware that, unless you stick your neck out, you're never going to make progress.

> In the beginning
> there was a great tortoise
> who supported the world.
> Upon him
> all ultimately rests ...
> He is all wise
> and can outrun the hare.
> In the night his eyes carry him
> to unknown places.[9]
> (William Carlos Williams)

Coaches in Hard Hats

> *The two workmen, Eddie and Fred, in hard hats are sitting on a plank high up on the scaffolding of a building. It is lunchtime and they're eating their sandwiches. They both complain, "Damn. Peanut butter again". Eddie says, "I will ask my wife for something else".*
>
> *The next day they're back up on the plank at lunchtime. Eddie unwraps a tasty sandwich with cheese, lettuce, salmon and tomato. Fred complains, "Damn...*
>
> *peanut butter again".*
>
> *"Didn't you are ask your wife to make you something appetizing"? asked Eddie.*
>
> *Fred responded, "You don't understand. I live alone and make my own sandwiches".*

Being a coach means realising that you don't always have the answers for every situation and every person. Often you will have to explore and discover, by trial.

Story, imagery, metaphor and archetype have a number of roles to play in the coaching interaction. These roles include establishing rapport, forging emotional connection, raising awareness, showing empathy, conveying insight, extracting meaning, facilitating reflection, unveiling possibility, eliciting metaphor to aid expression, fostering visualisation, enabling reframing, encouraging journaling ....

To sum up: always remember that all your *coachees* will be different. Some don't know that they need to change, some don't want to. Learning takes place at different rates and in different ways, so be patient. Don't be afraid to risk as this will be a very real part of your own learning and growth.

A coach is perhaps like the man with the blue guitar, quoted as preface to this chapter. To his observation that things are changed in the playing, the people respond:

> But play you must,
> a tune beyond us, yet ourselves.
> A tune upon the blue guitar. [1]

---

[1] Stevens, Wallace. *Collected Poems*, Knopf, NY, 1990.

[2] Czikzentmihalyi, M. *Flow: The psychology of optimal experience,* Harper Collins, NY, 1991.

[3] Cameron, Julia. *The Artist's Way*, Pan Books, Oxford, London, 1993.

[4] Zeus, Perry and Skiffington, Suzanne, *The Complete Guide to Coaching at Work*, The McGraw-Hill Companies, Inc, Columbus, Ohio, 2000.

[5] Grisham, John, *Bleachers*, Century, 2003, Copyright © by Belfry Holdings, Inc, 2003.

[6] Belasco, James A, *Teaching the Elephant to Dance,* Hutchinson Business Books, London, 1990.

[7] De Vries, Manfred Kets, *The Leadership Mystique*, Financial Times/Prentice Hall, Great Britian, 2001.

[8] O'Connor Joseph and John Seymour. *Introducing NLP,* Thorsons, London, 1995, citing Gregory Bateson, *Steps to the Ecology of Mind,* Paladin Books, 1980.

[9] Williams, William Carlos. *Collected Poems of William Carlos Williams*, New Directions, NY, 1986.

Chapter 18

Mindfulness

*Authentic connection is the core of quality
relationships and mindfulness is a practice that
opens and deepens our capacities for connection* [1]
Surrey

Being in the Moment

A man approaches a teacher, who is sitting meditating.

He asks, "How can you sit there when there is so much pain, suffering and grief in the world?"

The teacher picks up a drinking glass and holds it in the air. "You see this glass? Look how it catches the light". Then she fills the glass with water and runs her finger around the rim. "Listen now how the glass makes music".

She puts the glass on a shelf behind her. "But I could easily knock this glass off with my elbow or the wind could take it. And it would be shattered into a thousand pieces. So I presume that the glass is already broken, and I enjoy every moment of it".

To be in the 'flow zone' and perform effortlessly, we need to find real purpose, meaning and bliss in the work that we do. We need also to practice mindfulness while we work and especially during our interactions with others and when listening to their troubles, triumphs and tales.

Being mindful means being 'present', being calm and relaxed, being focused – in order to be attentive, concentrated and empathetic.

100

In the Eye of the Storm

GTE Airphone operator Lisa Jefferson would probably like to forget what was going on at the other end of the phone that morning (of September 11th) when she spoke to Todd Beamer, a passenger on the hijacked United Flight 93. It was his plane that crashed into a field in western Pennsylvania after passengers bravely decided to charge the hijackers.

Knowing he was going to die, Todd tried to call his wife from the plane. But he had a problem with his credit card and was connected to Lisa. According to news reports, they spoke for 13 minutes during which Lisa took details of the hijackers, consoled Todd and promised to call his wife. Finally, she prayed with him before the air phone connection was terminated. Lisa told the authorities she heard passengers wailing in the background. Later she called Todd's wife to relay her husband's heroic final moments and message.

How was Lisa able to keep herself together in those harrowing and unprecedented 13 minutes? Service professionals understand the importance of remaining calm, strong and focused.[2]

Darwin Awards

We live so much in distraction. Sometimes in a crisis our minds move to past or future. Remember the monk who drank soy sauce then said he had drunk water? What if that had been paraffin? Not being mindful can cost us our lives – literally and figuratively.

The Darwin rewards "salute the improvement of the human genome by honouring those who remove themselves from life. Of necessity, this honour is generally bestowed posthumously".

The Darwin Awards website carries many stories about not being present. In one of them in 2003, a Brazilian worker was responsible for cleaning out the storage tanks of petrol tanker trucks. He began filling a tanker with water, a standard safety procedure that forces flammable vapour out of the container. When he returned an hour later to check, he lit a cigarette lighter so he could see into the tank. The vapour explosion threw him 100 meters. He died from severe burns, and an injury to his head.

Monkey Mind, Puppy Mind

Meditation teachers often liken our restless minds to a monkey or an untrained puppy. The monkey chatters and leaps from branch to branch. The puppy wanders everywhere. If you have tried to sit quietly emptying your mind from thought, you will have experienced just how difficult this practice is. This poem illustrates how easily we are distracted.

Puppy Mind

the puppy runs wild
    after the smell of rabbit,
    sniffed down a hole.
    whines and scratches
    at the fluff beyond reach.

runs barking at the past
revisits a tree, leg-lifts,
then pants back
into the future,
drinking a mirage.

I must train this Labrador,
call it to heal, to connection.
to be where my feet shift,
for it is a
guide dog
and I am blind. [3]

Mindfulness and Science

Eastern religions, as did early Christianity, have long practiced meditation in order to become grounded in the present, be aware and become mindful of what is happening within and around, to themselves, their environment and others. Western research is now slowly discovering the scientific validity of such practices:

- mindful meditation practice increases activation in an area of the brain associated with compassion [4]

- mindfulness practice enhances the capacity for attention [5]

- empathy is a function of attention (cognitive) and compassion (feelings, attitudes). [5]

Awake, Aware, Alive

We repeat a story told in Chapter 5:

> *A young girl approaches her father and asks, "Is it true that when we are asleep, we can wake up?"*
>
> *Her father assures her, "Of course it is true".*
>
> *"Then," says the girl, "it must also be true that when we are awake we can wake up more".*

Our purpose in this consideration of mindfulness is not to teach techniques that may help increase mindfulness – mindful breathing, tai chi, yoga – but rather to challenge you to strive to find your own way to become always mindful. This is what enables us to develop self-understanding and acceptance and relate better to others. We learn over time to

- know ourselves by being aware of our own feelings, anxieties, drives

- become content, happy

- keep our wits about us at all times

- be present for and focused on others

- exude calm, peace and acceptance of others.

Spiritual mindfulness

Spiritual mindfulness is an emerging notion. It is much more than simply raised awareness. Mindfulness shares with spirituality an internal focus and outward execution, habitual practices, and simply being human. Spiritual mindfulness can be seen to include an appreciation of wide interconnectedness (and a resultant other-orientation), finding meaning (intrinsic motivation), transcendence (a higher world view, seeing a bigger picture) and development of our inner selves. Such spiritual mindfulness fosters authenticity and brings positive virtues to the fore in ethical situations – or enhanced ethicality. It means:

- as we traverse the web of life we become a positively healing (integrating rather than fragmenting) force. We bind rather than sever.

- we become contemplatives in action, enter the flow zone and contribute warm-heartedness and love to a humanity that is in strife and disarray. Futurist John Naisbitt (who has laid down and advocates the balancing principle that more high-tech demands more high-touch) puts it this way: *"The most exciting breakthroughs of the 21st century will not occur because of technology but because of an expanding concept of what it means to be human,"*[6] and therefore our *"learning how to live as compassionate human beings in a technologically dominating time."*[7]

- We learn to think non-dualistically (AND instead of BUT/OR – especially in our relationships), and thus see wisdom and possibilities in paradox, ambiguity and (apparent) contradictions. In our brains, synapses are the gaps between neurons. Connection-activity in the synaptic space is vital. Using the brain neuron and synapse analogy, psychologist Louis Cozolino coined the term *'social synapse'* to refer to the gaps between people, and the vital importance of our gap activity. [8]

- Counter-intuitively, as our focus moves away from self at the centre of the web towards others, we give to ourselves. For example when we're feeling helpless we purposefully help others, when we're lacking something we give that to another, when we're down we seek to lift someone up ....[9]

Chris Lowney, a former Jesuit and top J.P.Morgan executive, tells the amazing story of the Jesuit organisation and its 450-year old guiding principles.[10]

Founded by St Ignatius of Loyola they achieved astounding growth, world-wide reach and enviable influence, overcoming incredible obstacles, all based on the 'Jesuit Way,' his Spiritual Exercises and four interrelated principles of:[11]

- *self-awareness (spiritual mindfulness)*

- *ingenuity (resilience and innovation)*

- *love*

- *heroism (in pursuit of a higher purpose)*

In short, whole-person leadership. They believed strongly that leadership was about being, a way of living. They also mentored and coached their members on a non-directive basis. [11] (No one else can provide our personal self-awareness, and the first person who we lead is ourselves).

These Jesuit virtues have relevancy for business leadership today. A mindfulness that transcends the ego (possessions, position, pride) and our shadow-side *"the divisions we feel within our very selves"*, [11] is the entering point for *being* which gives rise to effective *doing*. In order to contribute to bringing about peace (or love, resilience, authenticity, trust ...) we must first *be* that which we desire to see.

A Large Space

When we live in the present we live expansively because the present expands. Time seems to become irrelevant.

> *A teacher asks a student to fetch a glass of water. He goes to a nearby farmhouse and knocks on the door. The farmer opens the door. Behind the farmer stands the farmer's daughter. The man thinks, "I will work for this farmer".*
>
> *He works for several years, courting the daughter. Eventually they marry and have children – one, two, three. The man works the rice fields for his father-in-law.*
>
> *One day he is out in the field and is caught in a cloud burst. He finds himself waist deep in water, holding a glass of water. Suddenly he remembers.*
>
> *The man hurries as fast as his legs will carry him to the teacher and pants, "I am sorry I took so long".*
>
> *The teacher looks at him and replies, "You were only gone a moment".*

This story takes about twenty seconds to read. Yet as we read it, we travel through many years to far off places. Story time, like dream time, is expansive time. It is possible to increase our efficiency when we operate from such a space.

---

[1] Surrey, quoted in Germer, Christopher K., Siegel, Ronald D., Fulton, Paul R. (eds), *Mindfulness & Psychotherapy,* The Guildford Press, NY, 2005.

[2] Dawes, Gary. *Customer First : Front lines (Vol. 3 No. 7. 2002).*

[3] Haarhoff, Dorian. *Drawing Water,* Leopard Press, Durban, 2006.

[4] Davidson, R. J., Kabat-Zinn, J., Schumacher, J., Rosenkranz, Muller, D., Santorelli S., et al, *"Alterations in brain and immune function produced by mindfulness meditation"* Psychosomatic Medicine, Vol. 65, 2003.

[5] Germer, Christopher K., et al (Eds). *Mindfulness & Psychotherapy,* The Guildford Press, NY, 2005.

[6] Naisbitt, John *Megatrends: ten new directions transforming our lives* Warner Books 1984

[7] Naisbitt, John with Naisbitt, Nana and Philips, Douglas *High Tech High Touch: technology and our accelerated search for meaning* Nicholas Brealey Limited UK 2001

[8] Cozolino, L *The Neuroscience of Human Relationships: attachment and the developing social brain* Norton & Company, Inc. NY 2006

[9] Walsch, Neale Donald *The Complete Conversations with God: an uncommon dialogue* Hampton Roads Publishing Company, Inc. and G.P. Putnam's Sons NY 2005

[10] Lowney, Chris *Heroic Leadership: best practices from a 450-year-old company that changed the world* Loyola Press. A Jesuit Ministry. Chicago 2003

[11] Fleming, David L. S.J. *The Spiritual Exercises of St. Ignatius: a literal translation and a contemporary reading* Smyth Sewn Paperback The Institute of Jesuit Sources, St Louis 1978

Section C
Art and Craft:
Story-telling Guidelines

For it is not the story that counts.
What matters is the way you tell it [1]
Oom Schalk Lourens
(Herman Charles Bosman)

This section offers a guide through storyland with maps, travel tools for your saddle bag (horse or dragon) and tips aplenty. Story telling is not a talent. It is a learned skill available to anybody. Story telling and listening is not primarily a set of techniques and rules but a question of being transparent, vulnerable, passionate – about being real. It is about learning to breathe consciously.

Anansi the Spider, the trickster figure in west African folklore, acquires story-telling from the great god in the sky. Like Anansi we can acquire stories.

We offer suggestions on how to

- create a story-telling culture
- make up and structure the content of a story
- source stories
- remember the story/ learn stories off by heart
- learn what to include and what to leave out (how much is enough?)
- tell a story (climb inside and tell it from the inside)
- breathe and modulate your voice
- use your body in the telling
- work with silences.
- apply story ethics

Stories can start simply. "By the way, I was having a conversation with someone the other day and he asked me an unusual question". This takes people into story mode as they relax and become more open.[2]

For it's also about creating a receptive setting – physical and emotional – from the boardroom to the beachwalk and the braai. It is about harnessing the huge power of story (teller, listener and the story) to create understanding, awareness, energy, movement, excitement, passion. Story power surprises, brings fresh perspective and lessons. Stories challenge our beliefs, values, attitudes, ways of relating and behaving.

According to Pulitzer prize-winning author, Michael Chabon, Will Eisner (creator of the comic book character Spirit in the 1940's) rightly believed that "comics were a medium capable of doing stuff no other medium was capable of – intertwining words and images and coming up with something greater than either one on their own".[3] It's interesting that one of the best-selling business books ever is cartoonist Dilbert's *Management Principles*.[4] So we hope that we, you, the stories themselves and the illustrations will serve to carry you into your imaginary and real business Camelot. A place of beauty, adventure, learning, challenge, leadership. A place of best practice.

In ancient India, the throat chakra was about truthful expression, but blockages can occur. (The noose). The crown chakra is about being fully in touch with yourself and others and elevates all other chakras. (The halo). May you tell your stories with crown chakra energy.

---

[1]   Bosman, Herman Charles. *Mafeking Road and Other Stories,* Human and Rosseau, Cape Town, 1947.
[2]   Smart, Jamie. *NLP Tips* www.saladltd.co.uk.
[3]   Chabon, Michael. In *Will Eisner: A Spirited Life,* Mpress, Milwaukee, 2005.
[4]   Adams, Scott. *The Dilbert Principles,* Harper Business, NY, 1996.

Chapter 19
Story Patterns

Heroes and broken contracts can only be referred to by
virtue of their prior existence in the narrative world[1]
Jerome Bruner

The Use of Maps

We know that the map is not the territory. Yet maps, if drawn to scale and if updated when the landscape changes, can offer us context and insight. Stories provide this kind of map in that they offer us connections and patterns, insights and a bird's eye view that cannot be seen from the actual terrain.

> *Tortoise rested at a waterhole. Eagle landed next to it. Tortoise said to Eagle, "Look at this huge waterhole and these huge reeds. This is all there is".*
>
> *Eagle flapped his wings and ascended, bearing Tortoise in its claws. Tortoise saw the pond slipping away, becoming smaller and smaller. He saw the other animals running across the plain. Eagle flew so high that Tortoise saw the curve of the earth.*
>
> *Then Eagle set Tortoise down back at the waterhole. Tortoise travelled as fast as he could go to tell his tribe about the world he'd seen when he ascended on Eagle's wings.*
>
> *The other tortoises said, "Nonsense, you were dreaming. The waterhole and the reeds – that is all there is".*
>
> *But one tortoise asked, "Where can I find that eagle?"*

Stories also place what happens to us in a larger context. Through offering us a pattern, they connect to our work experience and locate us in the process. Paradoxically by being transported to a higher plane we become more grounded. This is one of the ironies that enriches our experience. This chapter offers a number of these story maps, models or patterns.

The Eight P's

You can hang a personal or organizational story on eight words beginning with the letter P – people, place, progress, problem, process, plan, possibility, product, e.g. somebody starts a business in a small town. The business catches on. Gets too big. Takes on more staff. Structures break down. Leader and team meet to brainstorm and make a plan. This leads to new possibilities. A new product emerges.

A product here could be either a material object or a way of doing business.

The Four Circles

Another pattern strongly evident in fairy tales, mythology and in other ways of telling, involves four circles. This is an ancient Motif. This story illustrates this pattern or movement.

> *A pot stood on a shelf in the museum. Many came to admire it. The woman who worked there took special care of this pot. She dusted it carefully and arranged it so the light from the window fell on it. (First circle).*

> *One day somebody left the window open and a gust of wind knocked the pot off the shelf. The pot lay in a thousand pieces. When the woman came to work the next day, she put her face in her hands and grieved for the broken pot. (Second circle).*

> *Then piece-by-piece she began to reassemble it. The woman glued pieces together and searched in the cracks between the floorboards. Those pieces she could not find, she measured and made. (Third circle).*

> *When she had glued the last piece, she stood back to gaze at her handiwork. Then she placed the pot back on the shelf. Despite its cracks many came to admire it. (Fourth circle).*

The creation story of *Genesis* also mirrors this pattern. Circle one is about perfection – the perfect beginning. Paradise (The Womb). The story hasn't started yet. If a story remains in the womb, there is no story:

> *A prince wanders into the forest and meets a princess. They gaze at each other mind-to-mind, eye-to-eye, heart-to-heart. They link hands and run to the palace. The Queen and King say, "Of course, you can marry". And they live happily ever after.*

Most people respond with the word 'boring'. Nothing happens. There is no movement. Nothing to resolve.

It seems that one of the necessary events of a story is the fall from grace and out of wholeness. Stories exist to help us make sense of the difficulties, challenges, brokenness. There are many versions of a person approaching the Enlightened one to ask, "Why is there so much pain and suffering in the world?" The Enlightened one responds, "To thicken the plot".

In the story something happens. The pot breaks. Time and death enter the world. We have fallen out of paradise into the second circle (The Wound). Grieving for a loss, a retrenchment, is attending to the wound. Appropriate shock, immobilisation, grief and despair can introduce the third movement.

In the third circle, we begin to respond – begin to move (The Work). We accept, we wander. We set forth on a journey. We desire to restore what has been broken, to recover and heal.

In a fairy tale this is often the longest and richest part of the journey – the hero travels far and encounters many dangers, enters many bargains with helping creatures, fights transition battles, grows in stature. And brings back to the kingdom the quality or the thing necessary for transformation. This is what mythologist, Joseph Campbell, refers to as the Hero's Journey.[2]

The fourth circle is about transformation (The Wonder). This is also about wholeness. About alchemy. Out of the dross of pain, loss and setback comes the gold of strength, value and reward.

The fourth circle is not the first circle. We cannot get back into paradise. In *Genesis*, the angels bar the gates with a flaming sword. And we have been on the poet William Blake's journey from innocence to experience. We think of the velveteen rabbit's journey from abandonment and heartache to becoming real. Here is the universe's principle of attraction when things tend towards wholeness.

The four circles repeated constitute a spiral – which takes us away from the concept that corporate time is only linear.

The Four Circles and a Client

In workshops we present many images and patterns to the group. This enables them to select the one that makes sense to them and then for them to work with this.

Sometimes it is necessary to allow the people in the wound to acknowledge and to name their grief. The first step for movement often involves the freedom to grieve. Note that one doesn't necessarily need to do anything about it nor have the power to solve it. And this active listening sometimes releases the person who is stuck at the start of the journey, if they so choose.

A CLIENT EXPERIENCE

In one case, working for a bank, participants cottoned on to the words 'wound' and 'work'. They saw the problems of their organization in terms of these stages in the story. Some people were still stuck in the wound, feeling a sense of betrayal. Some employees were hankering back to the paradise – to 'the good old days' – to the beginnings of the bank, when it was the blue-eyed boy (first circle). Others in the group were on the journey (third circle) but were not sure how to motivate their wounded colleagues (second circle), to take charge of the work.

Simplifying and Making Profound Through Story

Story patterns can help us keep things simple and in perspective. We once read of a suicide where a person had left a note saying, "I could not simplify my life". Einstein suggested we make things as simple as possible, not oversimplify them.

In another workshop one group seemed lost in the details. Their work story seemed to be over-complicated. After dividing the participants into four groups representing each of the four circles, each group was asked to say in three sentences what story was contained in that particular circle.

The first group described the Halcyon days of the company.

"What happened? What caused the fall from grace?" we asked the second group. They responded with three words, "Greed, arrogance and dishonesty".

The third group described briefly the restorative work they were doing.

The fourth group offered their vision in a clear, simple and easy to understand way.

This links to the idea that stories help us witness what happens to us and help us to move forward boldly, with courage. The old Spanish word Ultreya, meaning 'go forward with courage' is often heard on the El Camino Santiago de Compestelo pilgrimage.

The Comic and the Tragic

Some consultants apply Shakespeare's plays to modern business. Shakespeare, of course, wrote both tragedies and comedies. Some understanding of these two forms offers us another pattern.

How do we read what happens to us in our relationships at work or at home?

What expectations do we have of the future? Do we see the outcome as tragic or as comic? What do we understand by the words tragic and comic?

We're perhaps clearer on the word tragedy as meaning some inevitable calamity caused by natural disasters or human agency. The concept of comedy is a little more difficult to grasp. Comedy does not necessarily mean funny. When Dante uses this term and calls his great work, *The Divine Comedy,* he is working in a tradition that says that the road might be difficult.[3] There might be death and destruction. But the outcome is benign. Hopeful. This understanding of comedy arises from a belief that the forces of re-membering (putting together again) are greater than the forces of dis-membering (taking apart).

Tragedies seldom end with the death of the great ones – Hamlet, Lear, Macbeth. So -called minor characters carry on the business of living and complete the story. As one elderly professor once said, "These characters sweep up the entrails of the great". After the office volcano, life goes on.

There is something cyclic at the heart of the view that life is ultimately a comedy. This is how the cycle of nature works and how the seasons work. It seems that we are tuning in to a greater rhythm.

It seems that when we focus on human life and achievement as being the large picture

Draw two circles. In the first draw a large stick figure of a person that fills the space. In the second circle, draw a tiny stick figure. Which represents tragedy? Which represents comedy?

or the only picture, we tend to lean towards the tragic. When we position human beings and their achievements as part of a larger ecology in which they are among forces working outside our command and control, then we perhaps are in a better position to appreciate office politics and life as comic. In the sense of *comedia*.

So ultimately, whether we approach life as tragic or a comedy is a choice. The comedy mode does not deny suffering, hardship, dealing with the unexpected, – "the thousand natural shocks that flesh is heir to", to quote Hamlet. That means that we position this in a process. In this way tragedy becomes a 'cleansing' experience. It cleans us out for something else. A little like Rumi in his poem, "this being human is a guesthouse". Rumi invites us to welcome thieves who break into our home and steal our possessions as guests who might be cleaning us out for something new – another version of the farmer and the neighbour in the 'you never can tell' story.

When we misread the tragic, the temptation is to conclude the story as absurd, and meaningless. Our response can become negative, cynical and despairing. When we embrace the comic, we become watchful. We don't have answers to the questions, but we come to understand that unanswered questions sharpen the eye for the road.

Heroes and Broken Contracts

In *Making Stories*, psychologist Jerome Bruner, suggests that many terms we use have their origins in narrative, that is in the beginning is the story. "We refer to events and things and people by expressions that situate them ... in a narrative (world): 'heroes' to whom we give medals for 'valour', 'broken contracts', where one party has failed to show 'good faith'. [1]

Irony

If you watch the surface of a river, sometimes the current appears to be moving in one direction. In reality deep down the current is moving the other way and what you are observing is the effect of wind on surface water. Irony which offers another way of reading story patterns, works like this. On the surface there might be small successes but the company is moving swiftly towards disaster. Or vice versa.

Stories captivate. The revered psychiatrist and hypnotherapist, Milton Erickson, used story-telling in his therapy, making use of metaphors in order to overcome the barriers of the conscious mind and assist patients to achieve a relaxed and trance like state, and reach their unconscious.[4] During business story-telling listeners become less critical, more open to positive suggestion.

The plot and process of story, parable, fairy tales unveil metaphorical comparisons that illuminate what may be unseen or unthought and unlock an unconscious search for understanding, resolution of internal conflict, new ways of thinking, meaning. As O' Connor and Seymour put it, they create a journey from present state ('Once upon a time ...') to desired state ('... and they lived happily ever after').[4] They allow listeners to become captivated and to reframe fears and challenges – so an ugly duckling becomes a beautiful swan, a struggling organization becomes driven by a new vision, poor Cinderella is transported into a new world, a difficult problem becomes an opportunity, a frightening transition becomes an adventure. As Diarmuid O'Murchu reminds us in *Evolutionary Faith*, "Telling stories as a lure to the future is an ancient strategy of sages, philosophers and great religious leaders".[5]

In the 80's one of us was employed by a firm that faced enormous financial difficulties and price-cutter competition. I remember well our fears and sadness as things became worse and worse. We were on the brink of shutting up shop. It reminded me of waiting for someone very ill to die. Somehow in the midst of all the chaos and uncertainty new alliances were forged, new creative ideas began to emerge, new possibilities came to the fore. We worked long hours, sometimes not sleeping, to come up with new products and different and better marketing strategies. Many of us gave up our annual leave. A strong team was formed. With nothing to lose we went all out, released new campaigns, visited every one of our customers to share what was happening. It seemed like ages, but before too long we were again growing and thriving – not only the firm, but we too as people.

In a way stories are like jokes, where the punch line reframes what has gone before. They allow us to jump out of patterned, habitual thinking.

Story-telling skill relates closely to social intelligence, which is about being socially adept and managing interpersonal connections by good self-presentation, tuning in, building rapport, engaging others, showing genuine empathy, influencing positively.[6]

To raise the Story IQ at work, we need to become conscious of how much story patterns impact on and contextualise our working life.

---

1   Bruner, Jerome. *Making Stories, Law Literature and Life*, Farrar Straus and Giroux, NY, 2002.
2   Campbell, Joseph, *The Hero with a Thousand Faces*, Bollingen Series, Princeton University Press, NY, 1972.
3   Luke, Helen. *Dark Wood to White Rose, Journey and Transformation in Dante's Divine Comedy*, Parabola, 1993.
4   O' Connor, Joseph and John Seymour, *Introducing NLP,* Thorsons, London, 1995.
5   O' Murchu, Diarmuid. Evolutionary Faith. Orbis, NY, 2002.
6   Goleman, Daniel. *Social Intelligence,* Hutchinson, London, 2006.

Chapter 20

Shape, Song, Substance and Setting
Creating Stories

The life so short the craft so long to learn [1]
Chaucer

Sad is the man who is asked for a story
And can't come up with one [2]
Li-Young Lee

Oom Schalk Lourens – the Bushveld Story-teller

Herman Charles Bosman's creation, Oom Schalk Lourens, is a master storyteller. In *Mafeking Road* he observes:

"When people ask me – as they often do – how it is that I can tell the best stories of anybody in the Transvaal," Oom Schalk Lourens said, modestly, "then I explain to them that I just learn through observing the way that the world has with men and women. When I say this, they nod their heads wisely, and say that they understand, and I nod my head wisely too, and that seems to satisfy them. But the thing I say to them is a lie, of course.

For it is not the story that counts. What matters is the way you tell it. The important thing is to know just at what moment you must knock out your pipe on your veldskoen, and at what stage of the story you must start talking about the school committee at Drogevlei. Another necessary thing is to know what part of the story to leave out.

And you can never learn these things". [3]

The wily Schalk is protecting his territory. We *can* learn these things. We can also learn how to structure a story. And though Chaucer suggests in the quotation prefacing this chapter, that it takes a long time, there are ways of learning quickly. A kind of paying attention that speeds up acquiring the skill. A way of placing ourselves in the way of a story so that it finds us. And a belief and acceptance that there is part of us that knows how to tell the story. Remember the story of Edgar Bergen asking the puppet Charlie McCarthy questions and getting amazing answers?

This is an ancient ancestral part that reminds us that we have storytelling in our genes and that we come from a long line of story-tellers. And our brain is wired for storytelling. "We are all endowed as story-tellers; there is a mystic in every one of us," writes theologian Matthew Fox.[4]

Practise, Practise, Practise

So how do we reacquire this gift? How do we remember?

> *A man is wandering around New York looking for the famous music concert venue, Carnegie Hall. He asks directions but no-one seems to be able to tell him where it is. Eventually he sees an elderly woman with grey hair carrying a cello and concludes she must surely know how to get to the place. So he approaches her.*
>
> *"Excuse me, Ma'am, can you please tell me how to get to Carnegie Hall?"*
>
> *The woman puts down her cello on the pavement, shakes her white hair and looks him in the eye.*
>
> *She answers, "Practise, practise, practise".*

Develop the habit of practising. Each story you tell will support the next one.

The Punch Line: How to Remember

> *Years ago a farmer lived in the area where Finland and Russia met. It was a time when national pride was running high. The authorities were determining the border and this ran right through the middle of his farmhouse.*
>
> *The map maker, a burly Russian, approached the farmer and asked, "Do you want to be in Finland or in Russia?"*
>
> *The farmer answered, "In Finland".*
>
> *The map maker questioned aggressively, "And why is that?"*
>
> *The farmer had to think quickly. "Because I could not endure another Russian winter".*

Jokes work on punch lines. The last line carries the point of the joke. We prefer to call jokes stories. Joke implies that we're expecting the reader to laugh, whereas story gives them the freedom to do so or not to do so. Sometimes the last line offers a sideways movement or a surprise. An unexpected ending. A sudden shift in frame of reference. Creative or lateral thinking is also about shifting frames of reference and the same part of the brain is involved – a link between aha and ha ha.

If we can remember the last line, we can remember the joke. The stories are like that too. If you have the last line in place, you can find your way there. It doesn't matter if you can't remember the exact words en route. We construct it backwards.

We absorb a story via osmosis. As with dreams, when you pay attention to a story, the story begins to pay attention to you.

A word about ownership – our feeling is that stories belong to anybody. So many are ancient and have been retold through generations. If you know where they come from, acknowledge your source.

When telling stories, remember that each telling will be different. You will be adding your own particular slant to the story – bringing in your creativity. And the next time you tell it, the story will be different. Once again no one jumps into the same river twice.

And then there is the joy of making up your own story and adapting it to the circumstances of the telling. You can use the chapter on story patterns in this section to construct simple stories. (One of us made up the snake story in the chapter on Listening, chapter 2).

MORE TIPS

A. See the story

There is a saying if you can't see the story, you can't tell it. Often when you look at a storyteller, you will see that while they are in your presence and looking at you, part of them is seeing the story. Playing out the drama moment by moment as it happens. They see the young man approaching the old cello player. They see her shaking her white hair.

B. Remember the story

Three ways of choosing a story and remembering it:

- learning by heart

- tell one you know

- make up your own.

We can learn a story by heart. In pre-literate days we were like the child who can recite the Koran. We passed on our information through memory. One of the casualties of literacy is memory. Fleeing from Indonesia, the poet, Li-Young Lee's father, who was personal physician to Mao Tse-tsung, taught the family mnemonics so they could remember. "Slender memory stay with me," writes Lee.[5]

C. Build up a bank of stories

We can build up a bank of stories. Source them from others, the Internet. Type in an entry such as 'Sufi stories' (over 500,000 entries on one search engine alone), and see what you get. Some story collections appear in the bibliography. The stories that you're likely to remember are those that carry energy for you. That speak to you. That touch you in a deep place. Use these because then you'll be involved in the story and tell it from an authentic place. Just as your dreams reflected your current circumstances, so will your choice of stories.

Be aware of two traps here. One is to make the story too literal. Stories that are too similar to our work circumstances often don't have much impact. The distancing of setting in time, place and circumstance is necessary to create the conversation between the life depicted in the story and the life depicted in our office. (Refer to the *Enchanted Tapestry* told later in this chapter).

The second trap is to add a moral in order to manipulate behaviour. Stories empower people because they allow them to work out their own ethics and viewpoint. Remember the debate around the Clay digger who lost the stone but did not tell the captain? Trust the moral to emerge from the story. A debate around ethical issues and differing viewpoints encourages cooperation and development of a work community.

Building a Story

You will have noticed that this is a book of cross references. This is because a story is like a cut diamond refracting light. It is 'hard' and endures for ages, has great value and many facets. One story serves many purposes and nearly every story could be part of any chapter. So we're dealing with a rich substance.

Stories carry five basic elements:

- *a plot* – events linked through causation

- *the story line* – what happens next, the action, conflict, resolution

- *characters* – often a main one the protagonist who drives the story and an antagonist who opposes her or him

- *setting* – in time and place

- *themes* – the deep down pattern in the story, hidden message.

It is possible to use these elements to build a story so that it relates to certain issues we want to address. Bear in mind that stories, because they have access to the unconscious, address many issues.

Say I want a story that will touch on merchandise, quality, exchange and value (theme). I choose an eastern carpet, which is sufficiently removed from the company's product. I choose a protagonist who sells the carpet – the salesman. I bring in a friend, the antagonist (character). A wise fool archetype. I create a name sufficiently unfamiliar, say Horat and Himra. I choose a place for the transaction – the marketplace and a hut (setting). I choose a currency – say gold pieces. 100 gold pieces – a whole number, a mythical number.

Such fictional choices widen the appeal of the story. The protagonist sells something (story line) and the antagonist challenges him. I need some form of conflict to give the story energy – say the difference of opinion about the transaction between the two characters (plot). I think of a way of creating an unexpected last line. As I am a busy executive, I need an 'economical' story. It's something that will stimulate discussion. I come up with this one.

Himra comes home to her hut from the marketplace and meets her friend Horat.

"Horat I have sold my Persian carpet for 100 gold pieces".

Horat's face falls. "Is that all you've got for that beautiful carpet?"

Himra responds, "Is there a number higher than 100?"

Not only does the story address your immediate need for the particular story, it also opens up unexpected areas such as challenge and limitation. It also speaks in the silence. We're not told whether Himra is proud of her transaction or what her motive was.

Nancy Mellon in *Storytelling and the Art of the Imagination* tells of being asked to create a story for a teacher and her class. The context was that the teacher was leaving the school. Since she and her class were close, there was sadness at the parting, and her legacy needed to be recognised. Mellon found out that the teacher was passionate about foxes. So she created a mythical character, a fox fairy, who helped children lost in the forest at night.[6]

Presidents, preachers, teachers, sales executives all need to find ways to make their ideas take hold.

In their well-researched book, Chip Heath, Professor of Organizational Behaviour, Graduate School of Business, Stanford University and Dan Heath of Duke Corporate Education, previously a researcher at Harvard Business School, have identified six "Success" principles:

Simple

Unexpected

Concrete

Credible

Emotive

Stories [7]

Apply these principles when presenting, persuading, engaging, telling your stories:

- simple, hard-hitting and profound captures attention

- the unexpected taps into people's curiosity, gets their attention and interest

- when thoughts are not abstract but rather communicated in concrete terms, so that the listeners are able to see, hear, feel them – they are clearly understood, received, remembered

- what is heard as carrying authority, is believable, credible – is noted and accepted

- people will care about what is told to them if it touches them emotionally

- telling stories enables people to visualize, imagine and identify. Stories stimulate by providing insight, they inspire listeners to action, contribute to the development of skills.

So use the Heath's findings as a checklist when refining your own stories.

Elemental Setting

In the 100 gold pieces story, the marketplace and the forest carry a certain energy. Part of the energy is an accumulation of stories that have been told about such places.

This Chinese folk tale, *The Enchanted Tapestry,* speaks, inter alia, of the setting for a story.[8] Once more a setting removed from the ordinary business day in time and place can invoke much possibility.

> *A poor widow weaves tapestries to provide a living for herself and her three sons. Li Mo, Li Tu and Li Ju. One day she begins a tapestry of a garden, stream, bridge and a house with a welcoming red door. The tapestry catches her imagination. Her two eldest sons argue that she should hurry up and complete the work so it can be sold for gold to buy rice.*
>
> *But the widow carries on weaving. She weaves her dreams, hopes and tears into a fish pond brimming with fish. When she pricks her finger, she creates brilliant red flowers and a glowing sun. The youngest, Li Ju, understands that this is her vision. So he cuts wood for the family, while his mother carries on working. She weaves herself and Li Ju into the tapestry.*
>
> *One day, while the eldest sons are arguing, and the mother is distracted, a mighty wind lifts the tapestry off the wall and sweeps it off into the east. The widow takes to her sick bed and pines.*
>
> *Each of the older brothers in turn sets out reluctantly to recover the tapestry. They in turn meet an old woman with a stone horse who offers them a choice. If they will prick their fingers and drop 10 drops of blood onto the horse, it will come alive and take them to the tapestry. Or they can have a bag of gold instead. Both brothers take the gold and disappear.*
>
> *After the two older brothers have failed in the quest, Li Ju sets out to find the tapestry. From the old woman, he learns that the fairies of Sun Mountain have taken it. He pricks his finger, mounts the horse and gallops through the flame mountains and the icy sea to the land of the east. There he meets a woman dressed in red. She offers to return the tapestry, but instructs him, "You need to rest first, for you cannot cross to mortal lands by night".*
>
> *The next day Li Ju returns with the tapestry folded close to his heart and pins it to the wall. His mother rejoices and recovers. As the sunlight from the east strikes the tapestry, it enlarges. The widow and Li Ju step into it and walk in the gardens, stand on the bridge and admire the fish. As they approach the red door, it opens. The mysterious woman, who had woven herself into the tapestry while Li Ju slept, waits to welcome them. Two beggars appear at the gates. The wind blows them away.*

The setting, both domestic and wild, invokes something elemental. These are archetypal settings. Mellon suggests other archetypal settings such as lakes, inland seas, swamps, dark towers, doors, gateways, mazes, the high seas. To these one could add palaces, caves, planets, deserts. In such settings the landscape becomes a character, a moving, driving force that operates beyond rational logic. Where transformation can take place. And in such a setting we begin to see each other in the words of Marianne Williamson, "mythically, not pathologically".[9]

Shape

The Enchanted Tapestry, a story about passion for work, also moves through seasons of the heart – death, quests, greed, transformation. It is also a good example of how to shape a story. Here are some aspects of that shape, translated into corporate terms. We could read it as a company graph. We could see it as a four-part shape (Refer to the Analysis box at the end of this chapter).

You could build your own story based on this pattern. One way to learn to structure a story is to slot your version into an existing pattern.

The Beachwalk, the Braai, the Boardroom

What is the best setting for a story? Stories absorb the atmosphere around them.

Stories are about creating ritual space. Stories can be told on the trot, as it were. You can walk with a story through a forest or along the beach. This is particularly useful when a group has become stuck. Physical movement induces the flow of ideas.

If that section of the brain that regulates physical movement is the same as the section that regulates mental movement, then it makes a great deal of sense for one or more people to go for a walk, and to pace up and down together, when they have a problem to solve or an issue to resolve. They would be silly to just sit in a rigid position in the boardroom expecting to make real progress, connect, unearth a creative solution, wouldn't they?

Beach walks take place next to unbridled nature and that symbol of the collective unconscious – the sea. Braais depict the best of communal meals and breaking bread together. There is something biblical about a beach braai. So a story set in a context so different from the boardroom has every chance of attracting, engaging, engulfing.

When we tell stories around the night fire we evoke all those ancestral night fires that have gone before and all the stories that have been told. (We have told many Oom Schalk stories round many fires). One definition of a ritual is that it connects us to what happened before we arrived and what will happen after we have gone.

If we're not out in the wild but in the boardroom, markers can assist us in creating ritual space. To change and charge the atmosphere that might be fatigued by previous meetings.

We suggest you use markers. Markers indicate we are leaving tick-tock time. Going on a journey time. Perhaps dim the lights, light a candle, scatter a cloth, stand up, beat a drum. Orchestrate the story as you move your arms. Find a ritual that is appropriate for you.

Songs

Beyond the five elements listed in Building a Story, stories are about music and rhythm. Fairy stories have been compared to a ballet because of their symmetry. "A story may be experienced as a symphonic word picture circulating through the chambers of the heart," writes Mellon.

As you create stories may you hear the rhythm and conduct and orchestrate deftly. May you hear the music and thrill to the performance and concert.

ANALYSIS OF SHAPE

The *Enchanted Tapestry* story

1. Things getting worse, or an unexpected change, or a transition to be made

- financial struggles
- in house power struggles
- somebody's passion
- conflict about income
- loss of the product
- crisis
- a new leader
- announced restructuring
- threatening competition
- limiting legislation

2. Inertia

- unenthusiastic responses
- self-interest
- a coach offers a solution
- greed
- worsening crisis

3. A creative response

- a committed response
- someone risks the adventure
- cost (the blood)
- risk taking
- something dead comes alive
- fortune favors the brave

4. Success – new life, energy and hope

- a new expanded product
- a coming home
- a new partnership
- a dream come true

It is more about authenticity, passion and beauty than about technique, correct language, style and delivery.

As Margaret Wheatley says, "Knowing the steps ahead of time is not important; being willing to engage with the music and move freely onto the dance floor is what's key".[10]

[1] Chaucer. *Cantebury Tales*, Barnes and Noble, NY, 2007.

[2] Lee, Li-Young. In Moyers, Bill, *The Language of Life, A Festival of Poets*, Doubleday, 1995.

[3] Bosman, Herman Charles, *Mafeking Road and Other Stories*, Human & Rosseau, Cape Town, 1947.

[4] Fox, Matthew. In Simpkinson, Charles and Anne, *Sacred Stories*, Harper, San Fransisco, 1993.

[5] Lee, Li-Young. In Moyers, Bill, *The Language of Life, A Festival of Poets*, Doubleday, 1995.

[6] Mellon, Nancy. *Story Telling and the Art of the Imagination*, Element, Rockport, MA, 1992.

[7] Heath, Chip and Heath, Dan. *Made to Stick: why some ideas take hold and others come unstuck.* Arrow Books. London 2007.

[8] San Souci, Robert D. *The Enchanted Tapestry*, Methuen, London, 1987.

[9] Williamson, Marianne. *Being in Light*, Hay House, Carlsbad, California, 2002.

[10] Wheatley, Margaret J. *Leadership and the New Science*, Berrett-Koehler Publishers Inc, San Francisco, 1994

Chapter 21

Breathing In, Breathing Out
Techniques for Telling

Breathing in, I know that my actions of body, speech and mind,
are my only true belongings
Breathing out I know I cannot escape the consequences of my actions
Breathing in, I determine to live my days deeply in mindfulness
Breathing out, I see the joy and benefits of living in the present moment [1]

Thich Nhat Hanh

Story-telling is not a talent. It is an acquired skill. We learn through connecting to our experience, observation and imagination. We engage the discipline of learning how to tell – how to visualize and as Buddhist monk, Thich Nhat Hanh, reminds us, how to breathe. It is something that we do from birth to death and yet are so often unmindful of.

Story-telling is about using that musical instrument, the voice. How to develop a sense of timing. When to pause. When to increase tempo. When to draw out a word. When to spit it out. How to shape a story and give it weight and substance. How to test its length. How to begin. How to end.

This chapter offers an introduction to how you can become the kind a story teller that breathes life into stories and who enriches your own life while reaching and enabling an audience.

Voice and Breath

Story-telling is making music with our voices. Once sitting on a wooden bench listening to a friend with a deep resonant voice, we felt the wooden slats and our breast bones vibrating. We are musical instruments. There are in us resonating chambers and strings to vibrate sound and a cavity to amplify that sound. The human voice can set up such a vibration that listening becomes a healing and enchanting experience.

Shakespeare's King Lear, at the death of his daughter, Cordelia, laments, "Her voice was ever soft, gentle and low, an excellent thing in woman".[2] And of course in men too. The human voice can also screech discordantly and shatter glass. Notice how sometimes when we're stressed, feeling uncomfortable, ill, anxious or fearful, we speak from the top of our throats, not from the belly. Our breathing changes, speeds up, becomes shallow, interacts in a different way with the rest of our body and our vocal chords.

A story rides on the tide of our breathing. It is centred in the breath. Before we begin, if we slow our breathing and breathe deeply, this will calm us and align us with the story. When we pause, like a singer we take in breath and the story rides on the out-breath.

There is a new diagnostic tool to read the health of the body. Voice Bio. You speak into a microphone about something that stresses you, something that delights you and something you feel neutral towards. Your voice is analysed according to the musical scale and the resulting graph reveals which aspects of your body are at optimal health and which are under stress.

It might be an interesting exercise to tell a story into the voice bio machine and to see what tendencies towards wholeness occur in the body. It may also be interesting to be mindful of your breathing next time you listen to a story or watch a movie – how does it change at different times and during different scenes? Does it match and mirror the drama, excitement, tranquillity, silence, violence, love, indifference, action, pause being enacted or told to you?

In Gay and Kathryn Hendrick's *Conscious Loving*, there is a couple's exercise for harmonising the breath.[3] A couple sit opposite each other, and in turn, tune into

---

RESEARCH

Voice Bio

The keynote frequencies found in the body are the very same frequencies found in music. And just as the note of C appears several times on a piano keyboard at varying octaves, the note of C appears many times in the body. The voice, being the composite sound of the human being, is representative of all of the frequencies in the body.

Until now, we might have been tempted to consider the human voice to be one sound, distinctive certainly from person to person, but definitely not revealing 12 individual sound frequencies. However, through the technology of VoiceBio©™, the independent frequencies can be captured, translated and sorted onto a voice print chart, giving a highly accurate indication of physical function.

and match each other's breathing. In stories too teller and listener can synchronise breathing.

Stage Fright

> *A crowd gathers under a tree where Nasrudin is playing a lute. He plucks one note, then he plucks the same note again. After ten minutes he's still plucking the same note. People begin to drift away. After an hour everybody has left and Nasrudin is alone under the tree.*
>
> *He sighs, "I can't understand it. I have found the one perfect note and nobody wants to listen".*

We sometimes dream of opening our mouths and of no sound arriving or of speaking and no one listening. Some of us experience nervousness and the accompanying symptoms – shaking hands, voice tremor, dry throat – when faced with a group of people. This could be true of speaking in public or telling a story. We don't have Nasrudin's confidence, nor his cheek.

Part of the way around this, is to shift the emphasis from performance to participation, from impressing to expressing. Modern physicists tell us that we live in a participatory universe. We also live in a universe were the story is larger than the teller. The attention is not on us but on the story. We are offering a gift as we enter this mystery. Even if we are standing in front of a crowd of people, there is a sense that we are really standing next to our audience and pointing not to ourselves, but through ourselves to the story.

An elder once told us it helped him to imagine putting on the cloak or robe associated with whatever role he was to assume. In the same way as a Professor might don an academic gown, a priestess her garments, a king his robe or a nurse her uniform.

These lines from Shakespeare's *King Lear* are pertinent in a story-telling context.

KENT : You have that in your countenance which I would fain call master.

KING LEAR: What's that?

KENT : Authority.

With the donning of the story-teller's mantle, authority arrives. We settle into a space. (Note that authority is not authoritarianism).

In Native American lore there is a poem by David Wagoner which answers the question, "What do you do if you are lost in the forest?" The concluding lines are:

Stand still. You are not lost
The forest knows where you are
Let it find you.[4]

When we tell stories we are in the presence of something greater than ourselves. Octavio Paz reminds us:

I too am written
and at this very moment
someone spells me out.[5]

Pauses and Pace

A young lion club is thrown into a fenced enclosure where there are other lions. He shakes himself off and begins to wander around curiously. He comes across groups of lions engaged in some activity and asks them, "What were you doing?"

One group is pushing around a stone. "We are the soccer players," they tell him. Another group of four is sitting with small stones in their paws and a pile of stones in the middle of the circle. "We are the poker players," they say.

Then the lion cub comes across an old lioness gazing out into space. "And what are you doing?" the cub asks. Without shifting her gaze the lioness responds, "I am studying the nature of the fence".

If you were to tell this story, where would you pause in order to pace the story? There is obviously no right answer to these questions as different tellers might pause in different places.

Here is one possibility.

SP = short pause; LP= longer pause.

A young lion club (SP to allow the listener to orientate) *is thrown into a fenced enclosure with other lions.* (LP allowing yourself and your audience to breathe). *He shakes himself off and begins to wander around in great curiosity.* (LP) *He comes across groups of lions engaged in some activity. He asks them, "What are you doing?"* (LP)

One group is pushing around a stone. "We are the soccer players," they tell him. (LP) *Another group of four* (SP) *are sitting with small stones in their paws and a pile of stones in the middle of the circle.* (LP) *"We are the poker players," they say.* (LP. An even longer pause if there is laughter but don't anticipate it).

Then the lion cub comes across an old lioness (SP) *gazing out into space* (LP). *"And what are you doing?" the cub asks.* (LP to slow down the story) *Without shifting her gaze the lioness responds,* (LP allowing time to build up the punch line) *"I am studying the nature* (SP) *of the fence".* (LP to wrap the story in silence and allow digestion).

Which words would you emphasize? Where would you speed up? Where would you slow down? Apart from pauses there will be inflections, a rising voice or falling voice. The best way to understand this is to appreciate the story as a piece of music. Note where a teller pauses, draws out the story, drops the voice, increases the volume. Once again this all involves personal choice because we all tell the same story differently.

Pause before the story. This acknowledges that we are engaging in something important. It gives you and the listeners time to go to that place where stories live.

Pause at significant moments so the silence can surround your words.

Keep eye contact. People's faces will tell you where they need you to slow or increase the pace and where to pause. So it will be different with different audiences.

May you acquire the skill so that you're able to slip stories in past the rational guard in the left lobe of the brain. And bring healing and prosperity. And be like the poet Li-Young Lee's father:

> To pull the middle splinter from my palm
> My father recited a story in a low voice.
> I watched his lovely face and not the blade.
> Before the story ended, he'd removed
> The iron sliver I thought I'd die from.[6]

In the end, apart from the techniques of telling, and the practicing, tell a story you love and connect to. Tell it from your heart and not as if you are an actor, an entertainer. Your passion and enthusiasm will carry the day. They will breathe life into the stories that you tell. Remember the Psalm 23 story?

---

[1] Hanh, Thich Nhat. *Breath! You are Alive*, Parallax Press, Berkeley, 1996.

[2] Shakespeare, William. *King Lear.*

[3] Hendricks, Gay and Kathryn. *Conscious Loving, A Journey tot Co-commitment*, Bantam, NY, 1994.

[4] Wagoner, David. *Through the Forest*, Atlantic Monthly Press, NY, 1987.

[5] Paz, Octavio "Brotherhood", in Moyers, Bill, *The Language of Life, A Festival of Poets*, Doubleday, 1995.

[6] Lee, Li-Young "The Gift", in Moyers, Bill, *The Language of Life, A Festival of Poets*, Doubleday, 1995.

Chapter 22
The Language of Work, the Language of Story: The Words we Use

I've got to use words when I talk to you [1]
Sweeney, in a T. S. Eliot play

Words are the source of misunderstandings [2]
Little Prince

Big Words, Small Words

A cruel neighbour wanted to borrow Nasrudin's donkey.

"I'll have to ask the donkey," Nasrudin responded. He disappeared to the stable then returned. "I am sorry. The donkey says he is endowed with prescience that the future does not augur well for your relationship".

"What does he see in the future then?" asked the neighbour. "What does he mean?"

He simply said, "Long journeys, short meals, sore bones and scuffed knees".

There is a cartoon where Hagar and Lucky Eddie are exchanging ideas. One says to the other, "I can't stand people who use big words. They are pretentious". The other asks, "What does pretentious mean?"

The language used in the donkey story – apart from Nasrudin's relay of the donkey's response – and in most of the stories that we have shared in other chapters, is simple and concrete. Stories surprise us through the simplicity and directness of the language. The words bring a freshness to our experience. This is partly why they energize us.

Simple words can express profound and complex ideas. In this line from poet William Blake – "to see a world in a grain of sand" – all words have one thing in common. They are all words of one syllable, that is, the simple words.

This chapter is aimed at raising an awareness of the words that we use at work, and their impact and effectiveness in furthering or hampering our communication.

Preferred Words

Words are the tools that we use to describe our thoughts to others in order to communicate. Our words reflect the way we think. Some of us unconsciously use words or predicates that are visual. This is because the automatic way that we think and internalize experiences – known as our preferred representational system – is visual. We tend to use words and phrases like illustrate, envision, 'I saw red', 'It looks good', more than others.

Others who have a different representational system don't picture things as much but are more auditory. They express themselves using 'hearing' words and phrases: shrill, loud, tell, 'It went off with a bang', 'I don't like his tone', 'It sounds right'.

And those who are feeling (or kinesthetic people) automatically use and relate to words such as touch, balance, 'weighty matter', 'grasping a new idea', 'It feels right'.

Then there is a small minority who have a gustatory (taste) or olfactory (smell) representational system. They tend to use predicates like 'I could eat you up' and 'I smell victory'.

RAPPORT WORDS

One of us is involved in providing language representational system software to businesses to help them take a quantum leap in customer service. These are firms and organizations that:

- want their customers to feel understood, related to, appreciated at an unconscious level – so that their perception of service received from them is even more positive

- want to reinforce their employees' rapport with their customers so that this becomes habitual

- want their customers to receive consistently excellent responses from all their service providers.

Clients are encouraged to use a state of the art, user friendly computer assisted language analysis system that enables better communication. We give them an automatic analysing, scoring and recording facility for written communications that facilitates responses that assist in building rapport and relational connectivity. They get guidelines for answering in a way that, using representational words and phrases (audio, visual, kinaesthetic, audio-digital, olfactory/gustatory) 'fit' the customer's usage patterns, and that the customer will relate to. They get onto the customer's wavelength and 'speak' to the customer in the customer's language. It works!

Of course we all use a lot of neutral words but depending on our preference for pictures, sounds or feelings, we may interpret those neutral words differently.

When communicating and relating to others, it is far easier to get on the same wavelength and establish rapport and connection if we mirror and match the sorts of predicates that they use. When talking to an audience and in the act of 'story-telling' then a good mix of predicates will enable you to reach the visualizers, auditory thinkers and feeler-thinkers.

Inclusion and Exclusion

The examples at the beginning of the chapter show how language can be used to include or shut out.

We can shut someone out by the level of difficulty in our communication. We need to be sensitive to this in an environment of many mother tongues, where the language of business is conducted in our tongue.

When we use a string of polysyllabic words, we create a wall of sound. (Example: endowed with prescience). The listener or reader bounces off a wall like this. Such words tend to draw attention to themselves not to the communication. Smaller words tend to be more like a window. (Example: he sees ahead). We can see through them as they point to the experience, communication or story that is being shared. Notice how in many stories in this book, your focus is not on the words but on what is being shared.

And it is not only the polysyllabic words and abstract concepts that can shut out people. Simple possessive two letter pronouns such as 'us and them' or 'my company' can exclude people too.

> *A student who has an appointment, knocks on the door and the teacher asks, "Who's there?"*
>
> *The student responds, "It's me".*
>
> *The teacher calls out, "Go away".*
>
> *The puzzled student retreats, thinks and then returns to knock on the door.*
>
> *Once more the teacher asks, "Who's there?"*
>
> *This time the student responds, "It's us".*
>
> *"Come inside".*

The student's knee-jerk response is about separation or duality. The considered response is about belonging. Oneness. We move between oneness and duality much like a car flicker. On...off...on. One...two...one.

Heavy and Light

Language can also be 'light' or 'heavy'. There is an Egyptian myth about our hearts being weighed against a feather when we die. Here are two verses from a poem *Feather Prayer,* which uses the myth to reflect on language:

in Egypt, Osiris,
Lord of the underworld,
weighed the hearts
of those who crossed over
against the plume of truth.

those light of heart,
lived in his chambers
endlessly. while the crocodile,
monster of the Nile,
devoured souls
heavy with matter.[3]

It is possible to convey a seriousness through use of 'light' language that does not deny the seriousness. It is also possible to use 'heavy' language that makes the situation seem more heavy than it is.

The Language of Work

It would be an interesting exercise to pay attention to the words people use at work – the register – across the office desk, in the corridor and in the boardroom. Listen to the way people talk about what's happening in the business.

If language is seen as a ladder leading from the concrete to the abstract, quite often business words are high up the ladder, reflecting a degree of abstraction. Obviously abstract concepts have their uses. They save time as they collect objects under one name.

Yet problems arise when we assume that we are talking about the same thing. The words of The Little Prince, quoted at the beginning of this chapter, come as a cautionary warning. The more we use abstract terms, the more we need to check that we are sharing a common meaning.

More than 50 years ago, Dr. Rudolf Flesch, renowned for his research into language psychology and the author of *The Art of Plain Talk,* invented his 'fog index'.[4] This was a formula for assessing the verbosity, level of difficulty and degree of abstraction used in written communications – and thus how comprehensible the communication would be to readers.

The Poetry of Business

Every profession has its jargon and language barriers. Poets often try and be as cryptic as possible and convey as much as possible with as few words as possible – 'less is more'. However, in the process they are in danger of becoming obscure and boring their readership.

Yet appropriate poetry can offer us insights. As early as 1994, Ralph Windle who has written the afterword to our book, edited a collection of poetry, *The Poetry of Business Life: An Anthology.* An extract from one of the poems reads:

A boardroom is a kind of den
Wholly redolent of men

> Which women mainly get to see
> When bringing in the lunch or tea.
> But one or two I would applaud
> Have brought a Lady on the Board.
> Either out of great acumen
> Or as their 'statutory woman'.[5]

Mandy de Waal who looks at the rising phenomenon of poetry in business, believes that poets will become a key to unlocking cultural meaning, building relationships and developing leaders.[6] She re-tells the story of the emperor with no clothes where everybody praises the clothing of the naked emperor, except the young boy who exclaims, "The Emperor has no clothes on". The moral of the story? The tailors were consultants and the young boy, a poet. De Waal refers to a cartoon which paints the picture of an office where people gawk from behind desks as the director walks in with a praise poet in traditional garb.

David Whyte, who uses poetry to bring understanding to the process of change, has helped clients such as Bristol-Myers Squibb, American Express, Boeing, Kodak, Toyota and Nedcor to understand individual and organizational creativity and apply that understanding to vitalize and transform the workplace.

An annual Art in Management and Organization conference attests to a growing interest in these approaches.

To Jargon or Not to Jargon?

Often we talk in code. An in-house language. While this is an effective way of saving time – using abbreviations, acronyms (e.g. CCP – company change policy) can complicate our language. There may be positive power in some jargon – by getting to know the jargon and norms and nuances of work language, some employees develop a stronger sense of belonging.

Jargon can also lead to assumptions that employees hold the same meanings for those package phrases. This can inhibit the process of change. Maybe this is why there is a fairly recent and ongoing effort to get rid of legalese and write contracts in plain language?

Coining Words

We use the same word for making new money as we do for making a new word. Coining. Language is a moving, changing creature. Phrases bud, come to ripeness, then they whither and fall off the tree. They become compost on the ground and new words pierce though the soil. Someone once defined language as decayed metaphor. Poet T. S. Eliot reminds us:

> Words strain,
> Crack and sometimes break, under the burden,
> Under the tension, slip, slide, perish,
> Decay with imprecision, will not stay in place,
> Will not stay still.[7]

Language is sensitive to over-use. Language is like a razor blade. It shaved my grandfather beautifully, my mother used it adequately to shave her legs but by the time it arrives in my bathroom, it is blunt. Someone in the company coins a phrase. People respond to it and use it. After a while a phrase can become a buzzword and people's eyes glaze over when we use it.

The energy has left the word. We could say it has died. Dead language can trap us inside dead thinking. When the company language is heavy, energy can be trapped. Sometimes the fatigue we feel after a meeting arises from the dead words that have been used in the meeting. We feel as if the Egyptian crocodile has eaten us.

Reinventing Words

Sometimes outside trainers deliberately adopt the company language in order to get participants to go along with them – 'to buy into a process'. While this has its uses, it can also be limiting. New ideas need new language. Our challenge is to make the language of business more conscious. Can we find a place for the language of story in our language of business? Sam Keen and Ann Valley Fox's observation about reinventing ourselves,[8] referred to elsewhere in this book, is equally applicable to our language.

We need to become far more aware of the words that we use and their impact or lack of impact and energy. We need to consider anew how we might reinvent our language to our benefit and the organization's benefit. When we communicate in a clear and fresh way, the words do not refer to themselves. They help to point us to where we need to go. WRC – Words create reality.

Finding Gold

> *When King Arthur was a boy, Merlin was training him in alchemy – the ability to turn lead into gold. Arthur's brother, Kay, motivated by greed, asked him, "Can you really change something into gold?"*
>
> *He put a lead pitcher down in front of Arthur who closed his eyes in concentration. An hour passed. The impatient Kay observed, "The pitcher is still lead".*
>
> *Arthur opened his eyes and said, "I am not focusing on the pitcher. I'm trying to change myself into gold".*

May you find the gold in your stories. Stories are a communication must.

---

1   Eliot T. S. *Complete Poems and Plays,* Harcourt, NY, 1957.
2   De Saint Exupery, Antoine. *The Little Prince,* NTC/Contemporary Co, 2000.
3   Haarhoff, Dorian. *Tortoise Voices,* Mercer Press, Cape Town, 2001.
4   Flesch, Rudolf. *The Art of Plain Talk,* MacMillan, London, 1962.
5   Windle, Ralph. ed. *The Poetry of Business Life,* Berrett-Koehler, San Fransisco, 1994.
6   De Waal, Mandy. *The Poetry of Business,* www.harmoniousliving.co.za, 20 February, 2006.
7   Eliot, T. S. *Four Quartets,* Harcourt, 1968.
8   Keen, Sam and Fox, Anne Valley, *Your Mythic Journey,* Tarcher, NY, 1989.

Chapter 23
Story Ethics

*Let your conscience be your guide – Jiminy
Cricket, Pinocchio*

Values drive behaviours

When a system is rules-based, the rules get broken. All the laws, rules, regulations, ethical principles in the world do not guarantee virtuous behaviour.

Ethics have a psychological origin

Our intended and practiced behaviour stems from BEING (who we are). What we do is based on who and what we are. As we grow and mature we move from self – interest, to meeting the expectations of others to gain their approval, to conforming to group law and order, and finally to becoming principled through independent reasoning and internalised values.[1] During this journey we are exposed to many influencing factors, unique experiences, conditioning and priming. We develop our persona, whether we attribute happenings (and blame) externally or internally (which is related to our locus of control), and our moral imagination (which includes factors such as empathy) and decision-making ethics. Our behaviours are value-based. Many develop a strong spiritual dimension and become mindful of the consequences of all of their thinking and actions. When confronted with an ethical choice they are able to transcend the situational challenge by seeing the bigger picture, and acting accordingly – with certainty and courage.[3]

When our thinking, feeling and acting is completely and consistently congruent, we remain true to our values, and can detect and withstand overt and covert manipulations from other individuals or groups. Our internal focus and external execution are in line.

What has this to do with storytelling?

Stories are a powerful form of communication, which may be abused in a number of ways. Some of the ethics around story are always to acknowledge original source if possible, to obtain permission from a person we use in a story (before the telling), to stay true to the truth as you know it, to listen respectfully to another's stories, to refrain from imposing our stories on others not willing nor ready to hear them .... But most of all, ethical story usage is based on the right values and motives. Terrence Gargiulo, MMHS, President of Making Stories[4], co-authored what follows.

Storytelling has taken off

The storytelling movement in business has really taken off. Hundreds of tertiary educational institutions offer programmes with story modules, a growing number of books on the subject are being published, many more businesses want to use story in their internal and external communications. This is good news. After all, our cultures and psyches have built-in mechanisms to relate to stories. Stories are natural. We find meaning in stories, and they fulfil many functions. Clarissa Pinkola Estes: *"Most are not used as simple entertainment....used in many different ways; to teach, correct errors, lighten, assist transformation, heal wounds, re-create memory"*.

But a lot of the focus is on telling to win

The emphasis is on:

- the creation of an organisation's story to convey its history, purpose and values in a way that appeals to, and forges an emotional connection with potential recruits, potential clients and other stakeholders - whether or not what is espoused is true

- teaching leaders to tell stories that convince and persuade followers

- teaching employees to use story in order to sell a concept, product or service

A recent book has the give-away title *'Tell to Win'*, and is endorsed by none other than ex-President Bill Clinton as follows: *"...............masterfully demonstrates that telling purposeful stories is the best way to persuade, motivate, and convince who you want to do what you need"*.[5]

Elie Wiesel tells how Israel's Golda Meir's unexpectedly and successfully obtained missiles from the USA's John F. Kennedy. The turning point came after she told a story ending with, *"....all were motivated by the same powerful dream: that one day our Temple would be rebuilt. Well Mr. President, the Temple is not yet rebuilt. We have only just begun. And if this beginning itself is destroyed we will not even be able to dream anymore'. Kennedy stared at her for a long moment and then, without a word, pushed a button and ordered one of his aids to set in motion the administrative process that enabled the Pentagon to supply Israel with its first Hawk missiles. 'What do you think of that?' Golda asked, beaming. 'See?' I replied. 'A good story can get you anything. Even missiles'"*.[6]

On a much larger scale, 'astrosurfing' (which takes propaganda to another level) is an attempt to promote self-interest and orchestrate opinion by attributing the views of a few to many. The intent is to manipulate, deceive, 'imitate' grassroots' opinion. The term derives from Astro Turf - synthetic carpeting. Dave Snowden: *"A lot of story-telling practitioners are so wrapped up in the work they do that they believe story is inherently good and fail to realise that it's the core of propaganda and manipulation of ideas. We see the pattern at a nation-state level and in companies where orthodoxy starts to create a pattern into which everyone has to fit, a dangerous change to attitudes and ideation from where tyranny will always develop".*[7]

As with so many things, intention influences the way we use stories – to build up or diminish, to create or destroy. A storytelling-to-win focus carries potential for misuse - to manipulate others into doing what you want, telling in order to serve self. In short, used in only this way they become tools for the Machiavellian, narcissistic, even sociopathic. (a noose)

It's time to exercise caution

It is sometimes in order to use story to motivate, persuade, impress, trigger a modification of behaviour, feeling or thinking - but we advocate a wider focus and more noble intention. We like the idea of a self-regulatory traffic light system for storytellers:

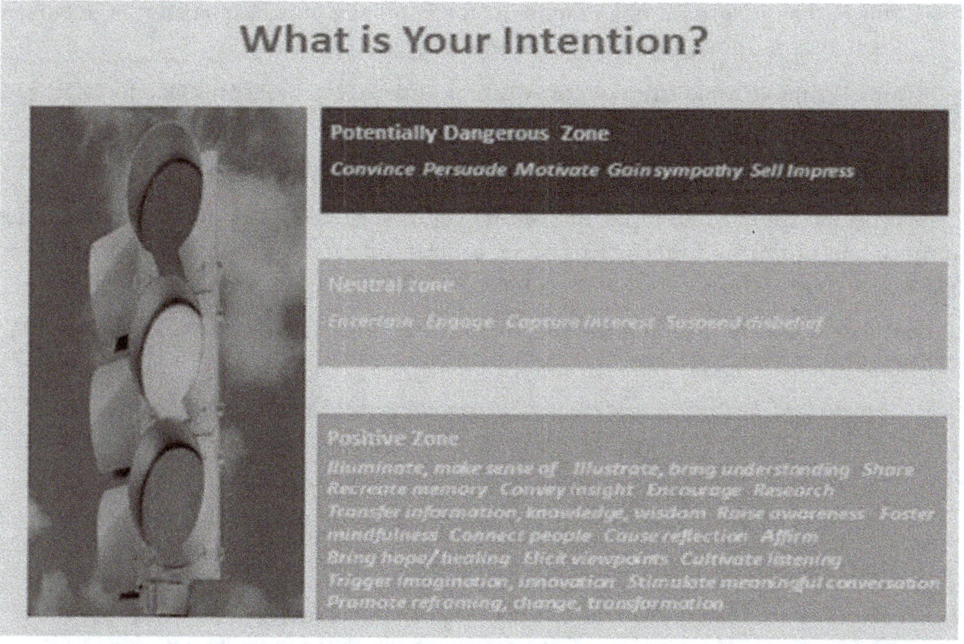

Stories themselves are by nature in the neutral (amber) zone. In this zone caution is needed. An entertaining story or joke, for example, is often told with the intent and expectation of eliciting a pre-determined response from the listener.

With wrong intention, tactlessness or deliberate misuse we can end up in the potentially dangerous (red) zone. Here we are in danger of trying to impose, manipulate, self-serve – and we lose credibility. We rob listeners of their freedom to interpret. Even right intention (or end) does not justify being in the red zone and manipulating (means).

Far better to strive to be often in the positive (green) zone, where the stories that are shared belong to both teller and listeners, create synergy. They invite the sharing of stories in return; an exchange. They are non-directive. An open, honest, vulnerable, real sharing happens. Dialogue takes place. Snowden believes that *this is key to micro-narrative approaches, creating multiple interaction between many people and their stories*.[7]

When people are glued together by listening and sharing, there is no need to impress, convince. A real emotional connection takes place. Things happen naturally. (a halo).

"People are best convinced by reasons they themselves discover". Benjamin Franklin *"A parable never tries to convince you. It takes you unawares, it persuades by tickling you deep inside"*[8]. Snowden points out that *"a parable always carries with it ambiguity"*.[7]

(Mark 4:26 *"With many such parables he (Jesus) would give them his message.......He never spoke to them except in parables....."*)

Thus before proceeding with our story telling we need to ask ourselves:

- – Is our aim or intent to gain or/and to share?

- – Can we introduce elements or motives from the positive zone – for example can inspiration and motivation come via the promoting of reframing, can we sell by bringing understanding, can we convince via the transfer of accurate, authentic purpose, information, knowledge and wisdom?

- – Can we move away from one-way telling and instead create a space for dialogue, feedback?

- – What can we do to improve our approach?

These 'checks' apply to all types of stories, fictional or real, and situations. It comes down to maturity, an other-orientation, a clear intent to co-create and build, to *"enlarge, enlighten, enliven"*.[9] .... and enable.

Authentic story sharing creates attention, interest, has impact, and attracts loyal clients and colleagues.

> *A committed disciple travelled each day to be mentored by his Guru, crossing a stream to get there. One day the rains poured down, the stream flooded and became a river.*
>
> *There was no way of getting across and the disciple sat down in despair, with his head between his hands. A sudden thought struck him: why not invoke the Guru's power?*
>
> *And so he stood up, chanted "Guru, Guru, Guru........." and walked across the river.*
>
> *The Guru was hugely impressed. When the disciple had left, he went down to the river, chanted "Me, Me, Me.....", stepped into the river and sank like a stone.*

20 years ago, as mentioned elsewhere in this book, I was entranced by a Maggie Smith performance at the Globe Theatre in London.

> *Lettice, a tour guide, shows people around 16th century Fustian House, one of its features being a Tudor staircase to which the public is denied access. The Fustian family motto is "by a fall I rise", derived from an incident where the visiting Queen of England trips on the hem of her dress at the first stair at the top of the 15-step staircase and nearly falls, but her escort John Fustian takes hold of her arm and saves the day.*

Initially her descriptions are straightforward and factual, resulting in disinterest and boredom.

So she responds by embellishing the story. The staircase becomes "The Staircase of Advancement!" Now the Queen's dress has 100 precious pearls sewn in, a gift from a Sultan, and the heaviness of the dress caused her to stumble. Fustian rushes to the rescue, and is given a knighthood for his noble act.

Lettice's story continues to grow as she succeeds in giving her tourists a more interesting and memorable experience. The staircase becomes "indisputedly the most famous staircase in England!". The Virgin Queen of England is garlanded by diamonds gifted by Czar Ivan the Terrible. Now when she trips and is sure to be maimed or killed, John Fustian leaps from the bottom to the top in a single, mighty bound to save her, "catches her in his loyal arms, raises her high above his head, and rose-cheeked with triumph cries up to her: 'Adored Majesty! Adored and Endored Majesty! Fear not! You are safe!", much to the enjoyment of the tourists, who applaud loudly.

Lettice is found out, and fired for her unethical behaviour.

What matters most to me after all these years is the unforgettable watchword handed down to Lettice by her mother: *"Enlarge! Enliven! Enlighten!"* [9]   As well as how we get there! Surely these should be the guiding principles for all corporate storytellers?

---

[1] Oberlechner, Thomas *The Psychology of Ethics in the Finance and Investment Industry* The Research Foundation of the CFA Institute 2007 citing Kohlberg, L., C. Levine, and A. Hewer *Moral Stages: A Current Formulation and a Response to Critics* In *Contributions to Human Development, Vol. 10.* 1983 Edited by J.A. Meacham. New York: Karger

[2] McGhee, Peter & Grant, Patricia *The Influence of Managers' Spiritual Mindfulness on Ethical Behaviour in Organisations* Journal of Spirituality, Leadership and Management, 2015, vol. 8, no. 1, pp. 12-33 http://www.slam.org.au/wp-content/uploads/2015/07/JSLaMvol8no1_McGhee.pdf

[3] Pascale, Richard; Sternin, Jerry & Sternin, Monique *The Power of Positive Deviance* Harvard Business Press Boston 2010

[4] *http://www.makingstories.net*

[5] Guber, Peter *Tell to Win: Connect, Persuade, and Triumph with the Hidden Power of Story* Crown Publishing Group (division of Random House Inc.) NY 2010

[6] Wiesel, Elie *All Rivers Run to the Sea* Alfred A. Knopf Inc. 1995

[7] An email exchange between Graham Williams and Dave Snowden, Founder and Chief Scientific Officer of Cognitive-Edge Pte Ltd May, 2009

[8] Osho *The Man who Loved Seagulls* St Martin's Griffin NY 2008

[9] Shaffer, Peter *Lettice and Lovage* Andre Deutsch, London 1998

Section D
Carrying on the Conversation

In this section we continue the conversation in more depth for those who

- wish to explore more reasons for the use of story in business, a conversation started in chapter 1

- would like a fuller discussion of modern leadership competencies, begun in chapter 3

- seek answers to the challenge of finding meaning in the work that they do, an exploration that was introduced in chapter 4.

- consider containment and story as container

Story, leadership, meaningful work, containers... The thread that ties these conversations together is the necessary high-touch connection between story tellers and listeners, leaders and followers, people and the work and colleagues they engage with. A thread that is assuming increasing importance as our world becomes more high-tech.

Chapter 24

More Reasons for Story in Business

The business world is in the throes of a major revolution:
we are seeing changes in technology, information and
knowledge systems, business models and processes,
legislation, the nature of work, the social contracts
between organizations and employees and the use of power.

The Scale of Change

The scale and pace of change is set to accelerate. How we relate to each other, how we communicate, view authority, conduct business, decide what to contribute or withhold and on what basis, how we formulate appropriate beliefs and values – are all outcomes of this revolution. Communications technology is facilitating the spread, not only of information and knowledge, but also of values and aspirations.

These changes seriously challenge organizations and individuals, who now experience higher stress levels, choosier customers, more demanding shareholders, increasing diversity, more and different competition, brand new business models, a shift away from 'command and control' cultures, and greater and greater pressure to deliver more with less.

Business can only meet these challenges by attracting and mobilising competent employees to carry out the changes needed. A sure way to do this is to make use of story in the workplace.

So Why Stories?

Stories nourish the health of an organization. David Whyte, a poet active in corporate America, has worked in South Africa. He writes:

> This is not the age of information...
> This is the time of loaves and fishes...
> People are hungry[1]

Stories offer us alternatives – other ways of responding to changing and challenging circumstances. They remind us that we have the resources. Stories offer us a place to embrace change from within, for in hearing and responding to the story we are changed. And as we work with stories, a new organizational story is born.

Here are more responses to the question – why stories?

- stories open troubled organizations to lateral thinking and to imaginative solutions

- stories know no boundaries, have limitless possibilities, touch both our left and right brains, and synthesise them

- stories invoke a new kind of leadership because they hold multiple meanings. No one meaning is 'right'. Collective answers are richer than those arriving top-down. Stories create tolerance and cultivate the arts of listening and of respect for another's point of view. A story is a store-house of the collective wisdom of the organization and a place to draw from for the next business adventure

- stories are open-ended. Stories start a conversation with ourselves and with others, and meet us where we are in personal and work circumstances. Who knows where that conversation might lead? Staff can identify and invest in a story that moves as the company moves

- stories raise awareness – the spiritual IQ of a company. They encourage personnel to reflect on past actions. A recipe for something that succeeded last time may this time fail dismally

- stories arrive in a pliable ever-changing form. If you re-tell a story you will add your own details and insights. Your own voice. Re-telling encourages personal identification with the story

- stories offer a context for change. They hold what is happening to us – they become the proverbial life boat in a stormy sea. An organization with a story is in a stronger position to survive and make the safety of the shore

- stories are the way of the future. An article in *The Futurist* describes the ages we have lived through – gatherer-hunter, agricultural, industrial and information (the current age).[2] The writer predicts that the next age will be the story telling age. Part of his reasoning is that there is an information overload. How do we contain it? We store it in a story – that seemingly simply yet highly complex form – a form containing infinite meaning and interpretation

- stories facilitate the engagement and commitment of employees. Stories provide the means to inform, reach, equip, inspire and mobilise people by appealing at an emotional, subconscious level and conveying meaning through analogy, surprise, transportation and enjoyment. Indeed stories touch the whole person: physical, intellectual, social, emotional and spiritual. Stories widen the circle of belonging.

The Story Triangle

Stories create a trialogue (you, me and the story), not a monologue. Another form of triangle is found in Chinese philosophy. One point represents Chi – the energy of the environment – the office air we breathe, the location of our work, the inputs that we receive from others. (Nurture).

The second point of the triangle, Ying, represents sexual energy or inheritance. This could refer to what we have inherited from our parents or mentors about ways of working in the world. Attitudes passed on through the genes. (Nature).

The third point, the one that interests us, is called Shen. This wild card concerns your vocation, your calling, your reason for being in the work in the first place. Shen is about purpose, meaning, passion and energy.

There is a Platonic myth about our birth. The soul has work to do in the world, so it takes on a body. And it goes through the river of oblivion. We are born forgetting why we're here. In the Hebraic tradition, there is a story about the indent between the lips and nose. According to the myth, this is where the angel placed its finger so that we would not talk of our previous existence. We begin by forgetting. Our task is to find out what are we meant to be doing here on earth. When we discover our Shen, we discover out unique gift to our work.

The River of Stories

We work in a river of stories. Stories hide in mission statements. They influence work performance and ethics (for better or for worse). Strategic planning invokes the next chapter in a story. Retrenchments involve stories of loss and repositioning. Mergers bring two streams of story together. A brand is an encoded story. Company reports are stories. When you look up from your office desk, stories stare you in the face.

Frank Delaney's novel *Ireland* tells of a story teller who traverses the country telling of Ireland's past – tales of courage, of rebellion.[3] The travelling storyteller is present in your business. He regales the sales force with tales of how your product and service became a legend. She mentors the newly appointed manager and encourages and inducts new employees. And so the stories themselves begin to travel and a culture, values, behaviours are born and grown and woven into the fabric that is your organization.

To work in stories (telling, repeating and listening), is to work in the *Mare Ignotum*, that is, the sea of mystery. The meanings of a story are inexhaustible, because they speak to us where we are in the circumstances of our lives.

Stories raise awareness, stimulate thinking, facilitate leadership, offer flexibility and possibility, nurture and engage. The telling of story helps us to take responsibility, clarify, become real, express what we believe in and value most, connect with others. In listening to story, and this is one of the most powerful things we can do, we pay homage to and acknowledge the value of the other, gain new information and knowledge and perspective, learn, become motivated, find common ground and become enriched.

Doris Lessing's Nobel Prize Acceptance Speech 2008 - An Extract

"The storyteller is deep inside every one of us. The story-maker is always with us. Let us suppose our world is ravaged by war, by the horrors that we all of us easily imagine. Let us suppose floods wash through our cities, the seas rise. But the storyteller will be there, for it is our imaginations which shape us, keep us, create us – for good and for ill. It is our stories that will recreate us, when we are torn, hurt, even destroyed. It is the storyteller, the dream-maker, the myth-maker, that is our phoenix, that represents us at our best, and at our most creative".

---

[1] Whyte, David. "Loaves and Fishes", *The House of Belonging,* Many Rivers Press, Langley, Washington, 2002.

[2] *The Futurist,* World Future Society, Bethesda, USA, May/June 1996.

[3] Delaney, Frank. *Ireland,* Time Warner Books, London, 2004.

Chapter 25

Head, Heart and Hands Leadership

Heading For Success

Three key competencies at the strategic, continual learning or 'head' level (if you want to mobilise and engage followers) are those of:

- – envisioning

- – steering transition

- – revolutionising.

Vision

As the Cheshire cat taught Alice: if you don't know where you're going, you're not going to get there.[1] A vision should be inspirational, clear regarding purpose, convey a sense of destiny, and above all: it must be measurable.

Those who believe in the veracity of vision know and understand that contemporary brain researchers have proven the links between having a future orientation and the ability to handle current complexities. That those who undergo a sound visioning process develop a bird's eye view and a worm's eye view, the ability to see the big picture and the interconnectivity of constituent parts.

A vision needs to be shared. If people are involved in formulating the vision, then they are likely to commit to it, to use it as a constant 'rallying point', to refer to it as a guide to all of their activities, behaved values and actions. So, as a leader, it doesn't help much to simply 'give them' your vision.

Visionary leaders are open to new insights, spend time reflecting on and anticipating the future, hold scenario conversations often, read widely on all sorts of subjects, and express their aspirations and excitement freely.

Reflecting on stories increases a company's reflecting capacity. Visions create company myths – in a major sense.

144

Transition

Organizations only change and grow if the people in them change and grow. This means we need to be equipped with coping mechanisms so that we can meet change challenges, be comfortable with and exhibit self-control when going through transition. It's important to realise that different people will be in different places at any one time during the same transition: the 'marathon effect'. As a participant in one of our workshops said, "I see story as a honeycomb, a structure to hold the honey".

The butterfly is often evoked as a symbol for transformation. In 1972 Trina Paulus wrote and illustrated the parable *Hope for the Flowers.*[2] Two caterpillars, Stripe and Yellow, in their striving for success, climb a kind of corporate "caterpillar pillar". In the end, surrendering to the cocoon, they finally fly. We have referred life coaches working in transformation to this book.

Leadership is about moving people from one point to another (not necessarily physically). So the steering of transition successfully is another key 'head' competency. A recurring theme in African animal stories such as the tale of the lion trapped in a hunter's net, suggests a way to success. The hyena is distracted, and the bird is sent to fetch help, while mouse begins to gnaw at the net.

Part of our leadership story is to

- prepare thoroughly (more important than mere planning)

- communicate frequently and openly

- foster close teamwork

- focus on the most affected 'animals' (that is, key stakeholders: employees and customers), and on the most important tasks to be done

- get rid of or sideline persistent detractors or saboteurs

- align all elements of the transition plan so that the desired outcomes are reached. These elements may include the clear definition of purpose, building organizational capabilities, establishing new communication channels, redesigning business processes, and the monitoring of team and individual behaviours.

This is akin to sinking a putt – taking account of the weather, slope of the green, distance and strength, selecting the right equipment, co-ordinating the physical and the mental, confirming with the caddy, coping with spectator behaviour, having confidence in the result, and then just doing it.

Are you adaptable and nimble? Do you appreciate the creativity inherent in turmoil and complexity? Do you focus on the people aspects during any transition? Story can be a calming word-picture during times of transition.

Revolution

In today's fast-changing, challenging world of business, leaders need to promote a climate of revolution. This does not mean the encouragement of disruption, instability or mavericks. It does mean a spirit of adventure, constantly seeking new models (new stories) for the business and its mission-critical processes, developing new game rules, and healthy, objective and penetrating enquiry. Like the athlete, striving for a faster, higher, better 'personal best' for the organization. Story can play a big role here.

Ganesh, the God with the elephant head in the Hindu pantheon, is a fine example of the kind of leader we envisage. He is the son of the goddess Parvati and the god Shiva.

> *Ganesh and his younger brother are highly competitive. If there are many pawpaws in the forest and only one mango, they will both want the mango. Mother and father god, tiring of this sibling rivalry, think of a way of settling this. They call them together. "First one around the world can have the mango".*

> *The younger brother travels on the back of peacock. In a flutter of feathers he's off round the curve of the world. Ganesh travels on a small white mouse. He hops on the mouse, circles his parents, hops off and holds out his hand for the mango.*

Since revolution comes from the word revolve, the metaphor of going around the revolving globe is appropriate.

Like a revolutionary leader, Ganesh (known as the one with the big brain, remover of obstacles), does not get locked into any one mind-set, but rather thinks outside of the normal grooves. He works with ambiguity, instils rhythmic innovation and wins the hearts and minds of followers so that they value revolutionising. He is prepared to take risks. To stand trembling at the brink of the precipice, but making the leap anyway – 100% of the way.

But most of all, the revolutionary leader is customer-focused, and knows deep down that customer expectations continually increase, that there is ultimately only one route to success; to build and keep customer loyalty by ever-improving service. This way the business is sustained and grown.

You Gotta Have Heart

An adult elephant's heart weighs around 50 kilograms. Those who study elephants tell us that the matriarch has 40 ways of communicating and the male elephant only six. And much of that communication is heart to heart.

Sometimes in business emotional factors are viewed as 'soft'. Feelings are written off. The hard-nosed leader, supposedly devoid of personal feelings, is still admired. But this stereotype is fast becoming a dinosaur. Beliefs, values and feelings drive behaviours. Good leaders share their hearts with the hearts of their followers and customers.

Enhancing relationships is a key 'heart' competence. Relationships are not hard-wired into technology, and "no man is an island". [3]

Good relating impacts on teamwork, productivity, creativity, networking success and customer satisfaction.

In *The Maiden Tsar*, an ancient Russian fairy tale:

> *A golden woman instructs Ivan, the young hero, to cut off the head of his tutor for his tutor has betrayed him. The tutor (the educational system) has separated head*

from heart. Thus begins Ivan's journey that ends with his marriage to the golden woman.[4]

In which ways do these two guru stories suggest a heart model for leadership? One of the messages is about trust in relationships. Increasing mobility, diversity, independence, new social norms, and different communication media call for sound relationships. Hi-touch relating skills include respect for the other's importance, self-worth and security, effective listening, courtesy, open and clear expression (using story where appropriate in conversation and presentations), empathy, reliability, responsiveness. Leaders need to create a climate that in turn creates motivated personnel. We know that results are a function of both competence and motivation. Leadership is about allowing followers to mobilise themselves to perform and achieve. It means building creativity, pride, perseverance, shared vision, harmony and co-operation.

This happens in a climate of trust and supportiveness.

Harnessing Diversity

In *Letters to a Young Poet,* Rainer Maria Rilke, meditates on questions:

> "Be patient toward all that is unsolved in your heart and try to love the *questions themselves* like locked rooms and like books that are now written in a very foreign tongue. Do not now seek the answers, which cannot be given you because you would not be able to live them. And the point is, to live everything. *Live* the questions now. Perhaps you will then gradually, without noticing it, live along some distant day into the answer".[5]

Here are two challenges:

- the global marketplace and workplace is rapidly becoming more diverse

- the best performing workgroups are the most diverse. That is, where energy is focused positively on how differences in physical attributes, thinking styles, culture, views and talents can be beneficial.

Here are two questions arising from those challenges – questions to live now.

Do you and your organizations have the competence to go beyond coexistence?

Do you understand that diversity is not managed, but harnessed? Story bridges divides between people.

The effective modern leader thrives on *forming partnerships* – with peers, subordinates, suppliers, customers, shareholders, competitors – and fosters appropriate alliances on an equals basis and stays on the lookout for joint ventures, collaborative partnering, cross-functional team opportunities.

How good is your 'partnershipping'?

Do you break down 'silos' between departments?

Do you maintain a network of 'banked goodwill' for when it's needed, expand thought boundaries through varied relationships?

Are you transparent, looking always for complementary and 'win-win' situations?

'Heart' competencies create motivated employees and beneficial collaboration, relationships that foster loyalty and advocacy. They release untapped human capital.

Essentially, heart leadership is about caring for others, eschewing mediocrity, being a role model, being non-competitive, welcoming difference. You've got to have a heart for success.

Letting Go: TheHandy Leader

One of W. H. Auden's poems ends, "selfhood begins with a walking away and love is proved in the letting go".[6]

Sometimes during tough times leaders have to roll up their sleeves and muck in – be 'hands on'. Most times though, effective leaders are those who are 'hands off'. They are able to 'let go'. Old style managers find it hard to allow employees the freedom to err, learn. Perhaps a progressive approach might be part of the answer.

> *A teacher, working with autistic children, was teaching them to walk. She tied a thick rope between two chairs. The children walked between chairs holding on to the rope. Then the teacher replaced the rope with string and the children walked the length of the string. Then she replaced the string with cotton and the children followed the cotton. Finally the children walked between chairs without holding on to anything.*

Why surrender over-control, delegate, stop holding on? In order to value subsidiarity. First enunciated by Pope Leo XIII, it means allowing power where it belongs. *The Concise Dictionary of Theology* describes subsidiarity as "a principle according to which decisions and activities that naturally belong to a lower level should not be taken to a higher level".[7] In short: let the people who do the work do the work – not undermining them but empowering them.

Another good reason to 'let go' is to escape from the trap of over-control. In the US military, there is increasing awareness of the "tyranny of the command post". Instead there is a focus on field commanders, a move away from arrogant, positional leadership towards a philosophy of "to lead is to serve" and "the spotlight should be on the led and not the leader".[8]

Letting go embraces the equipping and nurturing of those 'lower authorities' who are expected to take responsibility.

We need to remove organizational blocks to the taking of responsibility, and overcome constraints within self (fear of losing control, of achieving perfection, of worry, of not getting the credit). It's showing trust and respect and allowing others to gain meaning, become fully engaged, achieve breakthrough performance.

Another question. In the group that you lead, who generally takes the responsibility (and the credit) for developing vision, deciding values, strategy and policy, setting priorities and targets, developing plans, assessing and measuring progress, solving problems, making the big decisions and addressing obstacles when necessary?

The 'hands' leader displays true servant-hood and role-models the competency of serving both internal and external customers: 'follower-centric' leadership. She truly recognises the importance of people and their potential.

Some old-style managers find this to be counter-intuitive and difficult to grasp – so they fail to effectively coach and mentor, seek the best interests of the other, give of self, free others to learn and grow, take the bossiness out of being the boss.

> *In a close community, a young woman fell pregnant. In order to protect the identity of her lover, she told the elders, "The father is a monk who lives at the top of the hill". The indignant elders marched up the hill and handed the baby over to the monk saying, "This is your responsibility. You look after this child".*
>
> *"Ah so," the monk responded. He received the child into his hut.*
>
> *The monk looked after the child for five years. The mother in a fit of guilt confessed to the real identity of the father. The elders marched back up the hill and told the monk the story. "You need to return the child".*
>
> *"Ah so," the monk responded as he handed over the child.*

Servanthood is not a soft, sentimental concept. It is not about being a doormat to gain popularity and approval. It is about serving and not about being subservient. About releasing people and power. By serving others, leaders serve themselves and their organizations by building other's confidence, sharing leadership wherever possible. Working at developing the significance, self-worth and inner-security of others, concentrating on serving the valid needs of others. Another important hands competency is the ability to help others to grow.

The effective leader understands and practices appropriate reward and recognition consistently and fairly. From a position of self-knowledge and acceptance, he or she inspires and facilitates self-development in others.

These leaders are deft at using information/communication technology to extend the reach of communication and influence, promote inclusiveness, and obtain 'virtual' involvement and connectivity. The leader encourages and imparts basic business skills such as:

- time-management
- decision-making
- problem-solving
- priority-setting
- effectively contributing to meetings
- taking responsibility.

More questions.

Do you see the latent potential in others, feel genuine joy when they succeed, take opportunities to encourage, reward, praise – fairly and consistently, encourage self-directed learning? And do you get results?

Do you measure the right things in the right way (outcomes-based), use good or not so good results to foster learning and improvement, have a strong achievement–motivation, intuitively spot strategic opportunities, strive for 'relaxed excellence' rather than frenetic activity, and selectively involve external customers in just about everything?

Today's effective leader gets results. Results are only achieved through people.

Bringing Head, Heart and Hands Together

Head, heart and hands competencies are interconnected, and so the lines between them should not be seen as rigid boundaries.

The points of the triangle below show what 3H-leaders deliver. The sides repeat those competency sets that 3H-leaders use to make things happen. What followers need in order to produce the outcomes drives the entire model. The model can be viewed in two ways: Firstly, as a set of competencies or properties. Secondly, as a leadership process, where the 'Head' formulates a desired future and sets the agenda, then the 'Heart' is engaged in order to mobilise and obtain the commitment of followers, and the 'Hands' close the loop by achieving the desired outcomes. Again, the points of the triangle (what leaders deliver) can also be viewed in process terms (create the environment – make the vision to action leap – create the future).

Applications of the Leadership Model at Different Levels in the Organization

The 3H-framework is intended to cut across outdated paradigms of roles in the new-millennium organization. We discard the notion that:

- only top management can see the whole, formulate concepts and devise strategy

- middle management is the glue that holds the organization together and the oil between the moving parts above and below, and consequently that they need to

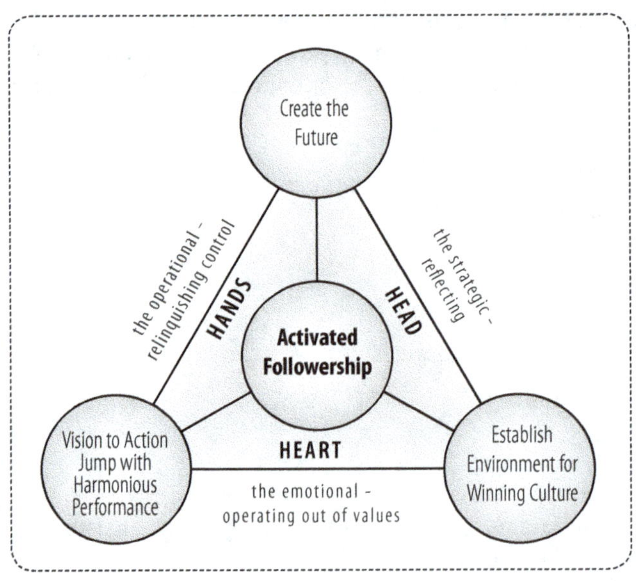

be equipped best in the area of human relationship skills

– workers at the bottom need simply to follow orders and get on with the job.

For example:

Jack Welch eulogises about the success of GE's "workouts" where key ideas of how to remove unnecessary work, to improve efficiency and effectiveness, and sound strategic thinking often surfaced from the lower levels of the organization.[9]

Peter Brabeck seriously questions one of the 'heart' strengths of middle management – the 'glue' of collaboration: "But where you have the layer of concrete heads is in middle management. They feel that we are taking away their hierarchy, that they are losing power. Many of them are not willing to collaborate, and some of them don't know how".[10]

A traditional approach to leadership is that it facilitates a situation where people in the organization rise to their level of incompetence. There is no guarantee that an extremely competent 'hands' worker will become a good 'heart' worker, nor that a good 'heart' worker will prove to be a good 'head' worker. The balanced 3H-model facilitates movement, both horizontally and vertically, and spreads desired values and behaviour congruently throughout the organization. In addition, all three competencies are brought to each job and to each person, making for a leadership ethic which adds a valuable dimension to performance. All levels need competency development in each of the three areas of leadership. Diagrammatically, we can depict how we have moved this way:

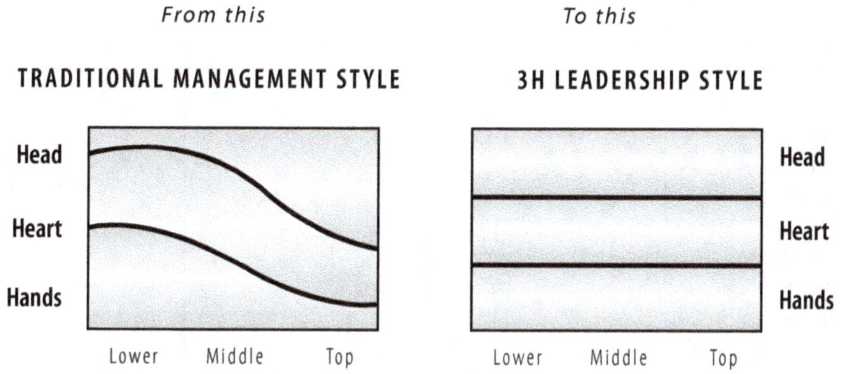

From this   *To this*

TRADITIONAL MANAGEMENT STYLE   **3H LEADERSHIP STYLE**

Organizational Head stories, Heart stories and Hand stories abound or can be created. Use them to infuse balance into your organization and all its leaders.

---

1   Carroll, Lewis. (Charles Dodgson) *Alice's Adventures in Wonderland* and *Through the Looking Glass*, Barnes and Noble, NY, 2005.
2   Paulus, Trina. *Hope for the Flowers*, A Newman Book, Paulist Press, NY 1972.
3   Donne, John. *John Donne's Poetry*, Norton, 2006.
4   Bly, Robert and Marion Woodman. *The Maiden King, The Reunion of Masculine and Feminine*, Henry Holt, NY, 1999.
5   Rilke, Rainer Maria. *Letters to a Young Poet*, Random House, UK, 2001.

6 Auden, W. H. "Walking Away", *Collected Poems*, Random House, NY, 2007.

7 O' Collins and Farrugia. *The Concise Dictionary of Theology*, Harper Collins, London, 1991.

8 Clancy, Tom with Franks, Fred, Jnr. (General, Ret.), *Into the Storm : A study in command,* Sidgwick & Jackson, London, 1999. Copyright © C. P. Commanders, Inc, 1999.

9 Welch, Jack. *Jack: what I've learned leading a great company and great people,* Welch, Jack, CEO, General Electric with Byrne, John A., Headline Publishing, Great Britian, 2001. Copyright © 2001 The John F. Welch, Jnr. Foundation.

10 Brabeck, Peter. *The Business Case Against Revolution*: *An interview with Nestlé's Peter Brabeck,* Harvard Business Review, Boston, February 2001.

SELF-ASSESSMENT

Effective 3H Leadership Assessment

	Areas of clear strength	Areas requiring some improvement	Areas of relative weakness
Head: *Learning Continuously* Visionary Transition champion Revolutionary			
Heart: *Relating Behaviours* Motivating Building partnerships Enhancing relationships Harnessing diversity			
Hands: *Achieving Breakthrough Performance* Displaying true servanthood Growing others Getting results			

Chapter 26

Meaningful Work

We had the experience but missed the meaning [1]

T. S. Eliot

We are all searching for meaning.

Harold Kushner, Rabbi and writer, points out that we humans share a craving for significance – the need to know that we are worthy and that our lives and choices have meaning.[2] We need to find something concrete and specific that gives us purpose in who we are and in the life that we lead.

Yet many feel lost or trapped in their situations.

We dread the thought expressed in Dante's *Divine Comedy*, "I woke to find myself in a dark wood. The right road was wholly lost and gone".[3] In a review of Caroline Myss' book *Sacred Contracts*, we read, "Myss has found that people often don't understand their purpose, which has led to a spiritual malaise of epic proportions. This metaphysical disease in turn leads to depression, anxiety, fatigue, destructive relationships and eventually physical illness".[4]

We under-rate the centrality and importance of meaning at our peril. We all need a reason for being. We need clarity on who and what we really are, where we are headed and how we have been gifted (by our in-built competencies – motives, attitudes, traits and self-concept) to be and to do.

Robert Johnson, Jungian analyst, suggests that the parameters and values driving living today have an impact on our feeling function.[5] When this is harmed by our failure to take care of our necessary inner work, our sensitivities and ability to find purpose and meaning are also harmed. Generally, the male drives to "slay dragons, rescue damsels in distress", achieve, create, gain prestige, power, position and wealth inevitably lead

153

to a loss of feeling function. We become cold, analytical, logical, precise, isolated from others. Similarly, the female archetype is about a drive to be accepted, to attract, to conceive and produce, to do what is really worthwhile – and the feeling function is damaged when these drives are frustrated or perceived to be frustrated.

All too often work is a means to an end and about the pay packet rather than about a passionate involvement in something truly worthwhile, that engages us, that uplifts, allows self-expression and gives joy and fulfilment.

We become slaves to a person or the system rather than serving what we love. We distance ourselves emotionally rather than seeking engagement. At the unconscious level we may even prostitute ourselves, our relationships and our behaviours in order to give ourselves apparent security or status. Equally often we unconsciously disempower ourselves in order to protect and preserve the status quo – through various acts that support our victim–standing, or sabotage our thoughts about making positive changes. We lock ourselves into our situations. According to Myss, people "...remain in jobs that make them miserable or sick, violate their ethics, or make them feel bad about themselves..." [3]

In the world of work, large numbers of people who work in worlds devoid of warmth exhibit a built in fear that someone else is waiting to take advantage of them or to outwit them. In managers this often manifests in a command and control style (in reality a defence mechanism).

Many workers caught up in such a pressure cooker environment feel more and more helpless. And this is happening at the very time that they need to look after themselves by developing a sure identity and strong self-estimation. People need to answer, "Where am I in this dark wood?" "How do I find my way?" By overcoming survival anxiety, internal organization conflicts and silos, envy, resentment, uncertainty and denial, by shaping my own career, making the right choices, and finding that my interactions with others reinforce and validate my self-worth, my significance, and my purpose.

And our identity trauma may well be exacerbated by workplace dynamics.

The Tyrant at the Gate

A King had gallows erected on a bridge outside the city wall. He commanded his soldiers, "When anybody approaches, ask them a question. If they lie, hang them. If they tell the truth, admit them to the city".

Nasrudin came along on his donkey. A soldier challenged him, "Where are you going?"

Nasrudin responded, "I am going to be hanged".

The soldier was confounded.

"If I hang you, you will have spoken the truth. If I let you into the city, you will have lied".

As if our own struggles for meaning were not enough of a challenge, sometimes managers and supervisors can be absolute tyrants. And unlike Nasrudin, we're not always able to subvert their demands.

Manfred Kets de Vries has much to say about the unconscious motives, power plays and pathologies of leaders.[6] Even those who resort to 'fail-safe' and totally 'rational' management approaches carry danger. 'Method' that is not mindful of the needs of the heart and that ignores deeper sensitivities and needs, is prone to neglecting the soul.

For example, a 'quality' management concept and method such as 'zero tolerance', may well be appropriate for reducing payroll errors, maintaining product quality and ensuring workplace safety. However, if carried to the extreme, it can be counter productive where there is a need for business process flexibility or to fully engage employees.

Ken Blanchard, quoted by Kushner, "warns managers that employees who feel they are ill-used and unappreciated as people will find ways to 'get even' – by taking excessive sick leave, pilfering company property, or giving less than their best effort at work".[2]

Questions that searchers ask in various ways and at various times about their workplace, are:

"What is the spirit of this place?"

"Do people love their work?"

"Will I be treated as a real, unique person here?"

"Is there genuine community?"

"Is what I am doing worthy of my long hours of work and commitment?"

"Will I be able to exercise my special areas of giftedness?"

Catching the Wrong Train

A porter approached a woman at the Johannesburg railway station and asked, "Where are you going?"

The woman glared at him and responded, "Cape Town".

The porter indicated the relevant platform. The woman climbed into the Cape bound train.

As the train pulled out of the station, she leant out of the window, and yelled at the porter, "You nosey parker, I'm in fact going to Durban".

Bottom-up employee pathologies can also induce workplace toxicity and blur the search for meaningful work. People unwittingly carry their history, defence mechanisms, vulnerabilities, projections and unresolved issues to work. We can become agents for various restricting, constraining and undermining activities. In the serving and helping professions (and this applies to the customer service arena) a high percentage of workers unconsciously seek to repair and heal their own past aggressions, hatred, injury and suppressed hurts – by doing good. [7]

Work as Opus

In his *Work as Opus*, Jungian therapist, Thomas Moore, points to work as probably the most unconscious of all of our daily activities, yet potentially the most important soul component of our spiritual lives.[8] (This is not about religiosity but about the essence of what it means to be fully human, with all of our contradictions, paradoxes, fallibility, how we relate to others, and how we access meaning).

He sees that work can be something "that both awakens and satisfies the very root of our being". It is a soul aspect that lies outside of ourselves, and mirrors back to us who we are, and what we can be.

When we do what we are meant to do, this brings transcending intensity, passion, acceptance of self, peace.

Work becomes our "opus rather than aptitude".

Manfred Kets De Vries: "Work plays an important role in humankind's search for meaning. Work.... gives people a sense of significance and orientation and offers continuity in a world that's increasingly discontinuous. Work can give meaning, not only in the personal sense described, but also in the broader, societal sense of transcending one's own personal needs to improve the quality of life, help people in need, or contribute value to society". [6]

Is it possible that the customer service movement has some special discoveries awaiting searchers?

The answer is an unequivocal "Yes!" All service providers are at one level caregivers. Care giving is by definition an opportunity to find meaning in providing for other's needs. The not-so-subtle shift is that people begin to see meaning in what is expected of them to give, rather than what they should expect to receive from their work.

Robert Johnson: "The meaning of life is not in the quest for one's own power and advancement but lies in the service of that which is greater than oneself". [5] Viktor Frankl's findings support this assertion.[9] He also suggests that meaning can be found in creative work, the fulfilling experience of beauty, art and nature, and in suffering.

It is a good thing that many organizational leaders are becoming more aware of the power of service.

The Servant Leader

Richard Wilhelm who translated the IChing, the Chinese book of Changes, into German, writes of an experience with a rain maker in China. When we first encountered this story, we thought it was a metaphor and then we found it truly happened. Stories are like this. They change the nature of reality.

> *There was a long drought in a village. The people summoned a rain maker from the mountains. He arrived and asked for a hut so he could be apart. For days the villagers did not see him. Then the clouds built up and the rain came.*

> *When the rain maker emerged from the hut, the villagers asked him, "How did you make rain?"*

> *"I did not make rain. Your village has been in a state of disharmony. This affected me when I arrived. So I retired to the hut and centred myself. That is when the rain came".*

The rain maker offers us a leadership and a service model. He did not see himself as separate from the society and environment around him. Through his action harmony was restored and the rain fell.

One of the paths to greater 'spirituality' is that of servant leadership. Not the subservient doormat variety but rather a strong, empathetic, sensitive leadership and adult-to-adult serving based on a strong self-concept.

Many old-style managers who are used to driving, directing, watching and controlling find the notion of servant leadership to be counter intuitive and difficult to grasp. It requires genuine belief that people (customers and employees) are the organization's most important asset and that results are only achieved through people.

This leads to taking the bossiness out of being the boss, and focusing on the wellbeing of others in order to give them the freedom to perform. In this way we achieve breakthrough performance results. Servant leadership transcends self-serving and becomes other-serving (some have this more strongly as motive, value and attitude than do others), as reflected in a driving concern for individuals and communities, and in a demonstrated power to invoke meaning (new ways to 'be') for and in others.

Like the Chinese rain maker, the greatest leaders serve others. They mobilise their followers by giving them new possibilities and new opportunities for enlightenment, significance. This style of leadership redesigns and redefines work so that employees have an environment in which to redesign and redefine themselves.

At the same time they (healthily) maintain, serve and look after self. "Enlightened leadership is serving, not selfishness. The leader grows more and lasts longer by placing the well-being of all above the well-being of self alone".[10]

Circles of Satisfaction

There is growing recognition that customer service and 'other-orientation' offers opportunities to find meaning.

At all levels in the organization (that is, beyond leadership) Kushner's statement holds good: "I have always found that an effective cure for that feeling of insignificance is simply to find someone who needs our help and reach out to that person".[2] (This may be sharing excess wealth or extending a debt repayment period or providing surprising and unexpectedly good customer service).

The same sentiment, this time from *Fish! Tales*: "The only way to be happy in this life is to get outside yourself and serve others".[11]

Psychologist Nancy Cohn illustrates this simply. "One day I saw a nurse massaging a baby's chest with an adapted electric toothbrush to clear the congestion in his lungs. In response to my asking if the baby liked it, the nurse became more aware that the baby was indeed enjoying this, and she then seemed to enjoy the procedure more herself".[12]

This means, of course, that all providers of service, whether working in a customer call centre or internally with someone from another department, are each day presented with opportunity after opportunity to make a difference for someone else. No wonder the research shows overwhelmingly that satisfied customers lead to satisfied employees and that satisfied employees are more than likely to satisfy customers. A closed loop system.

Indeed, to make a positive difference in another person's life (by serving their needs and giving them a sense that they're important and worthy of care) is both a definition of meaning and a definition of customer service. The spiritual attributes of selflessness and empathy benefit everyone.

Viktor Frankl, creator of logotherapy (meaning-purpose-spirit-therapy) reminds us that we all need a goal or purpose of which we are worthy: "We who lived in concentration camps can remember the men who walked throughout the huts comforting others, giving away their last piece of bread. They may have been few in number, but they offer sufficient proof that everything can be taken away from a man but one thing: the last of the human freedoms – to choose one's attitude in any given set of circumstances, to choose one's own way".[9] To find meaning.

Out of the Wood

When we are lost like Dante in a dark wood, our being lost prompts two deep and important questions: "Where am I?" and "How do I get out of the forest (home)?" There is an eastern tale about a woman lost in the forest. She looks down and sees the footprints of an animal. She follows the footprints and is lead out of the woods.

In service organizations more acceptance happens and more opportunities open up as customer service momentum develops within an organization.

When a customer service ethic and supporting practices within an organization reach 'critical mass', then a 'virtuous cycle' kicks in. There is a fast rate of 'conversions'. New employees are chosen for fit, and quickly adopt the service values, attitudes and behaviours, and find meaning in their work. And our way out of the forest.

This has certainly been the experience of the Ritz-Carlton Hotel Group, world renowned for their service leadership. Their selection, orientation, training and continuous coaching processes are aimed at effectively identifying and developing people who have a natural service gift.

A related finding comes from Faith Popcorn who has identified an interesting and important trend: that the way in which women think and behave is impacting business and causing it to become more 'relational'.[13] This clearly fits with the move towards improving external and internal customer service, which is all about relationships. It is perhaps significant that the word money derives from the name of a goddess (Moneta), rather than after a god. For money is about exchange and about relationship.

Sometimes we remain lost in the forest through our humanness. It's human nature to concentrate on what's wrong rather than what's right. We sometimes show a group a flip chart containing about 10 simple sums. One is wrong. Without variation, the group will point out the error. We've yet to find a group that points out that 9 of the 10 sums are correct. We should perhaps focus more on our latent capabilities, capacities and potential to be of valuable service to others. See the gold rather than the dross. We want our lives to have significance, and not just be like a candle in the wind.

Conversions sometimes happen quickly, as was the experience in the movie of Amelie Poulain from Montmarte: "a surge to help mankind engulfed her", and of the Pike Place Seattle employee: "One day I realised that I was serving people, making them happy. This gave me a plus in my life and I want to do it more". [14] (This is discovering what it really means to be customer-centric).

Or it could happen more slowly. Lawrence Kohlberg, whom Kushner quotes, says that doing right develops as a progression – initially out of fear of punishment, then out of a feeling of community solidarity with others, and finally doing right unconditionally because it is right. [2]

The customer service progression for many may be similar. As Myss points out: "Your shadow aspects are primarily rooted in fear patterns that have more control over your behaviour than does your conscious mind. This limits your ability to make choices in which you are aware of your motivations". [4] So, without too much introspection, we think the point is not to delay but to start by learning and by applying the appropriate behaviours and habits – to go for it. And let the requisite attitudes, values and motives follow. And we believe stories can lead you there.

Full engagement with our work and finding deep meaning in it can be facilitated (as we've shown) by human story telling and story listening.

But, and this is critical, we must be prepared to be honest with ourselves in our search for meaning.

---

[1] Eliot T. S. *Collected Poems*, Faber and Faber, UK, 1963.

[2] Kushner, Harold S. *Living a Life that Matters*, Sidgwick & Jackson, London, 2001.

[3] Dante, Alighieri. *The Divine Comedy* tran. Henry Wadsworth Longfellow (www.everypoet.com).

[4] Myss, Caroline. *Sacred Contracts: awakening your divine potential*, Bantam Books, NY, 2002.

[5] Johnson, Robert A. *The Fisher King and The Handless Maiden*, Harper Collins, NY, 1995.

[6] De Vries, Manfred Kets. *The Leadership Mystique*, Financial Times/Prentice Hall, Great Britian, 2001.

[7] Nicholson, Nigel. *Managing the Human Animal*, Texere, NY, 2000.

[8] Moore, Thomas. *Care of the Soul: How to Add Depth and Meaning to Your Everyday Life*, Piatkus, London, 1994.

[9] Frankl, Viktor. *Man's Search for Meaning*, Washington Square Press, Simon & Schuster, NY, 1963.

[10] Heider, John. *The Tao of Leadership: Lao Tzu's Tao Te Ching Adapted for a New Age*, Humanics Publishing Group, 1986.

[11] Obholzer Anton & Vega Zagier, ed Roberts, *The Unconscious at Work*, Tavistock Clinic, Routledge, 1994.

[12] Lundin, Stephen C., Christensen, John and Paul, Harry. *Fish! Tales*, Hodder & Stoughton, London, 2002.

[13] Popcorn, Faith. *The Popcorn Report*, Doubleday, 1991.

[14] Lundin, Stephen C., Paul, Harry and Christensen, John. *Fish!* Hodder & Stoughton, 2001.

Chapter 27

Contemplating Containers

"In my experience, psychotherapy at its best is like dual meditation - it's like a container in which you can be compassionate and mindful toward yourself" – Jack Kornfield

"Sharp acids corrode their own containers" - Albanian proverb

Hamlet, 'I could be bounded in a nutshell and count myself a king of infinite ... No, I could live in a walnut shell and feel like the king of the universe - Act II Scene 2 (Shakespeare)

A wide ranging concept

Stories as containers carry meaning for our self-concept, well-being, interactions with others, world view, resilience .... But, to begin at the beginning:

When we go to the origin, the root of a word, it can reveal its secrets and guide us towards creating different responses.

CONTAIN (kən-tān)

1. a. To have within; hold: a bin that contains rice.

    b. To be capable of holding: These barrels contain 50 gallons.

2. To have as a component or constituent part; include: Does the soup contain meat?

---

3. a. To hold or keep within limits; restrain: I could hardly contain my curiosity.

    b. To halt the spread or development of; check: Science sought an effective method of containing the disease

4. To check the expansion or influence of (a hostile power or ideology, political or military) by containment.

5. Mathematics: To be exactly divisible by.

So we may speak of:

- a business strategy – for example, cost containment

- a theory in criminology (*"developed by Walter Reckless, stating that juvenile delinquency happens when moral and social forces fail to contain such deviant behavior"*)[1]

- *"the energetic space between you and your 'psychotherapist'. It's the atmosphere that the 'therapist' or listening person creates that conveys a sense of safety, allowing you to more comfortably move through your emotions"*[2]

- *"psychological containment is an aspect of resilience and refers to the capacity to internally manage the troubling thoughts and feelings and behaviour that arise as a consequence of stress. It is a concept that was developed within the psychoanalytic tradition by Wilfred Bion. It is said that his experience as a tank commander in World War II underpinned the formulation of the idea. In psychotherapy it may be seen as a therapeutic outcome to increase a persons ability to tolerate their feelings, say of guilt and shame, and in so doing to build self esteem and self confidence"*[3]

- Spiritual containment. *"Franciscan theologian Bonaventure (1217-1274) saw God as 'a circle whose center is everywhere and whose circumference is nowhere'. You fall into this Wholeness - which will actually hold you - when you stop denying or excluding things, even the dark parts of yourself".*[4]

- A product. In a metaphor - elicitation consumer study in Greece, the Netherlands and Germany: *"Coke was described as a container of positive emotions that flow into yet another container, the body".*[5] Happiness in a bottle.

- A place of creative tension as alluded to by Jed McKenna: *"The Yin-Yang symbol is generally viewed as illustrating the dual nature of reality, the equal and opposite nature of balancing forces, always in harmony. But there's more. There's the third element namely Containment, which means the circle - the whole and the finiteness. Without the element of containment, the opposite elements could not exist, much less maintain their balance. The container is what defines the whole, out of which black and white are the two aspects. That matters because duality is always finite. Duality is always contained and cannot exist outside of a finite sphere. It's the sphere that defines the context within which opposites exist".*

Personal containers

Our personal containers may be physical, psychological, and social. Our mind contains ideas, memories, knowledge, feelings, and thoughts. Over time we may collect and store (contain) that which distorts our self-image, self-worth and security–and influences how we relate to others and our 'red-flag' responses to criticism. So we adopt defence mechanisms, ways of presenting ourselves to make ourselves more acceptable, hide what we don't like about ourselves, hide our fears, fake being resilient, develop limiting beliefs. We bury (contain) our true selves. Allow darker parts of our psyche to take over. Yet we retain heart voids (cravings, deficits, things we lack) and heart hurts (spiritual wounds, experiences and conditioning that have shaped us). Sadly, as somebody has said: *"There are people who die without ever having been themselves"*. The good news is that we can again come alive in those dead areas, through re-storying. We can become who we were born to be, our original, untainted 'factory-settings', see the truth in the Psalmists' insight: *"I am fearfully and wonderfully made'*.

And as we become more secure in our own real self and latent potential, we can focus more on others and their stories. This is what Viktor Frankl refers to in his Logotherapy[7] as 'self-transcendence'. Whereas (contained) in the concentration camps most descended into being animals struggling to survive, a few would comfort others, give away their last piece of bread – because they hung on to their basic values and self-belief. Self-transcendence is obtaining meaning outside of selfishness – another person who is waiting for you, or that book still to be written, maybe joining a worthy cause. Discovering purpose. Becoming who we should be, and living in the present moment.

Russian philosopher Mikhail Bakhtia (1895 – 1975) talks in terms of a masked-ball or carnival as *"the people's second life, organised on the basis of laughter ..... an escape from the usual official way of life .... (people) for a time entered the utopian realm of community, freedom, equality and abundance"*. The carnival event was a temporary container (You put on a mask in order to take off your mask, were contained within the facade of the carnival in order to free for a while).[8] Oh that we could permanently escape from what Antoine de Saint-Exupéry calls *"the tyranny of petty things"*.

Dietrich Bonhoeffer wrote in Tegel prison in July 1944 of showing an outer calm, serenity, pride, poise, cheerful appearance, but masking an inside, containing at that time an entirely different life force, mind-set, soul state[9]:

> *'restless, yearning, sick, like a caged bird,*
>
> *struggling for life-breath as if I were being strangled,*
>
> *starving for colours, for flowers, for birdsong,*
>
> *thirsting for kind words, human closeness ...*

We need to empty ourselves of what doesn't matter. When that happens and our true self begins to emerge we are at our most useful. And we have room to let in what's new (ideas, insights, wisdom). Like a cup. Lao Tzu:

> *"If the greatest fullness is empty,*
>
> *Then it's usefulness is inexhaustible".*[10]

The Organisations We Inhabit

An organisation contains, holds the expectations and aspirations of its members – or a toxicity that prompts some to escape that container. The earth's biosphere may be viewed as a container. Are our actions (pollution, degradation, war, destruction, exploitation) causing it to crack. Like Humpty Dumpty's shell, will we be unable to put it together again?

A person with trouble approaches a guru. The guru tells him to pour water into a glass "Now add a fistful of salt." The person does so. "Now drink it "says the guru. The man does and pulls a face. "What does it taste like?" "Salty".

The guru leads the troubled one down to a nearby lake. "Take the same amount of salt and throw it into the lake". Guru hands the person a bag of salt. The person scoops up a fistful and adds it to the water. "Now drink it".

The person does, sighs and licks his lips. "What does it taste like?"

"It's so sweet."

"The difference" says the guru, "is the container".

Two dying men share a hospital ward. They become friends. One of them is near the door, while the other's bed is positioned at the window. Each day the man at the window describes in great detail to his companion what is taking place outside of their room/container. He tells of many things: a lake, swans, flowers, people, the weather, cloud patterns, changing seasons. And his friend loves and lives these commentaries.

Then there comes a time when the man at the window dies.

His companion asks to be moved to the window bed.

When he looks out of the window, there is only a stark, unpainted, ugly, brick wall.

Clinical psychologist Marie de Hennezel tells of a man who, while losing his mobility , smells the tree that is outside the bedroom window.[11] *"He exists in the branches and feels the wind caressing. Thus, while becoming progressively more paralysed, he experiments with a form of joyful freedom".* (The man happens to be the Professor in *Tuesdays with Morrie.* [12] (de Hennezel translated the book into French).   She also invokes the spirit of Richard Alport (Ram Dass) who had a stroke and was confined to a wheelchair. In Ram Dass' book, *Still Here, Embracing Aging, Changing and Dying*[13] he nicknames his wheel chair his gondola and enjoys being pushed around, *"Chinese emperors and Indian maharajas were after all transported on palanquins".*

Confined to a hospital room, being paralysed and being wheelchair - bound are also metaphors for the way our assumptions about how business should be conducted, or how we may respond to change and adversity, how our organisations may constrain/ contain us and keep us drinking salt from a glass. Or how we might change them and what they contain.

Story Therapy

Margaret Wilkinson talks about a therapists' ability to contain or hold a space in which the patient can safely access and examine what is painful and confusing, tolerate and engage with what was previously unbearable. The use of artwork, narrative reframing and metaphor can facilitate this engagement. Metaphors are a bridge between two apparently unrelated concepts. The therapist who pays attention to a patients' use of metaphor will glean emotional truth from implicit memory, usually not easy to access. A novel (not an oft-used and familiar metaphor) can lead to a greater understanding of previously repressed feelings. They can help to open up and expose what is 'hidden' inside.[14] She cites Pally (Pally, R *The mind-brain relationship* Karna London & NY 2000) on this right-hemisphere phenomenon: *"by containing within them sensory, imagistic, emotional and verbal elements, metaphors are believed to activiate multiple brain centres simultaneously"*. And she shares this example:

> *"Well, last night I dreamt of a vase and that I was trying really hard to clean it. What meaning could there possibly be in that? I replied more directively than I would ordinarily because I sensed the importance of making sense of the image for her. 'Well, for starters what does the vase symbolize? After a while I added, "Is it something to do with it being a container?'*

> *'Mm, maybe' she replied. I continued' 'Well, yesterday we were talking about the difficult relationship you had with your mother and how she made you feel you were a no good, bad baby from the beginning. It's been so difficult to know whether you were a bad baby or whether it was actually your mother who was having difficulties'. Holly answered anxiously, 'I was trying to scrub the outside – why the outside?' 'But isn't that what you are often trying to do, wanting to look good on the outside, trying to please the other person, just as you so longed to please your mother and for her to see you and to love you?'"*

Diane Heller in an interview with Tami Simon gives clues to what we learn from '*how psychotherapists can work to create a secure holding environment for the healing of attachment-based wounds*'. *"Part of secure attachment is containment. In an ideal world—which, of course, it isn't—our parents would have been able to contain whatever emotional, physical state came up for us as babies. In an ideal world, therapists are repairing whatever parents couldn't do by being able to contain and maintain presence and regulation for all the various states that come up in the client's process—and, of course, your own personal reactions"*. The process is to move the client out of the 'broken connection' of trauma and self-focus, into becoming interested in secure reconnection with others, from stress to relaxation, from passive to active - work that's done in a safe, positive, and loving space.[15]

Psychotherapists Michael and Cheryl Irving explain about having good boundaries in relation to our well - being.[16]

They may be identified on the basis of physical distance around and between ourselves and others (too far away, too close?), distinguishing between another's and one's own feelings and maintaining appropriate ego-boundaries, clearly separating past, present and future (not clinging onto past traumas nor being anxious, absorbed or obsessed by the future), solving space issues, *"not knowing that the place you are in is not somewhere else; for example, your home feels like the place where you were abused"*, or thoughts (recognising that criticisms and what other's think should not affect us detrimentally – so we shouldn't allow this well-being boundary to be crossed). Good boundaries allow us to create a safe haven, an inner container for ourselves.

1   Bernard, Thomas J. Walter Reckless: American Criminologist http://www.britannica.com/EBchecked/topic/1340936/Walter-Reckless

2   My Shrink: Therapy Lingo: *Containment* http://www.myshrink.com/counseling-theory.php? t_id=32

3   http://psychology.wikia.com/wiki/Psychological_containment

4   Rohr, Richard Centre for Action and Contemplation meditation: *Willfulness to Willingness* Monday, June 15, 2015

5   Zaltman, Gerald & Zaltman, Lindsay *Marketing Metaphoria: what deep metaphors reveal about the minds of consumers* Harvard Business Press Boston, Massachusetts 2008

6   McKenna, Jed *The Yin-Yang Symbol* Sacred Valley Tribe: holding the space for transformation http://sacredvalleytribe.com/think-whats-true/consciousness/yin-yang-symbol/

7   Frankl, Viktor Man's Search for Meaning Washington Square Press Simon & Schuster NY 1963.

8   Bakhtia, Mikhail *Carnivalesque* https://en.wikipedia.org/wiki/Carnivalesque

9   Bonhoeffer, Dietrich *Letters and Papers from Prison* Touchstone NY 1997

10 Wing R.L. *The Tao of Power: Lao Tzu's classic guide to leadership* Aquarion/Thorsons (Harper Collins Imprint) London 1986

11 de Hennezel, Marie *The Warmth of the Heart keeps the Body from Rusting, a French recipe for a Long Life, Well Lived* Penguin 2013

12 Albom, Mitch *Tuesdays With Morrie: an old man, a young man, and life's greatest lesson* Random House 2002

13 Dass, Ram Still Here, Embracing Aging, Changing and Dying https://www.ramdass.org/still-here/

14 Wilkinson, Margaret *Changing Minds in Therapy: emotion, attachment, trauma & neurobiology* W.W.Norton & Company NY, London 2010

15 Heller, Diane Poole Psychotherapy 2.0 (An Insights at The Edge interview with Tami Simon of Sounds True) 25th August, 2015 http://www.soundstrue.com/store/weeklywisdom

16 Irving, Michael C, Ph.D. and Irving, Cheryl, B.A. *Well Being and Quality of Life: Containment* http://www.irvingstudios.com/Containment.htm

Afterword
Ralph Windle

The Halo and the Noose should be seen as an exciting further step in the long process of reconnecting business life to the mainstream of human history, experience and potential.

In retrospect, the early twentieth century orthodoxies of 'scientific management,' pioneered by Taylor and others – with their mechanistic attributes of planning, hierarchic structures and control – have proved amazingly durable and resistant to the voices of 'humanization'. Rhetoric apart, its rigid command structures probably still predominate in our twenty-first century business landscapes. And, as the accountant's influence progressively grew, formal systems, tiered structures and financial control were the dominant imperatives for many 'business schools' and management programmes.

It was in the Seventies and Eighties of the last century that a more enlightened 'guerrilla' battle for the souls of our business organizations began to be waged; spasmodically, at first, but soon to be re-enforced by the explosion of information technologies, the Internet and the challenges of the so-called 'knowledge economy'. More flexible work and career patterns loosened the structures and made more transparent the need for individuality and creativity. For the first time, the obvious desirability of a more enlightened approach to people in business became also the new economic imperative of our times.

Guerrilla warfare compensates for lack of numbers by enticing the enemy on to unfamiliar terrain, and so it has been in the battle for minds in which *The Halo and The Noose* now engages. For, to an unprecedented degree, the critical exchanges are about the need to revitalise the language of business so as to enrich the quality of the new dialogue.

There are already some key figures in the debate. Gareth Morgan's *Images of Organization* gave us a more coherent account of the significance of metaphor in shaping our ideas about organizations just as, in our broader lives, we need metaphor to understand any element of our experience in terms of another.[1] His classification of organizations – as 'machines', 'organisms', 'cultures', 'psychic prisons' and so on, gave us new words and images to enliven the debate.

Charles Handy in *The Age of Unreason* and *The Empty Raincoat* extended the metaphors and articulated the paradoxes of change.[2] Like me, he had come to business from a classical education and used a rich provision of story, allegory and parable to draw a whole new generation of business readers into the dialogue. "If you put a frog in cold water and slowly heat it, the frog will eventually let itself be boiled to death. We, too, will not survive if we don't respond to the radical way in which the world is changing".

Perhaps one of the more important and unexpected contributions to this liberalisation has been the growing legitimacy of poetry on the business scene.

James Autry's seminal *Love and Profit*, with its novel mix of prose and poetry, was a work of great courage against the trend for the US President of the Meredith Magazine Corporation.[3] He described to me how stunned people initially were to hear the word 'love' used as an attribute of someone in business. Many, who listened first because of the novelty of his status, stayed to relearn that – in the words of William Wordsworth – "Poetry is the breath and finer spirit of all knowledge".

The worldwide network of new and established poets who contributed to my own 1994 anthology *The Poetry of Business Life* has helped maintain this momentum.[4] There are other exhilarating developments on the poetry-in-business front, but we need to be on our guard against the sentimental and the twee.

It was Professor Roy Doughty, at Berkeley, who best articulated the significance of poetic language in this liberalising debate. "The conventional language of business is predominantly a language of information – accounting, policy manuals, financial reports – aimed at delineating, defining, separating – for the purposes of measurement and control. It is a technical language, honed to its specific purpose, but constrained in wider, more complex applications".[5]

By contrast, Doughty continues, "the language of poetry is the language of evocation, and it is this language which best speaks about relationships". Business people were in need of this language because "the world of commerce, no less than the worlds of ecology and spirit, is a nest of inter-relatedness".

Significant breaches are being made in the ramparts of the 'machine' corporate legacy, but the battle is not yet won. That is why it is so important and encouraging to have Graham Williams and Dorian Haarhoff opening this further front, harnessing the power of the story to the cause of progress and understanding.

For, as philosopher A. C. Grayling has said, "throughout human history story-telling has been a central means of informing people about possibilities beyond their personal sphere, and inviting them to understand those possibilities better. These things matter for a special reason: they promise an enlargement of our sympathies and sympathy is the basis of moral community".[6]

In the context of his own "Organizations as Machines" metaphor, Gareth Morgan reports a story related by the 4th Century BC. Chinese sage Chuang-Tzu.

Traveller Tzu-gung encounters an old man struggling ineffectively to irrigate his vegetable garden.

Tzu-gung said, "There is a way whereby you can irrigate a hundred ditches in one day, and whereby you can do much with little effort. You take a wooden lever, weighted at the back and light in front. In this way you can bring up water so quickly that it just gushes out. This is called a draw-well".

Anger showed in the old man's face, and he said, "I have heard my teacher say that whoever uses machines does all his work like a machine. He who does his work like a machine grows a heart like a machine, and he who carries the heart of a machine in his breast loses his simplicity. He who has lost his simplicity becomes unsure in the striving of his soul, which does not agree with honest sense. It is not that I do not know of such things; I am ashamed to use them".

The authors set out their complex and important themes with an impressive directness and clarity. They achieve this, we progressively discover, by the simple, persuasive device of practising what they preach. For the narrative moves between argument and story in a seamless way which argues a deep but unobtrusive scholarship in the literatures, cultures and traditions of many societies.

They are well aware of the paradox – "that the written word lacks some of the electricity of the spoken" – but disarm the criticism by the integrity of its anticipation and some novel ways of bridging the gap. The result is that the listener ranks equally with the teller in this book's perceptive approach to 'story'. It salvages and legitimises another important tool in our search for the words, images, metaphors and understandings which may better reveal why we are what we are, and could be.

The authors are right to position their work in the context of the inter-relationships between the right and left cortices of the brain. I believe that it is important that we emphasise the connections rather than the separations between these aesthetic and intuitive approaches to human understanding and what is happening in the relevant sciences – particularly the neuroscience. 'Only Connect' as E. M. Forster advised.

The neuroscientist Vilayanur Ramachandran proposed in his 2003 Reith Lectures, that the future "lies in a more thorough understanding of the connections between the 30 visual centres in your brain, and the emotional limbic structures".[7] And once we have achieved a clear understanding of these connections, we will be closer to bridging the huge gulf that separates what C. P. Snow called the two cultures – science on the one hand and Arts, philosophy and the humanities on the other.[8] We could be at the dawning of a new age where specialisation becomes old fashioned and a new 21st Century version of the Renaissance man – and woman – is born.

What a story that will be.

---

[1] Morgan, Gareth. *Images of Organization.* Sage Publications, 1986.
[2] Handy, Charles. *The Age of Unreason,* Random House, NY, 1989, *The Empty Raincoat,* Arrow Books, NY, 1994.
[3] Autry, James. *Love and Profit,* Chapmans, New Haven, 1992.
[4] Windle, Ralph. (ed.) *The Poetry of Business Life,* Berrett-Koehler, San Fransisco, 1994.

5 Doughty, Roy. Centre for Ethics and Social Policy, University of California at Berkeley.
6 Grayling A. C. *The Heart of Things*, Orion Book, London, 2005.
7 Ramachandran, V. S. *Neuro-Aesthetics - The Artful Brain,* BBC Reith Lectures, 2003.
8 Snow C. P. *The Two Cultures*, Cambridge University Press, Cambridge, 1959.

Appendices

From IQ to IQ plus EQ and SQ (Emotional and Social Intelligence)

In his book *Emotional Intelligence* Daniel Goleman showed that each emotion prepares our bodies for different responses,[1] for example

- *anger*: blood flows to hands, heart rate increases, adrenaline-hormone, energy lifts

- *fear*: blood flows to large muscles, body freezes, pause, focus

- *happiness*: body quieting, rest and heightened creativity

- *love*: parasympathetic relaxation response (opposite of anger and fear responses), calm and contentment

- *sadness*: slowed metabolism, so saps energy and enthusiasm, withdrawal.

He reported some key research findings proving that those who underwent emotional and social learning became more skilled than their peers, socially and in the workplace, at:

- exhibiting better emotional *self-awareness*

- *managing their emotions* more productively, marshalling them for optimistic self-motivation

- recognizing other's emotions and showing *empathy*

- *handling relationships* and conflicts.

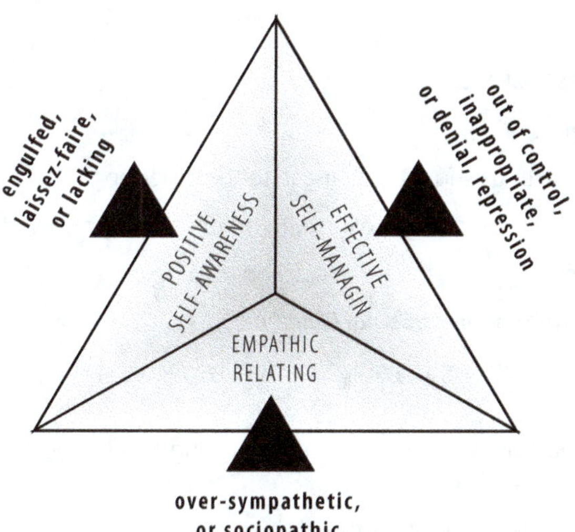

EMOTIONAL INTELLIGENCE

Goleman further showed that emotional healing, no matter how serious our historical emotional imprinting, is possible through the learning of positive behaviours and techniques, and practices such as meditation, that result in the physical alteration of established neural pathways.

He has since updated his review of research findings and adds to our knowledge in *Social Intelligence* the concept of social intelligence, which overlaps with emotional intelligence.[2] Whereas EQ is mainly about managing our own emotions, SQ is mainly about being socially adept and managing our one-to-one and group connections and relationships.

EMOTIONAL INTELLIGENCE	SOCIAL INTELLIGENCE
Self-awareness	Social awareness
Self-management	Relationship management

Social intelligence is the way that we apply a rational, moderating brake to our evolutionary-wired and memory-driven primitive, impulsive being. How we turn instinctive, impulsive perceptions and automatic reactions and responses into smooth effective interactions with others.

Arguably, the most important social intelligence expertise is empathy. Goleman: "As William Ickes, the University of Texas psychologist who has pioneered this line of research, contends, this ability distinguishes 'the most tactful advisors, the most

SUMMARY

SOCIAL INTELLIGENCE

Social Awareness:

> *Attunement.* Listening fully, tuning in to the other, engaging

> *Empathy.* Understanding, feeling with others, sensing non-verbal signals

> *Social cognition.* Being street smart, knowing how the social world works

Relationship Management/Social Facility:

> *Self-presentation.* Getting others to identify with us, gaining acceptance and trust

> *Concern.* Valuing the other. Sensing and caring about other's needs, and acting accordingly

> *Synchrony.* Interacting smoothly at the non-verbal level

> *Influence.* Building rapport and shaping social interaction outcomes

diplomatic officials, the most effective negotiators, the most electable politicians, the most productive sales persons, the most successful teachers, and the most insightful therapists' ".

A cursory examination of social intelligence attributes shows a close correlation with story-telling and story-listening attributes.

---

[1] Goleman, Daniel. *Emotional Intelligence,* Bantam Books, NY, 1995.
[2] Goleman, Daniel. *Social Intelligence,* Hutchinson, London, 2006.

Appendix II

The Tyranny of the Urgent
Managing Time and Energy

	SELF-ASSESSMENT						
	Effective Time & Energy Management						
	Score yourself from 0 to 5, where 5 = 'definite YES' and 0 = 'definite NO'. Add up total.						
1	Can you honestly say that you rarely experience symptoms of disorganization? (Frenetic activity, missed deadlines, lack of punctuality, missed meetings, out-of-control "in"- box)	0	1	2	3	4	5
2	Do you keep and use a diary/ time–planner?	0	1	2	3	4	5
3	Do you plan your time well in advance?	0	1	2	3	4	5
4	Do you periodically review how you have spent past time, and compare this to your overall goals and priorities (are they *in synch*)?	0	1	2	3	4	5
5	In planning your time, do you know and do you adjust to your own limits, gifts, rhythms?	0	1	2	3	4	5
6	Do you have a strategy for preserving energy and allowing for recovery time after emotionally draining events?	0	1	2	3	4	5
7	Do you regularly plan and budget your time?	0	1	2	3	4	5
8	Do you cater for a 'work, social, home, own – time' balance?	0	1	2	3	4	5
9	Do you use a continuous priority – setting mechanism?	0	1	2	3	4	5
10	Have you developed a strategy for unexpected crises, unscheduled interruptions and events?	0	1	2	3	4	5
11	Are you able to accurately assess how long a task will take?	0	1	2	3	4	5
12	Do you share your workload appropriately and timeously?	0	1	2	3	4	5
13	Do you work at overcoming procrastination (and doing those tasks you would prefer to avoid)?	0	1	2	3	4	5
14	Are you adept at conducting/attending effective and worthwhile meetings, efficient at solving problems, making decisions, working effectively and efficiently?	0	1	2	3	4	5
15	Do you stay focused on the single task at hand?	0	1	2	3	4	5
	YOUR % SCORE = The total score multiplied by 4, then divided by 3						

A Time and Energy Analysis

There is no false 'pass mark'. What you determine to be a 'good score' depends on you. This is how to interpret your responses:

Question 1. Self Awareness

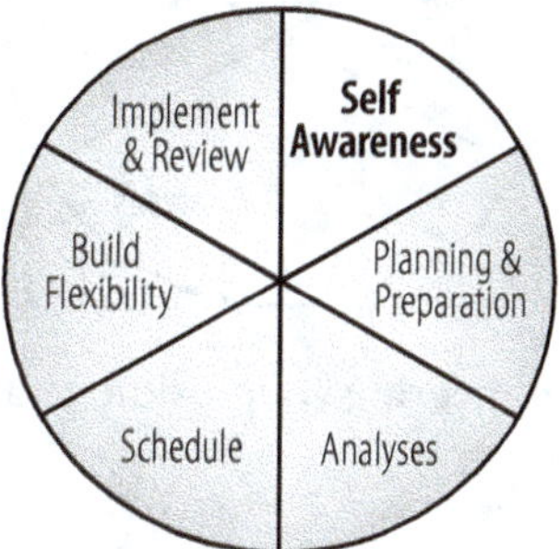

Your answer is a 'pointer'. Rely on your intuition here: if you've given yourself a 'low' score, then you're not happy with your time and energy management. Perhaps you can do something about it?

Questions 2 and 3. Planning and Preparation

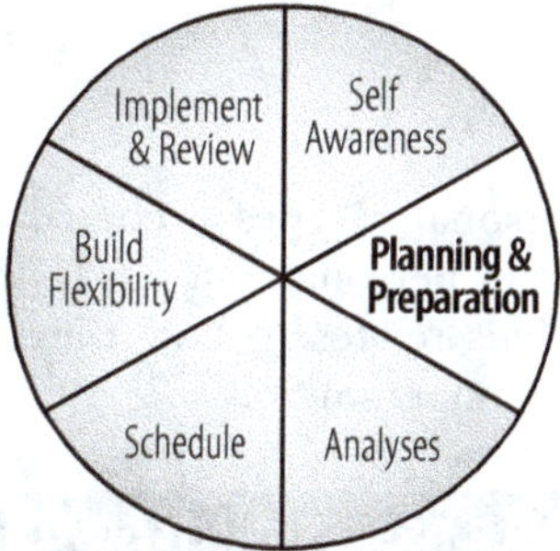

Are you in the *habit* of thinking ahead? If not, part of the solution may be to *not* look at your time-management in isolation, but to develop other aspects of your lifestyle and practices simultaneously. (For example, a healthier eating and exercise regime can impact positively on energy levels and motivation, and lead to better use of time and greater productivity. You will know what you need to do).

Simply being organized can be a good way of developing a more relaxed demeanour. Not being organized can be depressing. Not planning our own time makes us vulnerable to procrastination and reduced effectiveness, to being overtaken by events and the agendas of others, to losing the feeling of being in control. Moving ahead is a question of accepting and taking responsibility. Our choice.

Questions 4, 5 and 6. Analyses

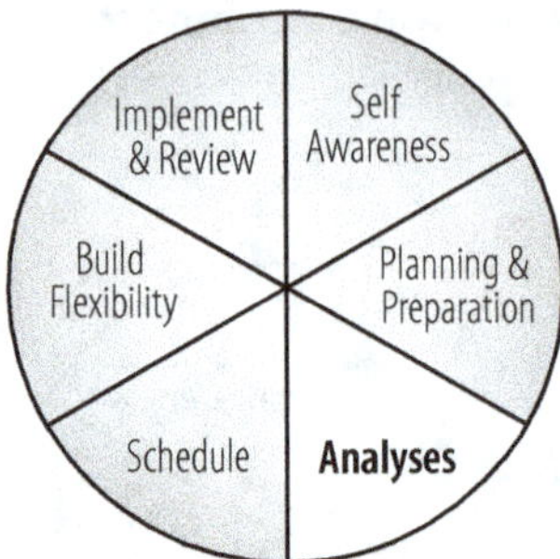

Are you focussing your time on meeting your vision, goals, priorities, energy levels and rhythm?

Day and Night Rhythms

Are you a morning, afternoon or evening person? Have you in the past planned key activities for those times during your day when your energy levels are high? When you feel at your best, when you're usually at your most productive? Do you know what you're good at and can do quickly and do you also know your limitations? The point is that when we are doing what we're meant to be doing, then we are, to coin a current 'in' phrase, flowing in the zone. So the message is simple: know who we are, what we do, plan time to do it, do it.

Time and Personality Type

Imagine a novel with all the personality types as characters. As in a story, actions arise out of our personalities. Different personality types tend to view and handle the time dimension in different ways. This relates to how they see the world, their thinking styles, relating preferences and temperament.

SELF-ASSESSMENT: GOALS

PHYSICAL   Health, Fitness, Finances, Assets

INTELLECTUAL   Learning, Stimulation, Hobbies

SOCIAL/EMOTIONAL/WORK   Career, Relationships, Pastimes/Activities

SPIRITUAL   Vision/Purpose, Values, Spiritual journey, Mindfulness

We suggest a Diary as a way of taking responsibility, for each chosen area, as we set goals, and match them with related actions.

In 1973 a well known study of the Yale University class of '53 found that the small minority of those who had as students *written down* their life goals and related actions to be taken, were the most contented and were the real achievers.

From a mechanistic, technical time management perspective, it may be that the ESTJ Myers-Briggs Personality type has an edge. Simplistically:

E's energy, focus and interest is directed outwards towards concrete things, people. (I's are introverted as opposed to extroverted, their focus being inward).

S's gather information through their five senses. They are interested in realities and facts, not concepts, theories, possibilities. (N's are intuitive, reliant on their '6th sense').

T's make decisions based on objective, logical considerations rather than feelings towards people and being harmony-driven. (F's are directed by their feelings).

J's lifestyle and approach is orderly, planned and they make quick decisions. (P's work with perceptions, concepts, connections and overviews, and don't readily distinguish between 'black and white').

INTP's try and keep their options open for as long as possible, and may be prone to procrastination. ESTJ's naturally master technical time management (although there are one or two aspects that they generally dislike – for example the practice of reflection).

From this mechanistic, technical view of time management, INTP's are the worst, being by definition the very opposite of ESTJ's. INTP's tend to be better at managing their energy though, take heed of their natural cycles and rhythms, and tend to be more spontaneous, adaptive, flexible and responsive when schedules change. (Some see Pope John Paul II as a ESFJ and Bill Gates as INTP).

Time Before, Time During and Time After

Many of us can identify with this sentiment: *"We haven't the time to take our time"*.[1]

Here are some questions to ask ourselves when scheduling an important activity that is likely to be energy-draining (a meeting about a key personal relationship, or to let someone know that their job is in jeopardy, or to deliver bad news, or visit someone newly bereaved).

Have you carefully allowed for preparation time? (Time to ready your mental and emotional state, to think ahead regarding the sorts of issues that may arise and how you will respond).

Have you allowed yourself recovery time following the event? (After events like this we need time to digest and recover. To set up back to back meetings *without* building in recovery time, simply reduces our ongoing personal effectiveness. In extreme cases this leads to a frazzled, disoriented state of being).

Have you allowed time to be present in the meeting?

There is a story in which an old peasant woman advises the people that if they seek contentment, they must allow tasks the time it needs to perform them.

Stress

A missionary in colonial Africa was hurrying between villages. A team of locals carried his belongings on their heads. At one point in the journey, at a signal from the head porter, the group put down their loads and sat under a tree. Nothing the missionary could say could get them to move. After some time, the leader nodded to the men. They all picked up their burdens and carried on.

The missionary asked the leader, "What was that about?"

The head porter responded, "We were travelling so fast that we left our spirits behind. We were waiting for them to catch up".

In managing negative energy (Stress) we might want to do better than the missionary. You may want to employ the diagram below as a checklist:

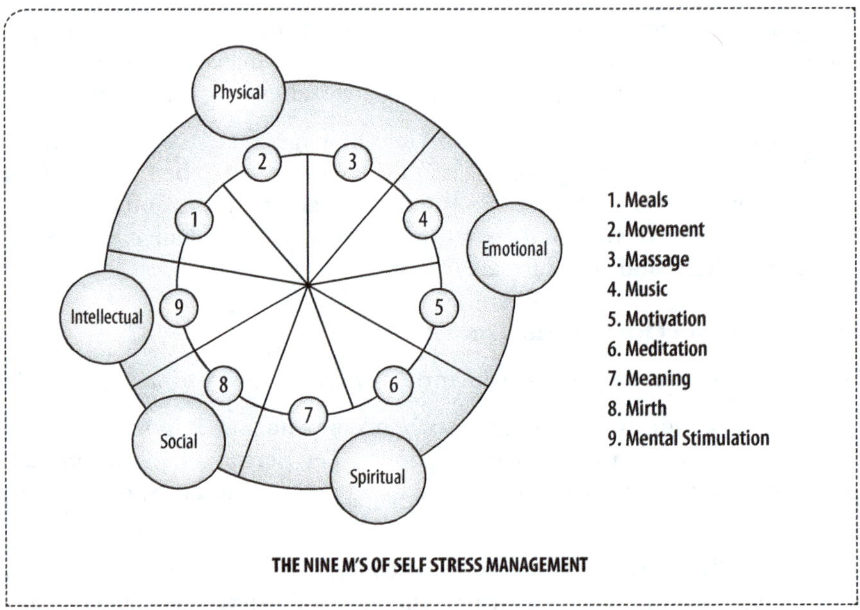

Questions 7, 8 and 9 Schedule Your Time

On a regular basis, 'budget' and balance your time according to your priorities:

Setting Priorities – A Process

- *seriousness* refers to the importance of the task, how much value it will add, how serious is it that the task must be executed

- *urgency* refers to the *real* urgency that applies – not someone else's 'manufactured crisis', not a response to who shouts loudest

- *volatility* refers to whether the task will have greater adverse consequences if left undone. (Some situations if left, 'go away'. Other problems grow worse/ become more serious if left for later).

Questions 10, 11 and 12. Build in Flexibility

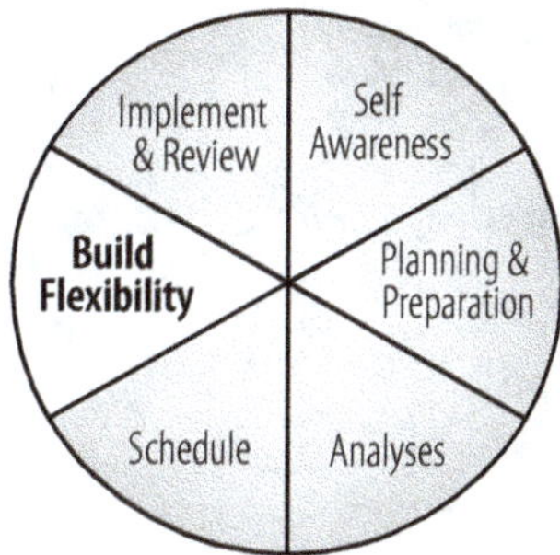

Remember the story of the farmer, the neighbour and the horse?

SELF-ASSESSMENT

1. List tasks to be performed
2. Give each task a seriousness, urgency and volatility score on a scale of your choice (1 to 5 is usually good enough)
3. These seriousness, urgency and volatility scores may be weighted if you prefer. (Often we are driven by urgency when seriousness is more important so you may wish to give seriousness a much higher weighting than urgency)
4. Add the scores (or weighted scores) for each task
5. Rank the tasks by order of score from highest to lowest.

LIST OF TASKS	Seriousness	Urgency	Volatility	TOTAL

There is a saying if you want to make God laugh, tell God your plans for the future. We cannot foresee the unexpected. The sudden arrival of something that demands our time, causes us to reset priorities and laughs at our carefully planned time. Scottish poet, Robbie Burns, reminds us that the best laid plans, "of mice and men gang aft aglay".[2]

Also, when we try and do too much, cram in too many activities – we're using a recipe for failure. So the purpose of this part of the time and energy management system is to encourage ourselves to be reasonable and realistic. And be kind to ourselves.

Questions 13, 14 and 15. Implement and Review

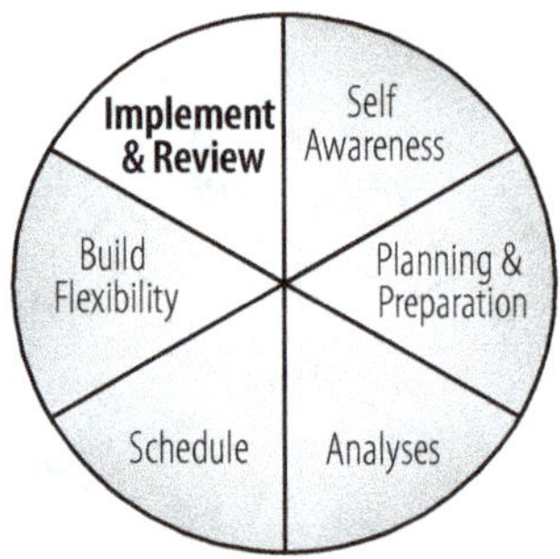

Lights, Action

Nasrudin was carrying a cage of roosters to a certain place. He let them out for a while so they could walk part of the way. The roosters scattered in all directions.

"Fools," shouted Nasrudin, "You know when it is going to be sunrise. How come you cannot understand where I am going?"

If a plan is not an *action* plan it's not a plan. We need to implement, do what we've scheduled, then review our effectiveness. This completes the cycle and commences the next cycle of activity: our time and energy management system is a closed loop system. Reviewing simultaneously improves our awareness, and thus our potential to continue learning and improving. It is also more than simply a 'technical' system, and embraces the 'whole person'.

If we value and esteem ourselves, we will also place a value on our time and use it productively. (Similarly, if others spend time with us it indicates that they value us). When we value ourselves, we apply self-discipline. If we procrastinate, fail to do what we intend to do (go fishing with our son when there is a free day, do a house repair that has been waiting for ages, stop smoking as a next new year resolution), or deliberately or unconsciously put off doing 'unpleasant', boring chores, even though they may be important, then we definitely have a self-sabotage, time-management problem. It may be deep-seated. We may be avoiding or postponing important activity because of

- *technical constraints* (awaiting full and proper information, entering new, uncertain 'territory', unclear project aims)

- *external/social factors* (an interfering, dominating boss, unexpected, unplanned for, unavoidable or avoidable crisis and distractions)

- *physical inhibitors* (chronic fatigue due to inadequate exercise, diet, sleep, time for relaxation/ fun/ reflection/ refreshment, and a negative, depressed attitude)

- *internal/ psychological factors* – by far the most important – fear of failure, ridicule, pain, the unknown, conflict, risk. Fear of finishing (before it's perfect!), fear of success (and whether you'll cope with your new position, power, money, responsibilities, glory, acquaintances – or arrive at your "level of incompetence"). Such fears can lead to a failure to start tasks and once started, to bring them to completion.

Remember American President F. D. Rooseveldt's famous remark? "We have nothing to fear but fear itself". Can we pinpoint our fears? This is the first step to overcoming them and in the process improving effectiveness and contentment levels. "Defer no time, delays have dangerous ends".[3]

Similarly, we may be prone to obsessive-compulsive behaviours (for example computer games that tie us up for hours and keep us from doing what needs doing).

Or have short concentration spans.

Or be disorganized, wasting time searching for car keys, 'lost' papers, the screwdriver or glue, a reference book, pen.

Or have 'an attitude problem': "I can't do this!", "I don't want to do this!", "Deep down, I don't care enough and therefore don't want to spend the time needed to mend this relationship", "I won't make the time to learn how to do this", "I will not 'let go' and let someone else do this", "I (secretly) enjoy being overworked and in demand even though on the surface I may complain". These are all examples of what are often inappropriate attitudinal problems related to time and energy management.

It may be that we need to hone our technical work skills – clearly if we're able to run an effective meeting, solve a problem clearly and logically, make good and lasting decisions, streamline the business processes – then we will use our time more efficiently (less direct time and less 're-work' time).

Other time traps include doing pleasant tasks and avoiding the unpleasant ones – even though they may be important. Becoming easily distracted. Not completing tasks. Being unpunctual. Striving for perfection to impress others or to (falsely) feed ones own needs to feel important and worthy.

The Key: Searching for Time

We can be neurotic about these problems (blame ourselves and make ourselves miserable, yet not fix it or seek help). Or like Nasrudin with his roosters, we can exhibit character disorder (blame the world, others, make them miserable and duck our own responsibility to fix it). We sometimes act like Cassim in this next story:

> *Cassim is on his hands and knees outside his house sifting sand through his fingers. His friend, Abdul, approaches.*
>
> *Abdul asks, "What are you doing?"*
>
> *Cassim answers, "I have lost my key".*

Without a word Abdul joins him in the sand and together they search in silence. After half an hour Abdul sits back on his haunches and asks, "Cassim, are you sure you lost your key here?"

"No, I lost the key inside the house".

"Then why are we searching here?"

Cassim responds, "Because it is too dark to look inside the house".

When we own the problem, take responsibility, be proactive and fix it, we begin to look for the key where we lost it. We get healed, we get organized. We save time.

When we are busy with a task, it's good to demonstrate 'stay-ability' and appreciate the power of focus. The channelling and focus of a ray of sunlight through a magnifying glass is what produces concentrated power sufficient to burn through heavy metal. Yet as the Cassim story suggests, we need to focus in the right place.

During each cycle, we may wish to keep a journal to record things of significance that have caused a deviation from what we had planned. This can be helpful in future planning, especially where this is repetitive.

Our diaries and work-plans are not primarily about events. They are about bigger life-goals that we are focused on achieving, and which are brought about by conducting certain events: an important distinction.

Becoming decisive not only enhances time utilisation, it also reduces worry and stress.

Being self-aware, setting realistic and achievable schedules, learning and improving, building in 'time–out', feeling in control, making time for story telling and story listening are all important de-stressors that can have a major bearing on our well-being.

Since so many poets have been preoccupied with time, some critics refer to a school of *Carpe diem* poets. The Roman poet Horace's line "Seize the day", was popularised in the movie Dead Poets' Society.

---

[1]   Ionesco, Eugene. *Exit the King,* Grove/Atlantic, London, 1994.
[2]   Burns, Robert. *Robert Burns, Selected Poems*, Penguin, 1994.
[3]   Shakespeare, William. *King Henry VI.*

Corporate Story Competence and Application: an assessment for organisations

"To evoke in oneself a feeling one has once experienced, and having evoked it in oneself, then, by means of movements, lines, colors, sounds, or forms expressed in words, so to transmit that feeling that others may experience the same feeling - this is the activity of art" - Leo Tolstoy

Story has been around for a long time

"There have been stories and messages delivered across different media ever since Cro-Magnon man figured out that mineral pigments like iron oxide and black manganese could be applied to the sides of rocks and caves. Whether chronicling life, communicating with others, or creating an inspirational image, there were stories being told".[1]

"For well over 100,000 years before written language, humans communicated all key information, histories, beliefs, and attitudes through oral storytelling AND archived (stored/remembered) all of that information in story form in human memory. 100,000 years of relying on story architecture as our primary storage and communications system has evolutionarily rewired human brains. We are all now born hardwired to think, to make sense, and to understand through story structure and by using specific story elements".[2]

Four of the compelling reasons why story is a must, are:

- Humans are still hardwired for story

- Story and metaphor have immense psychological power – our brains don't distinguish between imagination and reality[1] – Our cognitive functioning, the way we learn and grow, is via both abstract and narrative thinking[3]

- Many success stories have emerged of organisations who have made use of story for a range of business challenges (and around the world tertiary institutions are offering story modules)

Story touches the whole person

Our lives are stories, and filled with stories. We are immersed in story from womb to tomb, cradle to grave, sperm to worm, ancestry to after-life. We're touched by story emotionally, socially, physically, intellectually, and spiritually. Story connects us to our higher and deeper selves, and to others. It gives meaning, provides context, frees up our imagination and creativity.

> *"Stories have such a powerful and universal appeal that the neurological roots of both telling tales and enjoying them are probably tied to crucial parts of our social cognition".*[4]

Research shows that story is the way to establish rapport, engage and mobilise the disengaged; that listeners suspend disbelief, reality-testing and counter-argument during the telling; that people prefer reaching their own insights, and that well-told stories stick in the memory and stimulate big conversations and action. People respond far better to stories than they do to facts, figures, statistics, bar charts, bullet point presentations, jargon and business-speak. When a story is told we enter what psychologists term 'narrative transport'. Story plays a role in the development of important life skills – emotional intelligence, mindfulness, imagination:

– Jon Kabat Zinn, pioneer of mindfulness in the medical world and neuroscience, in a recent radio interview[5] pointed out that *"Those trained in mindfulness/awareness light up the narrative network in the medial region of the prefrontal cortex and harmonise with the experiential network grounded in the body"*.

– And the title of an article by PJ Manney needs no further explanation: Empathy in the Time of Technology: How Storytelling is the Key to Empathy.[6]

– We relate emotionally to metaphor words in stories. Researchers at Emory University found for example that *"when subjects read a metaphor involving texture, the sensory cortex, responsible for perceiving texture through touch, became active"*.[7]

– We live and breathe story. And as "Novelist Edmund White once wrote, *"When a person dies, a library is burned"*.[8]

In business, story has huge potential

Narrative has a key role to play in every aspect of business – every department, every business process, in our relating to suppliers, stakeholders, customers. In brand enhancement, knowledge management, training, making sense of issues and challenges, communication, sales connections, scenario construction, change/transition endeavours, presentations, coaching for reframing, narrative inquiry through theatre, conducting qualitative research (anecdote circles, metaphor elicitation ....).

Hence our development of this assessment instrument.

Using the Assessment

In these notes and within the assessment instrument, we have generally (in order to avoid tortuous and complicated descriptions) used *'Story'* an all-embracing term that covers narrative, metaphor, personal anecdote; and biographical, historical, mythological, metaphorical, wisdom stories; past, present, future stories; fact, fiction. Nor have we taken pains to distinguish between oral and written stories. These distinctions are of course necessary in certain situations - but should not blur the principle that what matters more than categorisation or 'academic accuracy' is the integrity and appropriateness of the use of story.

The assessment is in two parts:

- Story *competence* consistently displayed

- Story *application* deeply understood and used throughout the business

It reveals the organisations' strengths, weaknesses and opportunities - in the area of using story in order to advance corporate goals.

The assessment may be best completed in the presence of an experienced business story practitioner, so that the nuances and niceties of each of the questions is well understood before being answered. Interpretation and determining appropriate action will also benefit by a seasoned practitioner's perspective.

We hope that the diagnostic is used widely and wisely, adds to the professionalism of business story practitioners everywhere, and promotes and advances the effective and ethical use of story within organisations. Prominent story practitioners Karen Dietz and Lori Silverman refer to our assessment in their Business Strorytelling for Dummies.[9]

---

[1] Rutledge, Pamela Brown, PH.D., M.B.A *The Psychological Power of Storytelling* http:// www.psychologytoday.com/blog/ positively-media January 16, 2011

[2] Haven, Kendall Testing, *One, Two: how do I know they're listening?* © Kendall Haven 2011 Halo and Noose Articles Archive

[3] Bruner, Jerome *Actual Minds, Possible Worlds* Harvard University Press, Boston 1986

[4] Hsu, Jeremy *The Secrets of Storytelling: Why We Love a Good Yarn* Scientific American Mind, August 2008

[5] Kabat Zinn, Jon BBC World Service, The Forum 15/1/2011

[6] Manney, PJ Empathy in the Time of Technology: How Storytelling is the Key to Empathy Journal of Evolution and Technology Vol 19 Issue 1 Sept 2008 http:// jetpress.org/v19/manney.htm.

[7] Paul, Annie Murphy *Your Brain on Fiction* The New York Times March 17, 2012 http://www.nytimes.com/2012/03/18/opinion/sunday/the-neuroscience-of-you-brain-on-fiction.html?_r=1&pagewanted=all

[8] Baldwin, Christina *Storycatcher* New World Library, Novato, Canada 2005

[9] Dietz, Karen and Silverman, Lori Business Storytelling for Dummies John Wiley & Sons, Inc. New Jersey 2013

(1) THE LEVEL OF STORY *COMPETENCE* THAT IS CONSISTENTLY DISPLAYED IN YOUR ORGANISATION

	Never	Rarely	Some times	Often	Always
	0	1	2	3	4

Knowledge. All employees understand the psychological power of story to raise awareness, capture interest, engage, stimulate thinking, provide knowledge and insight, evoke responses and action, trigger sharing, improve personal and business performance. They know which types of story are appropriate for each business challenge. They know that outgoing and incoming stories serve to differentiate the organisation from competitors

Skill. Staff are able to access, construct, tell and write appropriate stories. Attentive listening is prevalent. People are able to reflect on story to get the most out of them. Story has a role in crucial conversations and conflict resolution. Levels of emotional and social intelligence are high.

Beliefs, values, attitudes, motives. Story, anecdote and metaphor is approached positively – to share, liberate, inform and convey feelings, provide insight ‑ and never with any intent to manipulate

Traits. A well-developed mindfulness, coupled with imagination, is applied to the listening to and telling of stories and anecdotes, and the meaning of metaphor. Respect for others' stories is present.

Culture. Story *is* 'the way we do, think and feel about things here', in all of the functional applications. We think and live story. Naturally. We are bent on continually learning to improve both functional application, and personal and organisational story competence. We understand that story can positively shape culture: it aids clarity of purpose and focus, is a catalyst for bringing new norms and behaviours into play, promotes mindfulness, imagination, listening, open‑ness, sharing

SCORING:	Level of Competence
0 – 7	*Not yet competent*
8 – 15	*Competent but not superior*
16 – 20	*Highly competent*

(2) *APPLICATION* - **THE EFFECTIVE USE OF NARRATIVE TO ADVANCE CORPORATE GOALS**

Do you use story in:

	Never	Rarely	Some times	Often	Always
	0	1	2	3	4

Living shared values spontaneously. Story is used to explain, illustrate and share the values. All participate and examples of positive behaviours are encouraged, recognised, shared, spread through personal stories and anecdotes. Leading is by example

Engaging with the future. Conversations take place at all levels and personal story and experiences are used to create a common vision, alternate scenarios, and alignment with strategies. People, planet and profit issues are openly debated and the benefits of increasing diversity are understood and welcomed. People think in terms of "possibilities" not "limitations"

External communications. The brand is strengthened via metaphor elicitation and customer dialogue, detailed attention to customer/stakeholder/supplier stories. People, planet and profit aspects are held in balance. Formal documents are infused with story, and interesting. The organisation embraces social media and is willing to engage openly with its publics. Messages and stories are clear, concrete, truthful

Internal communications. Community, belonging, teamwork, EQ, SQ and knowledge is built through story. Experiences are freely shared across departments and at all levels and the richness of diversity is harnessed. Presentations and meetings are enlivened by personal and wisdom stories. Presentations follow a story pattern. Formal and informal communications are built around story. People, planet and profit issues receive equal attention. Leaders are accessible and share openly. Story is the basis of knowledge management systems

Change and transitions. People are able to 'say the unsayable' in a trusting, safe place. Success 'war stories' arise spontaneously at all levels. Multiple viewpoints are encouraged. Story is used to promote resilience and adaptability. Appreciative Inquiry is used, people are involved.

Sense-making. Situations, decisions, problems are assessed, understood and responded to as a result of eliciting personal stories, consultation, capturing of diverse views, knowledge, experiences and perspectives. Consciousness is raised - using anecdote circles, clustering, analyses and feedback - rather than surveys and interviews, whenever possible

Learning. In formal training case studies and illustrative stories are widely used. Both successes and failures are used for learning purposes. Personal narrative reframing is used in coaching and mentoring. Reflection, piloting, lateral thinking, review and feedback are established practices. Stories play a role in bringing about new mental models.

Customer service and selling. There is an accent on listening to, understanding and responding to customer stories. Sales and supporting staff forge emotional-connections through story, metaphor and analogy. Social media stories are used to connect with customers, stimulate dialogue, build loyalty

SCORING:	Level of Competence
0 – 12	*Huge opportunities are being lost*
13 – 20	*Below average*
21 – 25	*Well developed application of story, with certain areas of potential that can be improved*
26 – 32	*Excellent application of story*

Bibliography

A World Café Hosting Guide http://www.empowermentinstitute.net/lcd/lcd_files/ World_CafevHosting_Guide.pdf

Adams, Scott. *The Dilbert Principles,* Harper Business, New York, *1996.*

Adichie, Chimamanda *The danger of a single story* http://www.youtube.com/watch? v=D9Ihs241zeg

Agnon, S. Y. *Book that was Lost and other Stories*, Schocken, New York, 1996.

Albom, Mitch Tuesdays With Morrie: an old man, a young man, and life's greatest lesson Random House 2002

Anecdote (Callahan, Shawn; Rixon, Andrew & Schenk, Mark) *The Ultimate Guide to Anecdote Circles: a practical guide to facilitating storytelling and story listening* www.anecdote.com.au

Armstrong, Lance. *It's Not about the Bike: My Journey Back to Life,* McGraw Hill, New York, 2000.

Auden, W. H. "Walking Away", *Collected Poems*, Random House, NY, 2007.

Autry, James. *Love and Profit,* Chapmans, New Haven, 1992.

Bakhtia, Mikhail *Carnivalesque* https://en.wikipedia.org/wiki/Carnivalesque

Baldwin, Christina *Storycatcher :making sense of our lives through the power and practice of story* New World Library, Novato, Canada 2005

Barks, Coleman. *The Essential Rumi*, Penguin, London, 1995.

Basho, Matsuo. *Matsuo Basho, The Master Haiku Poet*, Macmillan, London, 1983.

Bateson, Gregory. *Steps to the Ecology of Mind,* Paladin Books, London, 1980.

Bedier, J. *Romance of Tristan and Iseult,* Dover, NY, 2005.

Belasco, James A. *Teaching the Elephant to Dance,* Hutchinson Business Books, London, 1990.

Bernard, Thomas J. Walter Reckless: American Criminologist http://www.britannica.com/ EBchecked/topic/1340936/Walter-Reckless

Blake, William. "The Marriage of Heaven and Hell", *The Complete Poems*, Penguin, London, 1978.

Bleek, W. H. I. and Lloyd Lucy. *The Mantis And His Friends – Bushman folklore*, T. Maskew Miller, Cape Town, 1923.

Bleek W. H. I. and Lloyd, Lucy, *Specimens of Bushmen Folklore*, George Allan and Unwin, London, 1869, facsimile reprint, Cape Town, 1911.

Bly, Robert., Hillman James, and Meade, Michael. (eds). *The Rag and Bone Shop of the Heart*, Harper Collins, NY, 1992.

Bly, Robert and Woodman, Marion. *The Maiden King, The Reunion of Masculine and Feminine*, Henry Holt, NY, 1999.

Bonder, Milton. *The Kabalah of Money*, Shambala, Berkeley, 1996.

Bonhoeffer, Dietrich *Letters and Papers from Prison* Touchstone NY 1997

Bosman, Herman Charles. *Mafeking Road and Other Stories,* Human and Rousseau, Cape Town, 1947.

Brabeck, Peter. *"The Business Case Against Revolution: An interview with Nestlé's Peter Brabeck".* Harvard Business Review, Boston. February, 2001.

Bradbury, Ray. *Zen and the Art of Writing*, Bantam, NY, 1995.

Bruner, Jerome *Actual Minds, Possible Worlds* Harvard University Press, Boston 1986

Bruner, Jerome. *Making Stories, Law, Literature and Life*, Farrar Straus and Giroux, New York, 2002.

Burns, Robert. *Robert Burns, Selected Poems*, Penguin, London, 1994.

Cameron, Julia. *The Artist's Way*, Pan Books, Oxford, London, 1993.

Campbell, Joseph. *Pathways to Bliss,* New World Library, Novato, California, 2004.

Campbell, Joseph. *The Hero with a Thousand Faces,* Bollingen Series, Princeton University Press, NY, 1972.

Carroll, Lewis (Charles Dodgson). *Alice's Adventures in Wonderland* and *Through the Looking Glass,* Barnes and Noble, *NY, 2005.*

Chabon, Michael in *Will Eisner: A Spirited Life,* Mpress, Milwaukie, 2005.

Chaucer, Geoffrey. *Cantebury Tales*, Barnes and Noble, NY, 2007.

Childs, S. *Chicken Licken,* Ladybird, London, 1999.

Chuang-Tzu. *Chuang Tsu – Inner Chapters*, Random House, NY, 1974.

Clancy, Tom with Franks Fred, Jnr. (General, Ret.) *Into the Storm : A study in command,* Sidgwick & Jackson, London, 1999. Copyright © C. P. Commanders, Inc, 1999.

Cozolino, L *The Neuroscience of Human Relationships: attachment and the developing social brain* Norton & Company, Inc. NY 2006

Crawford, Tad. *The Secret Life of Money, How Money can be Food for the Soul,* Allworth Press, New York, 1994.

Crisp, Richard *The Social Brain: how diversity made the modern mind* Robinson Great Britain 2015

Czikzentmihalyi, M. *Flow: The psychology of optimal experience,* Harper Collins, New York, 1991.

Dante, Alighieri. *The Divine Comedy,* trans. Henry Wadsworth Longfellow, www.everypoet.com

Dass, Ram Still Here, Embracing Aging, Changing and Dying   https://www.ramdass.org/still-here/

Davidson, R. J., Kabat-Zinn, J., Schumacher, J., Rosenkranz, J, Muller, D., Santorelli S., et al, *"Alterations in brain and immune function produced by mindfulness meditation"* Psychosomatic Medicine, Vol. 65, 2003.

Dawes, Gary. "Customer First", *Front Lines,* Vol. 3, No. 7, 2002.

De Bono, Edward. *Serious Creativity*, Harper Collins, London, 1995.

de Hennezel, Marie *The Warmth of the Heart keeps the Body from Rusting, a French recipe for a Long Life , Well Lived* Penguin 2013

Delaney, Frank. *Ireland,* Time Warner Books, London, 2004.

Delio, Ilia *The Unbearable Wholeness of Being: God, evolution and the power of love Orbis Books, 2013*

De Mello, Anthony. *The Prayer of the Frog* Gujarat Sahitja Prakash, Anand, India, 1989.

Denning, Stephen. *The Springboard – how story telling ignites action in Knowledge-Era Organizations,* Elsevier, 2000.

De Saint Exupery, Antoine. *The Little Prince,* NTC/Contemporary Co, 2000.

De Soto, Hernando. *The Mystery of Capital,* Bantam Press, NY, 2000.

Deutschman, Alan. *Change or Die,* Fast Company New York. Issue 94, May 2005. ©2007 Mansueto Ventures LLC.

De Vries, Manfred Kets. *The Leadership Mystique,* Financial Times/Prentice Hall, Great Britain, 2001.

De Waal, Mandy. *The Poetry of Business,* www.harmoniousliving.co.za, 20 February, 2006.

Dickens, Charles, *Great Expectations.* Allen and Unwin, London, 2000.

Dietz, Karen and Silverman, Lori Business Storytelling for Dummies John Wiley & Sons, Inc. New Jersey 2013

Donne, John. *John Donne's Poetry*, Norton, NY, 2006.

Doughty, Roy. Centre for Ethics and Social Policy, University of California at Berkeley.

Dove, Rita. "To Make a Prairie", *The Writer*, Boston, Jan, 1995.

Eagleton, Terry. *Literary Theory*, Blackwell, London, 1983.

Eliot T. S. *Complete Poems and Plays,* Harcourt, NY, 1957.

Eliot T. S. *Collected Poems*, Faber and Faber, 1963.

Eliot T. S. *Four Quartets,* Harcourt, 1968.

Engstrom, Ted W. and Mackenzie Alec. *Managing Your Time* Zondervan, 1967

Estés, Clarissa Pinkola. *Women Who Run With the Wolves*, Rider, NY, 1992.

Fleming, David L. S.J. *The Spiritual Exercises of St. Ignatius: a literal translation and a contemporary reading* Smyth Sewn Paperback The Institute of Jesuit Sources, St Louis 1978

Flesch, Rudolf. *The Art of Plain Talk,* MacMillan, London, 1962.

Frankl, Viktor. *Man's Search for Meaning*, Washington Square Press, Simon & Schuster, NY, 1963.

Frost, Robert. "A Boy's Will", *Robert Frost Poems*, St Martin's Press, NY, 2002.

Frost, W. R. Nord. and L. A. Kefting, (eds.) *HRM Reality: Putting Competence in Context.* 2nd Edition, New Jersey: Prentice Hall, 2002.

Fukuyama, F. *Trust,* Penguin Books, London, 1996.

Gargiulo, Terrence http://www.makingstories.net

Germer, Christopher K., Siegel, Ronald D., Fulton, Paul R. (Eds.) *Mindfulness & Psychotherapy*, The Guildford Press, NY, 2005.

Gibran, Kahlil. *The Prophet*, Alfred Knofp, NY, 1923.

Gillard, Marni. *Story teller, Story teacher,* Stenhouse, Portland, 1996.

Goleman, Daniel. *Emotional Intelligence,* Bantam Books, NY, 1995.

Goleman, Daniel. *Social Intelligence,* Hutchinson, London, 2006.

Gray, Stephen. (Ed), *Modern South African Stories,* Donker, Johannesburg, 1983.

Grayling A. C. *The Heart of Things*, Orion Books, London, 2005.

Greenwood, Michelle. "The study of business ethics: A case for Dr. Seuss", *Business Ethics, A European Review*, Vol. 9 No. 3, July, 2000.

Grisham, John. *Bleachers*. Century, London, Copyright © 2003 Belfry Holdings, Inc, 2003.

Guber, Peter *Tell to Win: Connect, Persuade, and Triumph with the Hidden Power of Story* Crown Publishing Group (division of Random House Inc.) NY 2010

Haarhoff, Dorian, *Drawing Water*, Leopard Press, Durban, 2006.

Haarhoff, Dorian. *The Writer's Voice*, Zebra Struik, Johannesburg, 1998.

Haarhoff Dorian. *Tortoise Voices*, Mercer Press, Cape Town, 2001.

Handy Charles. *The Age of Unreason*, Random House, NY, 1989.

Handy, Charles. *The Empty Raincoat*, Arrow Books, NY, 1994.

Hanh, Thich Nhat. *Breath! You are Alive*, Parallax Press, Berkeley, 1996.

Hanh, Thich Nhat. *Going Home: Bringing Christ and the Buddha together in Daily Life,* Rider, Riverhead Books, Penguin Putnam Inc, NY, 1999.

Harpur, Patrick. *The Philosopher's Secret Fire, A History of the Imagination*, Penguin, London, 2002.

Haven, Kendall *Testing, One, Two: how do I know they're listening?* © Kendall Haven 2011 Halo and Noose Articles Archive

Heath, Chip and Heath, Dan. *Made to Stick: why some ideas take hold and others come unstuck*. Arrow Books. London 2007.

Heider, John. *The Tao of Leadership: Lao Tzu's Tao Te Ching Adapted for a New Age*, Humanics Publishing Group, 1986.

Heller, Diane Poole Psychotherapy 2.0 (An Insights at The Edge interview with Tami Simon of Sounds True) 25th August, 2015   http://www.soundstrue.com/store/weeklywisdom

Hendricks, Gay and Kathryn. *Conscious Loving, A Journey to Co-commitment*, Bantam, NY, 1994.

Hillman, James. "A Note on Story", Jeremiah Abrams (ed.), *Reclaiming the Inner Child*, Tarcher, NY, 1990.

Houston, Jean. *Trialogues at the edge of the West, Chaos, Creativity and the Resacrilization of the World*, Inner Traditions International, Rochester, 2002.

Hsu, Jeremy *The Secrets of Storytelling: Why We Love a Good Yarn* Scientific American Mind, August 2008

Hutchens, David *Circle of the 9 Muses: A Storytelling Field Guide for Innovators and Meaning Makers* John Wiley & Sons, Inc., Hoboken, New Jersey 2015

Hurst, Aaron (CEO of Imperative Group, Inc.) & Tavis, Dr Anna (Adjunct Professor of School of Professional Studies, NYU) *Workforce Purpose Index 2015* https://www.imperative.com/index2015

Ionesco, Eugene. *Exit the King*, Grove/Atlantic, London, 1994.

Irving, Michael C, Ph.D. and Irving, Cheryl, B.A. *Well Being and Quality of Life: Containment* http://www.irvingstudios.com/Containment.htm

Jaworski, Joseph. *Synchronicity, The Inner Path of Leadership*, Berrett-Koehler, San Fransisco, 1996.

Johnson, Robert A. *The Fisher King and The Handless Maiden*, Harper Collins, NY, 1995.

Johnson, Robert A. *We: understanding the psychology of romantic love*, Harper San Francisco, 1983.

Jung, Carl, *Psychological Reflections, Carl G. Jung*, Pantheon Books, NY, 1953.

Kabat Zinn, Jon BBC World Service, The Forum 15/1/2011

Kafka, Frans, *Metamorphosis*, Crown, 2003.

Katzenbach, Jon R. and Smith, Douglas K. *The Wisdom of Teams: Creating the High-Performance Organization*, Harvard Business School Press, Boston, 1993.

Keen, Sam and Fox, Anne Valley, *Your Mythic Journey*, Tarcher, NY, 1989.

King, Martin Luther Jnr, *A Testament of Hope*, Harper Collins, NY, 1990.

Kushner, Harold S. *Living a Life that Matters*, Sidgwick & Jackson, London, 2001.

Laurent, Andre http://www.speakers.co.uk/our-speakers/profile/andre_laurent

Lawrence, D. H. *Selected Poems*, Penguin, New York. 1989.

Lebow Company. *Lasting Change: the shared values process that makes companies great*, John Wiley & Sons, NY, 1998.

Lewis-Williams, J. D. (Ed) *Stories that Float from Afar*, Texas A&M University Press 2000.

Lopez, Barry. *Crow and Weasel*, North Point Press, NY, 1990.

Lowney, Chris *Heroic Leadership: best practices from a 450-year-old company that changed the world* Loyola Press. A Jesuit Ministry. Chicago 2003

Luke, Helen. *Dark Wood to White Rose, Journey and Transformation in Dante's Divine Comedy*, Parabola, 1993.

Lundin, Stephen, C., Christensen, John and Paul, Harry. *Fish!* Hodder & Stoughton, London, 2001.

Lundin, Stephen C., Christensen, John and Paul, Harry. *Fish! Tales.* Hodder & Stoughton, London, 2002.

Malherbe, Paul. *A Pragmatic Approach to The Creation of Value, Enrichment and Prosperity.* Author published. Cape Town, 2000.

Manganyi, Chabani. *Looking Through the Keyhole*, Ravan, Johannesburg, 1981.

Manney, PJ *Empathy in the Time of Technology: How Storytelling is the Key to Empathy* Journal of Evolution and Technology Vol 19 Issue 1 Sept 2008 http://jetpress.org/v19/manney.htm

Manning, Tony. *Making Sense of Strategy*, Zebra, Johannesburg, 2001.

McCallum, Ian. *Ecological Intelligence*, Africa Geographic, Cape Town, 2005.

McDermot, Gerald. *Anansi the Spider*, Holt, Rinehart and Winston, New York, 1972.

McGhee, Peter & Grant, Patricia *The Influence of Managers' Spiritual Mindfulness on Ethical Behaviour in Organisations* Journal of Spirituality, Leadership and Management, 2015, vol. 8, no. 1, pp. 12-33 http://www.slam.org.au/wp-content/uploads/2015/07/JSLaMvol8no1_McGhee.pdf

McKenna, Jed *The Yin-Yang Symbol* Sacred Valley Tribe: holding the space for transformation http://sacredvalleytribe.com/think-whats-true/consciousness/yin-yang-symbol/

Mellon, Nancy. *Story Telling and the Art of the Imagination*, Element, Rockport, MA, 1992.

Metzger, Deena. *Writing For Your Life, a Guide and Companion to the Inner World*, Harper, San Fransisco, 1992.

Miller, Arthur. *Death of a Salesman*, Penguin, London, 1998.

Monod, Jacques (translation by Austryn Wainhouse) *Chance and Necessity: an essay on the natural philosophy of modern biology* Collins London 1972

Moore, Thomas. *Care of the Soul: How to Add Depth and Meaning to Your Everyday Life*, Piatkus, London, 1994.

Morgan, Gareth. *Images of Organization*, Sage Publications, 1986.

Mountain Dreamer, Oriah, *The Invitation*, Thorsons, New York. 1999.

Moyers, Bill *The Language of Life, A Festival of Poets*, Doubleday, 1995.

Muller, Wayne. *Legacy of the Heart, the Spiritual Advantages of a Painful Childhood*, Simon and Schuster, NY, 1993.

My Shrink: Therapy Lingo: *Containment* http://www.myshrink.com/counseling-theory.php?t_id=32

http://psychology.wikia.com/wiki/Psychological_containment

Myss, Caroline, *Sacred Contracts, Awakening Your Divine Potential*, Bantam Books, NY. 2002.

Naisbitt, John *Megatrends: ten new directions transforming our lives* Warner Books 1984

Naisbitt, John with Naisbitt, Nana and Philips, Douglas *High Tech High Touch: technology and our accelerated search for meaning* Nicholas Brealey Limited UK 2001

Nicholson, Nigel, *Managing the Human Animal*, Texere, NY, 2000.

Oberlechner, Thomas *The Psychology of Ethics in the Finance and Investment Industry* The Research Foundation of the CFA Institute 2007 citing Kohlberg, L., C. Levine, and A. Hewer *Moral Stages: A Current Formulation and a Response to Critics In Contributions to Human Development, Vol. 10.* 1983 Edited by J.A. Meacham. New York: Karger

Obholzer, Anton and Vega Zagier, Ed Roberts, *The Unconscious at Work*, Tavistock Clinic, Routledge, 1994.

O' Collins and Farrugia, *The Concise Dictionary of Theology*,HarperCollins, London, 1991.

O' Connor, Joseph and Seymour, John. *Introducing NLP,* Thorsons, London, 1995,

Okri, Ben. *Birds of Heaven*, Phoenix, San Fransisco. 1996.

O'Murchu, Diarmuid. *Evolutionary Faith,* Orbis, New York, 2002.

Osho *The Man who Loved Seagulls* St Martin's Griffin NY 2008

Pascale, Richard; Sternin, Jerry & Sternin, Monique *The Power of Positive Deviance* Harvard Business Press Boston 2010

Paul, Annie Murphy *Your Brain on Fiction* The New York Times March 17, 2012 http://www.nytimes.com/2012/03/18/opinion/sunday/the-neuroscience-of-you-brain-on-fiction.html?_r=1&pagewanted=all

Paulus, Trina. *Hope for the Flowers,* A Newman Book, Paulist Press, NY, 1972.

People and Productivity. © *Investors in People UK,* October, 2001.

Perry, S. (ed.), *S T Coleridge, Interviews and Recollections*, Palgrave Macmillan, 2001.

Phillips, Jan. *God is at Eye Level, Photography as a Healing Art,* Theosophical Publishing House, Adjar, India, 2000.

Plato, *The Symposium*, Penguin, London, 2003.

Popcorn, Faith. *The Popcorn Report,* Doubleday, NY, 1991.

Ramachandran V. S. *Neuro-Aesthetics – The Artful Brain,* BBC Reith Lectures, 2003.

Rushdie, S. *Shame*, Viking Press, NY, 1985.

Rhoads, Dr. Gary and Whitlark, Dr. David. *Discover Engagement: what is engagement and why is it one of the most powerful emerging business concepts of the 21st century.* www. allegiance.com/Library (14th February, 2008).

Rilke, Rainer Maria. *Letters to a Young Poet,* Random House, NY, 2001.

Rohr, Richard Centre for Action and Contemplation meditation: *Willfulness to Willingness* Monday, June 15, 2015

Rohr, Richard. *Hope Against Darkness*, St Anthony Messenger Press and Franciscan Communications, Cincinnati, 2002.

Rohr, Richard Rohr Daily Meditation 25th December. 2015 Wisdom Lineage Summary: *Perfect Love Casts Out Fear*

Rowe, Dorothy. *Time On Our Side*, Harper Collins, London, 1994.

Rutledge, Pamela Brown, PH.D., M.B.A *The Psychological Power of Storytelling* http://www.psychologytoday.com/blog/positively-media January 16, 2011

Salpeter, Gali *The River Guide Book* www.storyandtherapy.com 2011

San Souci, Robert D. *The Enchanted Tapestry,* Metheun, London, 1987.

Schwartz, Delmore. *In Dreams Begin Responsibilities,* New Directions, 1978.

Seuss, Dr. *Lorax,* Random House, NY, 1971.

Shaffer, Peter. *Lettice and Lovage,* Andre Deutsch, London, 1998.

Shah, Idries. *The Pleasantries of the Incredible Mullah Nasrudin,* Jonathan Cape, London. 1968.

Shakespeare, William. *The Works of William Shakespeare.* Shakespeare Head Press Oldhams Press Ltd and Basil Blackwell MCMXLVII

Sinclair, Amanda *Possibilities, Purpose and Pitfalls: Insights from introducing mindfulness to leaders* Journal of Spirituality, Leadership and Management, 2015, vol. 8, no. 1, pp. 3-11 http://www.slam.org.au/wp-content/uploads/2015/07/JSLaMvol8no1_Sinclair.pdf

Simpkinson, Charles and Anne, *Sacred Stories*, Harper San Fransisco. 1998.

Simpson, Joe and Yates, Simon. *Touching the Void,* Vintage, London, 2004.

Smart, Jamie. Salad Seminars Ltd. www.saladltd.co.uk. Leics. 2008.

Smart, Jamie. *NLP Tips* www.saladltd.co.uk.

Snow C. P. *The Two Cultures*, Cambridge University Press, Cambridge, 1959.

Snowden, Dave (Founder and Chief Scientific Officer of Cognitive-Edge Pte Ltd) and Williams, Graham - *An email exchange* May, 2009

Sophocles, *Oedipus Rex*, Prestwick House, Clayton, 2004.

Stevens, Wallace. *Collected Poems*, Knopf, NY, 1990.

Stevenson, Louis. *The Strange Case of Dr. Jekyll and Mr Hyde*, Norton, NY, 2002.

Swift, Jonathan. *Gulliver's Travels*, Barnes and Noble, NY, 2003.

Teilhard de Chardin, Pierre. *The Appearance of Man*, Collins, London, 1965.

The Economist, "Better than People", December 24th 2005 – January 6th 2006.

The Futurist, World Future Society, Bethesda, USA, May/June 1996.

Tillich, Paul. *The Courage to Be*, Yale University Press, New Haven, 2000.

Toffler, Alvin. *Future Shock*, Random House, NY, 1970.

Toffler, Alvin. *Third Wave*, Bantam, NY, 1982.

Wagoner, David. *Through the Forest*, Atlantic Monthly Press, New York, 1987.

Walsch, Neale Donald *The Complete Conversations with God: an uncommon dialogue* Hampton Roads Publishing Company, Inc. and G.P. Putnam's Sons NY 2005

Welch, Jack. *Jack: what I've learned leading a great company and great people.* Jack Welch CEO, General Electric with John A. Byrne, Headline Publishing, Great Britain, 2001, Copyright © 2001 The John F. Welch, Jnr. Foundation.

Wiesel, Elie *All Rivers Run to the Sea* Alfred A. Knopf Inc. 1995

Wheatley, Margaret J. *Leadership and the New Science*, Berrett-Koehler Publishers Inc, San Francisco, 1994.

Whitney, John O. and Packer, Tina. *Power Plays*, Simon & Schuster, NY, 2000.

Whyte, David. *The Heart Aroused, Poetry and the Preservation of Soul in Corporate America*, Doubleday, NY, 1994.

Whyte, David. *Crossing the Unknown Sea, Work as a Pilgrimage of Identity*, Riverhead, NY, 1994.

Whyte, David. *The House of Belonging*, Many Rivers Press, Langley, Washington, 2002.

Wilber, Ken. *No Boundary, Eastern and Western Approaches to Personal Growth*, Shambhala, Berkeley, 1979.

Wilhelm, Richard. trans. *The Pocket I Ching*, Arkana Penguin Books, London, 1987.

Wilkinson, Margaret *Changing Minds in Therapy: emotion, attachment, trauma & neurobiology* W.W.Norton & Company NY, London 2010

Williams, Graham; Haarhoff, Dorian & FoX, Peter *The Virtuosa Organisation: the importance of virtues for a successful business* Knowledge Resources 2015

Williams, Graham. *Revelling in Transition.* Centre-ing Service, Cape Town, 1997.

Williams, Graham. *Centre-ing Customer Satisfaction*, Centre-ing Service, Cape Town, 2000.

Williams Graham. *Learning Reflections for 3h Leaders.* Centre-ing Service, Cape Town, 2000.

Williams, Graham. *"From Sweat Shop to Shop Window"*, Services SETA Research Journal, South Africa, October, 2003.

Williams, Margery. *The Velveteen Rabbit*, Egmont, London, 2005.

Williams, William Carlos. *Collected Poems of William Carlos Williams*, New Directions, NY. 1986.

Williamson, Marianne. *Being in Light*, Hay House, Carlsbad, California, 2002.

Windle, Ralph (ed). *The Poetry of Business Life*, Berrett-Koehler, San Fransisco, 1994.

Wing R. L. *The Tao of Power.* Aquarian/ Thorsons, London. 1986.

Zaltman, Gerald & Zaltman, Lindsay *Marketing Metaphoria: what deep metaphors reveal about the minds of consumers* Harvard Business Press Boston, Massachusetts 2008

Zeldin, Theodore *An Intimate History of Humanity* Vintage 1994

Zeus, Perry and Skiffington, Suzanne. *The Complete Guide to Coaching at Work*, The McGraw-Hill Companies, Inc, Colombus, Ohio. 2000.

Zohar, Danah and Marshall, Ian. *Spiritual Intelligence,* Bloomsbury, London, 2000.

The Authors

Graham Williams, CMC, B.Com Hons, B.A. is a certified management consultant, thought leader, speaker, executive coach – an associate of Change Partners, and author who has worked in a large number of countries and sectors around the world. An essential component of his 'motivational fingerprint' is to overcome severe organisational blockages by installing creative, healing solutions – from concept to implementation. He focuses on the use of narrative, anecdote and metaphor as critical contributors to successful business interventions. 

 Dorian Haarhoff is a poet, writer and mentor who is steeped in story. A former Professor of English, he now runs his own business Creative Workshops. He facilitates corporate story workshops for a number of companies in Africa and elsewhere and acts as a writing coach for local and international clients.

Additional Endorsements

5-stars. A valuable resource for those interested in the processes of organizational change and how to effect it using the power of story. While understanding that businesses can be looked at through the lens of numbers and statistics, Williams and Haarhoff make a persuasive case that it is even more powerful to look at them through the lens of story. This lens focuses on the soul of a business and sees its connection to the larger mythic themes of which we are all a part. Those connections provide both information and energy for business transformation and ultimately affect whether the business flourishes.

Drawing from a deep reservoir of stories from literature and folklore of global cultures, the authors tell these stories in workshops and in business consultations to expand listeners' thinking about the business issues they are faced with. By engaging us as storytellers and listeners at the mythic, soul level, they stimulate change that otherwise might not happen. The book presents case studies in which the process of telling a story well and listening to a story well has helped people come up with creative and innovative approaches to business issues.

"Stories raise awareness, stimulate thinking, facilitate leadership, offer flexibility and possibility, nurture and engage," say the authors. One of their workshop participants said, *"I see story as a honeycomb, a structure to hold the honey."* This beautifully written book takes us into a honeycomb of food for the souluseful information and inspiring stories. I recommend it to readers who would like to expand their ways of looking at themselves and the organizations with which they are involved.
  Carl Greer, PhD, PsyD Clinical Psychologist and author of Change Your Story, Change Your Life. USA

"This book offers pure enjoyment of reading the numerous stories, and practical application for all who work with people – coaches, facilitators, OD practitioners, HR, managers and leaders, AND this is not an instruction book. It is something to dip into and become submerged, because reading the stories takes you places, stimulates the imagination. The learnings are not laboured – most times you need to develop your own conclusions, metaphors, meanings and interpretations".
- **John Paisley, Procoaching**

"The stories are delightful and I love the skilful way in which you explain and illustrate the relevance and connection of stories to every sphere of our short earth walk.....congratulations for a fine and profound gift that will I have no doubt, weave its magic with all those you are fortunate enough to read it".
- **Bruce Copley, CEO of AAHA Learning International**

"I was utterly captivated by The Halo and the Noose, and now regularly recommend it when I am facilitating my Train the Trainer Presentation Skills courses. I am also experimenting with more use of stories in my training, and loving the fresh slant it brings to my education role (a real VitB-Injection after 20 years of doing what I do !)"
- **Roma Howard & Associates, Training & Development Practitioners, Leadership & Team Effectiveness**

"A great piece of work which stimulates one to look at life differently - very useful for consultants, trainers and coaches who can draw on the various aspects of storytelling."
Joel Ford, trainer and consultant.

"This is the best book about leadership and business that I have seen in a long time. It is fresh, interesting, needed and written to reach out and touch the toughest part of each of us. This is not about story telling, but more importantly, about how we can all change our story and create a future distinct from the past. Read this book".
Peter Block author (Flawless Consulting) and consultant partner in Designed Learning, USA. Masters Degree in Industrial Administration (Yale)

"A great piece of work which stimulates one to look at life differently - very useful for consultants, trainers and coaches who can draw on the various aspects of storytelling in ways that traditional methods simply cannot."
Angelo Kehayas, CEO Profweb, Fellow Certified Management Consultant, BSc, and MBA

Index